# PHP 8 for Absolute Beginners

## Basic Website and Web Application Development

## Third Edition

Jason Lengstorf
Thomas Blom Hansen
Steve Prettyman

Apress®

*PHP 8 for Absolute Beginners: Basic Website and Web Application Development*

Jason Lengstorf
No 392
Portland, OR, USA

Thomas Blom Hansen
Kirke Saaby, Denmark

Steve Prettyman
Palm Bay, FL, USA

ISBN-13 (pbk): 978-1-4842-8204-5
https://doi.org/10.1007/978-1-4842-8205-2

ISBN-13 (electronic): 978-1-4842-8205-2

Managing Director, Apress Media LLC: Welmoed Spahr
Acquisitions Editor: Steve Anglin
Development Editor: James Markham
Coordinating Editor: Mark Powers

Cover designed by eStudioCalamar

Cover image by Li Zhang on Unsplash (www.unsplash.com)

Distributed to the book trade worldwide by Apress Media, LLC, 1 New York Plaza, New York, NY 10004, U.S.A. Phone 1-800-SPRINGER, fax (201) 348-4505, e-mail orders-ny@springer-sbm.com, or visit www. springeronline.com. Apress Media, LLC is a California LLC and the sole member (owner) is Springer Science + Business Media Finance Inc (SSBM Finance Inc). SSBM Finance Inc is a **Delaware** corporation.

For information on translations, please e-mail booktranslations@springernature.com; for reprint, paperback, or audio rights, please e-mail bookpermissions@springernature.com.

Apress titles may be purchased in bulk for academic, corporate, or promotional use. eBook versions and licenses are also available for most titles. For more information, reference our Print and eBook Bulk Sales web page at http://www.apress.com/bulk-sales.

Any source code or other supplementary material referenced by the author in this book is available to readers on GitHub (https://github.com/Apress). For more detailed information, please visit http://www.apress.com/source-code.

Printed on acid-free paper

*This book is dedicated to every volunteer who provides open source code and training (videos and tutorials) for anyone who wants to improve their skills and learning. Without your dedication to help fellow programmers, we would not progress as an industry to providing the best, most reliable, and most secure programs possible.*

# Table of Contents

# About the Authors

**Jason Lengstorf** is a turbogeek from Portland, OR. He started building websites in his late teens when his band couldn't afford to pay someone to do it, and he continued building websites after he realized his band wasn't actually very good. He's been a full-time freelance web developer since 2007 and expanded his business under the name Copter Labs, which is now a distributed freelance collective, keeping about ten freelancers worldwide busy. He is also the author of *PHP for Absolute Beginners* and *Pro PHP and jQuery*.

**Thomas Blom Hansen** has extensive experience teaching web programming in the Digital section of the Copenhagen School of Design and Technology. When he is not teaching, you can find Thomas fly-fishing for sea-run brown trout in the coastal waters around Denmark or possibly hiking some wilderness area in southern Scandinavia. Thomas lives in a small village with his wife, three kids, too few fly rods, and a lightweight camping hammock.

**Steve Prettyman** is a college instructor on PHP programming, web development, and related technologies. He is and has been a practicing web developer and is a book author. He has authored several books on PHP including *Learn PHP 7* and *PHP Arrays* for Apress.

# About the Technical Reviewer

**Satej Kumar Sahu** works in the role of Senior Enterprise Architect at Honeywell. He is passionate about technology, people, and nature. He believes through technology and conscientious decision-making, each of us has the power to make this world a better place. In his free time, he can be found reading books, playing basketball, and having fun with friends and family.

# Introduction

Modern web development relies on the successful integration of several technologies. Content is mostly formatted as HTML. With server-side technologies, you can create highly dynamic web applications. PHP is the single most used server-side scripting language for delivering browser-based web applications. PHP is the backbone of online giants such as Facebook, Flickr, and Yahoo.

There are other server-side languages available for web application development, but PHP is the workhorse of the Internet. For an absolute beginner, it should be comforting to know that PHP is a relatively easy language to learn. You can do many things with a little PHP. Also, there is a thriving, friendly community supporting PHP. It will be easy to get help with your own PHP projects.

## Who Should Read This Book

This book is intended for those who know some HTML and CSS. It is for those who are ready to take their web developer skills to the next level. You will learn to generate HTML and CSS dynamically, using PHP and MySQL. You will learn the difference between client-side and server-side scripting through hands-on experience with PHP/MySQL projects. Emphasis will be on getting up and running with PHP, but you will also get to use some MySQL in your projects. By the end of the book, you will have created a number of PHP-driven projects, including the following:

- A personal portfolio site with dynamic navigation

- A dynamic image gallery where users can upload images through an HTML form

- A personal blogging system, complete with a login and an administration module

In the process, you will become acquainted with such topics as object-oriented programming, design patterns, progressive enhancement, and database design. You will not get to learn everything there is to know about PHP, but you will be off to a good start.

# How to Read This Book

This book is divided into two main parts. Part I will quickly get you started writing PHP for small, dynamic projects. You will be introduced to a relatively small subset of PHP – just enough for you to develop entry-level web applications. Part I will also teach you the basic vocabulary of PHP.

Part II is a long hands-on project. You will be guided through the development of the aforementioned personal blogging system, starting from scratch. Part II will show you how to use your PHP vocabulary to design dynamic, database-driven web applications.

# Source Code

All code used in this book can be downloaded from `github.com/apress/php8-for-absolute-beginners`.

# PART I

# CHAPTER 1

# Getting Ready to Program

## Objectives

After completing this chapter, you will be able to

- Understand how operating systems make programming easier
- Understand how PHP works with Apache and MySQL/MariaDB to create dynamic web pages
- Install a PHP test environment
- Determine if the test environment is working properly
- Create a simple PHP program
- Execute and test a simple PHP program

Welcome to the world of programming! Whether you have never attempted to write a program before or you have been creating programs for a while, we hope that this book will help you to understand the basics of program development. Every minute of your life has been surrounded by computers. From the monitors in the delivery room the moment you were born to the coffee maker that brewed your dark roast this morning (assuming you like coffee), computers and programs attempt to make our lives easier. Your interest in programming might have grown due to your ability to shine in the gaming world, from using social media applications, or, maybe, from watching entrepreneurs on TV pitch their inventions in an attempt to create a successful business. No matter the reason, you are here to discover how to create programs in the PHP language and, more importantly, determine if programming is something you want to do.

© Jason Lengstorf, Thomas Blom Hansen, Steve Prettyman 2022
J. Lengstorf et al., *PHP 8 for Absolute Beginners*, https://doi.org/10.1007/978-1-4842-8205-2_1

The IT (information technology) industry provides unlimited potential for you to be creative and a true pioneer. There is no limit to what you can design and create. Your creation could help save the planet or make life easier for a disabled person. It is truly up to you to determine what you will invent. You can choose to work for a large multinational corporation, a small startup, or venture out on your own. As your career progresses, you can change your path as many times as you need. You might start with a larger company to build up experience, slide into a startup once you discover your expertise, and finally develop your own application which will pave your way to retirement. The IT industry provides you the freedom to determine your path.

So, let's begin this adventure. Since we assume you want to start programming as quickly as possible (that is why you bought this book, right?), let's briefly cover some groundwork, so we can all start from the same level of understanding.

Here we go! First and foremost, "Computers are dumb." What? But they provide us with so many amazing tools, how can they be dumb? To keep it simple, computers only know two things, 0 and 1. This is based on the idea that a circuit either has electricity (1) or it does not (0). This is the basic building block of how computer *hardware* and *software* is designed. Hardware is what we commonly think of when someone mentions a computer. The physical components, such as the keyboard, screen, circuits, memory chips, and other internal components. The software is the actual programs (applications) that communicate with the hardware. Every computer has an *operating system* which provides the ability for an application (and possibly a human) to communicate with the hardware. The operating system is like a language interpreter; it converts the information it receives (from an application or human) into the language the computer understands. Just like a human interpreter can convert English to Spanish.

A *program* is usually defined as a set of code that accomplishes a task. An *application* (app) can be many programs, types of hardware, and even people working together to accomplish the task. However, don't get hung up on these definitions, because in the real world we tend to use these two words interchangeably. As you will note, we have already done so in this book. The application software is usually not designed to directly communicate with the hardware of the computer. It talks to the operating system, which then talks to the hardware.

As an example, think about the applications you use. When you want to print something from an application, a print window appears, giving you options for your task. If you were then to open up another application on your computer and print from that application, the same print window appears. Where did that come from? The operating system. Operating systems include coding for common tasks that applications request. These modules include blocks of code and the *interface* (graphical window) when required. An application uses an *API* (*application programming interface*) call when using one of these tools. An API is simply a line of code that tells the operating system what block of code to execute and what parameters (information) to use when executing the code.

The print API might request the operating system place the requested document into the *print queue*. The print queue is a list of documents waiting to be printed. Not only can the operating system talk to the printer, but the printer can also talk to the operating system. It actually sends a special signal (*interrupt*) back to the operating system letting it know when a print job is complete (or if there is a problem, such as out of paper). The operating system, once a print job is complete, will remove that job from the queue and send the next job to the printer.

We have greatly simplified the actual process. For example, when the requests are sent back and forth between the operating system and the printer, the instructions (language) are converted back and forth from what the operating system understands to what the printer understands. Where does this conversion happen? With the help of a little application called the *print driver*. Actually, we could dig into this even deeper, but the point is that the application, the operating system, and the hardware (including the printer) work together to accomplish tasks. Hardware is worthless without software (except maybe as a doorstop), and software can't exist without hardware (except maybe in our imagination).

Remember, we stated that computers only know 0 and 1. So how do they accomplish so much if that is all they know? As we know, computers have the ability to store information. They can store this information in the *memory*, on an *internal storage device* (*hard drive, chip*), or even on an *external server* (the cloud). Information that is stored by a computer is stored as a series of 0s and 1s. A *bit* is a single 0 or 1. A *byte* is a series of multiple 0s and 1s. The size (number of 0s and 1s) of a byte might vary depending on the computer (…, 32, 64, 128, …), but it accomplishes the same task of either storing information or executing a task. A *word size* is the number of bits that can be stored within a computer at one location (in memory or a storage device) or executed at one time. The larger the word size, the more information that can be saved or executed at one time. Computers with larger word sizes process information faster.

*Unicode* is a standard that combines bits together to represent many symbols and languages used throughout the world. Quite a task indeed! At one time, programming was mostly designed for English-speaking countries. However, today, programmers exist in all regions of the world. Let's look at an example of following a simple process of typing a character on the keyboard into a document. Assuming we have opened our favorite text processor (such as Microsoft Word), we can begin typing. When we click the letter "s" on the keyboard, it magically appears on the screen (in the document). How does that happen? When a key on the keyboard is pressed, the bit pattern (0s and 1s) for the letter is sent to the text editor via the operating system. However, most people don't understand patterns of 0s and 1s. So, when the text editor receives the information, the information that is displayed is converted on the monitor to the letter we pressed ("s"). Notice, we stated that the display is converted, not the actual data itself. When we store the data, it is still stored in *bit format*.

Again, we have simplified it, because the conversion actually involves memory, the text editor, its driver, the operating system, a graphics card, and the monitor and its driver. A lot goes on very quickly. Luckily, we can just understand that this all happens, without digging into the details. Just remember, what the computer understands, and what we understand is different.

In addition to being a language interpreter, the operating system is also a *memory manager*. In all higher-level programming languages (such as PHP), when data needs to be temporarily stored in memory or more permanently stored on a storage device (or cloud server), the operating system takes over. As a programmer, we ask the operating system to store data in memory by creating variables or constants. A *variable* is similar to the variables we used in algebra. In algebra, when A + B = C, A, B, and C are all variables. We know that they can represent any number. In programming, the same variables can also store numbers, or even characters, while, at the same time, informing the operating system to temporarily store these items in memory.

Most program languages (including PHP) reverse the algebra equation to C = A + B. Why? Glad you asked. While A, B, and C are variables, the equal sign in programming is actually an *assignment operator*. It takes whatever is on the right side (A + B) and stores it into whatever is on the left side (C). Thus, it takes the value (number) stored in A and adds it to the value stored in B and places the result into the variable C. All three of these variables reside in the memory of the computer.

The result of our addition program is stored someplace in memory, and we don't know where. What? We really don't care where, as long as we can use the variable C to retrieve it anytime we need it. We trust that the operating system has our back (it does the right thing by properly storing and protecting our information).

The operating system will either look at the values that are being stored in the variable or look at a *variable declaration statement* in the program code to help determine how to store the variable. Remember that bit patterns are used to represent all characters (including numbers) in a computer. When information is stored in memory or a storage device, it is stored in bit format. Thus, the operating system needs to know if a number is being stored or a character is being stored. There is a difference between the number 1 and the character 1. Basically, we usually don't do mathematics on a character, and we do on a number. Thus, the system needs to know if we might do mathematics. If we are going to use it in a calculation, it is stored in a format that allows us to do so. We will explore this more when we do calculations in PHP.

This also brings up another difference between us and the computer. We create numbers using the *base 10 system*. We count from 0 to 9 (ten different numbers). Then when we need to go to the next number, we add a digit to form the number 10. As you know, eventually we'll add a digit when we go to 100 (10 sets of 10). Computers, however, use the *binary system* (*base 2*) to store a 0 or a 1 (two different numbers). When the computer needs to store a number bigger than that, it adds a digit (10). You might have noticed when you are using a computer or shop for one that everything seems to actually be based on eighths (8, 16, 32, 64, …). Why? Actually, that occurs logically as we add more bits.

When converting from binary 0 to base 10 zero (or from binary 1 to base ten 1) is easy because they mean the same value (zero or one). However, a binary 10 is not the same as a base ten 10. A base ten 10 represents 10 values (ten fingers). In the last paragraph, we mentioned that when a binary number needs to go above 1, it needs to add a digit. A binary 10 is one more than 1; it is the number 2 in base ten (two fingers).

Confused? Let's look at some examples.

**Table 1-1.** *Comparing Base Ten to Binary*

| Base Ten | Binary (Base Two) |
|----------|-------------------|
| 0 | 0 |
| 1 | 1 |
| 2 | 10 |
| 3 | 11 |
| 4 | 100 |
| 5 | 101 |
| 6 | 110 |
| 7 | 111 |

Remember, the first digit (to the right) in binary is a 0 or 1. The second digit represents a 2. Thus, 10 is 2 (2 + 0). 11 is 3 (2 + 1). Since 11 is 3, we have to add a digit to produce a 4 (100). Five is 101 (4 + 0 + 1). Six is 110 (4 + 2 + 0). Seven is 111 (4 + 2 + 1). It takes some practice to get comfortable with this. Don't get hung up on the details; if you understand the basic idea, eventually you will have an "aha" moment as your programming skills increase. Notice that when we reach three digits (111), we have actually created eight values (0–7). This logically shows that bits can be collected based on eighths. 111 111 would be two sets of 8s (8 × 2 = 16). 111 111 111 is three sets of 8s (8 × 3 = 24). 111 111 111 111 is 32 (8 × 4). It becomes logical that we look at multiples of eight when determining how the computer stores information. Let's move on; we will look at this again later.

Let's return to our operating system discussion. The operating system also will determine where in memory a variable is stored. The *algorithm* (code) the operating system uses to determine where it stores the data is well refined and very efficient. It has been tweaked for many years and provides the best solution for storage of information. The operating system looks at a lot of factors (too many for us to explore in a beginner's book) to determine where to store the data. Some of what it considers is how frequent it might be used, what program is using it, how big the data is, and what type of data is being stored.

We hope you are now seeing that the operating system makes our lives easier as programmers. We don't have to worry about details of where to store information and even where our actual program runs in memory. The operating system will allocate locations in memory for everything our program needs. It will also try to protect our program from other programs trying to cause it harm and even handle problems when our program decides to crash. Depending on what caused our program to crash, it might even let us know, via *error messages*, what happened. For example, if there is not enough memory available to run our program (or continue running our program), it will let us know.

When a program ends (either because it is done or has crashed), the operating system will clean up the memory the program used and make it available for the next program that may need it. Actually, technically, it just sets a *flag* (bit) in the memory locations which declares them as available. When another program or data is stored in these locations, the old 0s and 1s are written over. It's not necessary to empty out the location before using it again because new code or data will be placed in that location. Thus, overwriting it anyway.

Let's look at one final thing that an operating system does to help our program. The operating system is a *task manager*. It decides on when and how long our program can run before it stops or gets interrupted. Let's do a quick exercise to look at tasks running.

**Exercise**: Locate the task manager for your operating system. You can do a search on your computer for "task manager," or if you are using a Microsoft Windows machine, you can click the ctrl (lower left of keyboard), alt (lower left of keyboard), and delete (upper right of keyboard) keys at the same time. Then click "task manager" on the list that appears.

Your manager should be similar to Figure 1-1. The chart presented gives us a hint of many tasks the operating system is maintaining on our computer. It is managing CPU, memory, disk, and network usage. This includes any applications we are using (like Microsoft Word). Other programs, which we may or may not have directly used ourselves, are also running in the background (such as Amazon Photos). As the tabs in your manager or in Figure 1-1 indicate, the operating system also manages performance and other services.

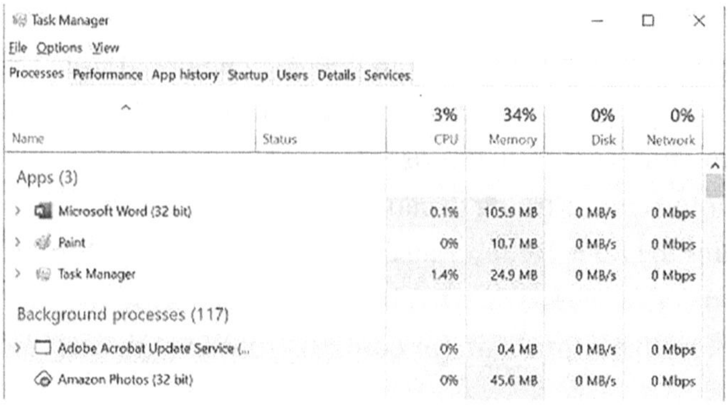

**Figure 1-1.**  *Task manager*

When we start a program, as stated before, the system will determine memory usage and memory location for the program. It will also determine when and how long the program will run before it stops or is interrupted. The system determines the *priority* of the program (system programs like the operating system itself have the highest priority) and how much of a time slice it will allow for the program to run. The system's algorithms are very accurate in determining *runtimes* for programs. However, outside factors can slow a program down, such as emergency system problems (might be a memory shortage). The operating system can *swap* out your program when necessary to run other programs with higher priority. But, normally, we never even notice because everything executes extremely fast.

---

**Note**    If you have been using computers for a while, you may have experienced using applications that never seem to work (they seem to be hung). This could be caused by a shortage of memory (or storage), which the system is trying to resolve by swapping programs in and out of memory to share what limited memory is available. However, it can cause the system to spend a lot of time swapping and allowing very little time for the application to run. It's important that you pay attention to the amount of memory (and storage) any application you install will need to run efficiently. Otherwise, not only might your application not run properly, but it could tie up your computer with constant swapping, so nothing will run properly.

---

We have only skimmed the surface of a very deep ocean when talking about how computers operate. There are many books, videos, and courses you can discover which can provide a much deeper understanding. Our goal, however, is to give us enough knowledge on how all of this affects any program we create. Hopefully, we have built a basic understanding of this, so let's move on to another subject.

Why start with PHP?

A very good question indeed. There are a lot of programming languages that we could choose. Why select PHP as our first experience? First, PHP is one of the easier languages to learn. You can accomplish a lot with just some basic commands and concepts. It is one of the more popular languages used because it can manage web pages and applications. It is commonly considered one of the skills needed to become a *full stack developer*.

---

**Note**    A full stack developer understands both the front end of a web application (the web page displayed to the user) and the back end (code used by the web page existing on the web server). They have knowledge of front-end tools, such as HTML, CSS, and JavaScript. They have experience using languages that can support the web page on the back end (such as PHP and Java). They also may use additional tools to manage the development cycle.

---

With *PHP 8*, the language has become much more efficient in operation and in computations than ever before. While, as of the creation of this book, PHP is not known as a language for developing gaming platforms or big data operations due to its previous limitations, the efficiency of the newest versions could soon make this a reality. There are some groups beginning development of smartphone applications using PHP. But even if it never becomes a gaming platform, there is plenty of work for PHP to accomplish by just hosting web pages and creating applications.

**Exercise**: Is PHP alive and well? Don't believe us. Go to your favorite search engine and ask the following question: "Who uses PHP?" or "Is PHP alive and well?" What did you find? The answer should tell you, "Yes, PHP is alive and well" and "Lots of organizations use PHP." What organizations are currently using PHP? What are they using it for? What does the future hold for PHP? You will discover that there is current development in creating big data dashboards, smartphone applications, and gaming applications, along with web applications. Lookout Python, PHP might be after your job!

# Setting Up a Development Environment

Getting a working *development environment* put together might initially be intimidating, especially for the absolute beginner. However, developers have created many types of software packages, which can install everything we need, with default settings. No longer do we need to go into the setup files to connect our environment together (unless we choose to do so). The environment is automatically linked together for us. To follow along with the projects in this book, we will need to have access to a working development (test) environment which contains *Apache* (*web server*), PHP, and *MySQL/MariaDB* (*database*). It's always desirable to test locally (on a single machine, not a server), both for speed and security. Doing this both shelters your work in progress from the hackers on the open Internet and decreases the amount of time spent uploading files to a *web server*. It allows you to completely test and secure your programs before placing them in a live environment.

PHP is a powerful *scripting language* that can be run by itself. However, PHP alone isn't sufficient for building dynamic website applications. To use PHP for a website, we need a web server that knows how to process PHP scripts. Apache is a free web server that, once installed on a computer, allows developers to test PHP scripts locally; this makes it an invaluable piece for a local development environment. Apache is the most popular web server used in conjunction with PHP.

Additionally, web applications need to store information. PHP code can be developed to store this information in a database, so it can be modified quickly and easily. This is the significant difference between a PHP application and an *HTML* site. Strictly HTML-only sites cannot store information. This is where a *relational database management system* such as MySQL can come into play. Many of the book's examples store information using the MySQL/MariaDB database systems.

---

**Note**   Without going into too much detail, MySQL and MariaDB are very similar systems. When Oracle purchased MySQL, some developers wanted to ensure that a free version of MySQL would still exist (although Oracle does still provide a free version as of the release of this book). MariaDB was the result of this collaborative effort. They ensured that no coding changes would be needed when creating programs using either database system. You will even discover some of the software packages still use the term MySQL when they are really referring to a MariaDB database.

---

# What Is PHP? How Does PHP Work?

PHP is a general-purpose scripting language that was originally conceived by Rasmus Lerdorf in 1995. Lerdorf created PHP to satisfy the need for an easy way to process data when creating pages for the *World Wide Web*.

---

**Note**   PHP was born out of Rasmus Lerdorf's desire to create a script that would keep track of how many visits his online résumé received. Due to the wild popularity of the script he created, Lerdorf continued developing the language. Over time, other developers joined him in creating the software. Today, PHP is one of the most popular scripting languages.

---

PHP originally stood for *Personal Home Page* and was released as a free, *open source* project. Over time, the language was reworked to meet the needs of its users. In 1997, PHP was renamed PHP: *Hypertext Preprocessor*, as it is known currently. At the time we are writing this, PHP 8.1.1 is the current stable version. Older versions of PHP are still in use on many servers. However, they might not be as secure. PHP 8 has provided many powerful changes to the language which has increased usability, speed, and security. All code provided in this book works with PHP 8 (or later). Some of the code will also work with previous versions. We suggest you install and use the most current version available.

HTML is parsed by a *browser* on the user's computer after the page downloads. The browsers determine how to display the information provided from the code provided by the HTML and CSS. Since, unlike HTML, PHP code is retained on a remote web server, browsers cannot process PHP code. PHP is processed by a *PHP interpreter* connected to a web server (such as Apache). The results of the execution of the PHP code (not the actual PHP code) are included in the document (web page) before it is sent to the user's browser to be interpreted. Because PHP is processed on a server, it is a *server-side scripting language*.

**Exercise**: Search for a company that uses PHP. Go to their website. View the source code of the main page of their site. You can view the code by selecting "View Source" within your browser. Did you find some PHP code? The answer is no. Why? Because your browser shows the results after the PHP code has been processed by the web server. You can see HTML, CSS, and JavaScript code, but you will not see any PHP code. Where can you see the PHP code? If you had access, you could view it on the server itself.

With PHP, you can create dynamic web pages (web pages that can change according to conditions). For example: When you log in to your Facebook account, you can see your content. When you log in to another Facebook account, you see different content. We are loading the same resource (www.facebook.com) and code, but we are served different content dynamically. This would be impossible with strictly HTML web pages because they are *static*, meaning they can't change. Every user would see exactly the same HTML page. We will soon explore many more examples of dynamic web pages in this book.

PHP is an interpreted language, which is another great advantage for PHP programmers. Many programming languages require that you *compile* files into *machine code* before they can be run, which can be a time-consuming process. Bypassing the need to compile every time you make a code change means you're able to edit and test code much more quickly. However, this also can cause PHP to be slower than compiled programs in a live environment. Compiled programs are already machine-level programs that the server can directly run. Script programs (like PHP) have to first be interpreted before they can run. With PHP 8, this disadvantage has been removed. PHP 8 includes a *JIT (just-in-time) compiler* which can be used to compile PHP code for live sites. This removes the delay.

---

**Note**    While doing initial testing of our code, we first are concerned with removing all syntax and logical errors. During this phase, we can test PHP using the original interpreted mode. After errors are removed, for heavily used web applications, we can use the JIT compiler to speed up the PHP application in the live environment. Since this is a beginner's book, most of our testing will be using the interpretive mode of PHP, to save debugging time and effort.

---

Because PHP is a server-side language, running PHP scripts requires a server. To develop PHP projects in a local development environment means we need to install a server on our local machine. The examples in this book rely on the Apache web server to deliver our web pages, since it is the most popular server used with PHP.

# Apache and What It Does

Apache hosts just under 40% of all websites that exist as of the release of this book. Apache is an open source server that runs on virtually all available operating systems. Apache is a community-driven project, with many developers contributing to its progress. Apache's open source roots also means that the software is available free of charge, which probably contributes heavily to Apache's overwhelming popularity relative to its competitors.

On the Apache HTTP Server Project website (`http://httpd.apache.org`), Apache HTTP Server is described as "an effort to develop and maintain an open-source HTTP server for modern operating systems including UNIX and Windows NT. The goal of this project is to provide a secure, efficient, and extensible server that provides HTTP services in sync with the current HTTP standards." The Apache Project provides billions of free lines of open source code for anyone to use.

As with all web servers, Apache accepts an *HTTP request* and serves an *HTTP response*. When you enter a URL (`www.apress.com`) into your browser, the browser transforms the information into an HTTP request. This information is sent to the web server (Apache). The server determines what has been requested (access to the Apress website). It then creates an HTTP response which includes the information requested (the main page for Apress) and sends that information back to the browser. While the server is creating the response, the web server sends any noncompiled PHP code to the PHP processor to be interpreted. All the PHP code is then executed, and the results are included in the response along with any HTML, CSS, or JavaScript. Along with displaying the results of the PHP code, the user's browser will interpret the HTML, CSS, and JavaScript code to format the web page requested within the browser.

# Storing Info with MySQL/MariaDB

MySQL and MariaDB are relational database management systems (*RDBMS*). Essentially, this means that they allow users to store information in a table-based structure, using rows and columns to organize different pieces of data. There are many other relational database management systems and *nonrelational systems* (such as *NoSQL databases*). Since MySQL/MariaDB is one of the most popular RDBMS systems, many examples in this book rely on them to store relational data.

Now that we are familiar with the tools that we need, let's get the ball rolling by installing these tools.

**Exercise**: Before starting the installation process, visit the PHP (php.org), Apache (apache.org), and MySQL (mysql.com) websites. What are the current stable releases of each? When determining which software package to install, look for one that has the most recent versions available.

# Installing PHP, Apache, and MySQL/MariaDB

One of the biggest hurdles for new programmers is starting. In the past, before you could write your first line of PHP, you had to download Apache, PHP, and MySQL/MariaDB, separately, then fight through installation instructions that are full of technical jargon you might not understand yet. This experience left many developers feeling unsure of themselves, doubting whether they've installed the required software correctly. Just trying to get each tool to communicate with the other was a major hassle requiring changing settings within the setup files that you had little knowledge or understanding about what the files accomplished.

This hurdle kept many new programmers from learning programming for months, even though they desperately wanted to move beyond plain ole HTML. It took many unsuccessful attempts to install PHP before being able to run the first command successfully.

Fortunately, the development community has responded to the frustration of beginning developers with many software packages that take all the pain out of setting up your development environment, whether you create applications for Windows, Mac, or Linux machines. These options include all-in-one solutions for setting up Apache, MySQL, and PHP. We refer to these packages as *LAMP* (Linux, Apache, MySQL/MariaDB, PHP), *WAMP* (Windows, Apache, MySQL/MariaDB, PHP), and *MAMP* (MacOS, Apache, MySQL/MariaDB, PHP) stacks.

As of the end of 2021, some of the most popular and best packages included

> *AMPPS*: Provides LAMP, WAMP, and MAMP versions –
> www.ampps.com
>
> *WAMPSERVER*: Provides only a WAMP version –
> www.wampserver.com

*XAMPP*: Provides LAMP, WAMP, and MAMP versions –
`www.apachefriends.org`

*Neard*: Provides a WAMP-only version – `www.neard.io`

*WAMP.NET*: Provides a WAMP-only version – `www.wamp.net`

*EasyPHP*: Provides only a WAMP version – `www.easyphp.org`

**Exercise**: Go to each of the preceding websites and explore what is included in each package. Many of these packages have additional tools to assist in program development. Compare the versions of PHP, Apache, and MySQL/MariaDB provided with each package. Currently is one more up to date than another? Does one package interest you more than another? In this book, we will use XAMPP. But you may find that one of the other packages meets your needs better. You will find videos on YouTube which will demonstrate the installation process for each package. We recommend installing XAMPP for now, but after you gain experience, make your own decision as to the package that is best for you.

It would be redundant to demonstrate how to install each of the most popular stacks available. Therefore, we will show the installation process for the package we used to create the examples in this book. The author's personal choice for PHP code creation and testing is XAMPP, which is one of the most common all-in-one free solutions; it has been available for many years. XAMPP is used by thousands of programmers across the globe to create dynamic PHP programs. XAMPP has earned an almost perfect five-star rating from its users for ease of use and reliability. It's a good choice for beginning programmers.

---

**Note**  Most Linux distributions ship with one flavor or another of the LAMP stack bundled in by default. Certain versions of Mac OS X also have PHP and Apache installed by default.

---

# Installing XAMPP

Enough background. You're now ready to install XAMPP on your development machine. This process should take just a few minutes and, hopefully, is completely painless.

**Note**   New versions of XAMPP are released frequently. If you discover that the current version of XAMPP has major differences than the version shown in the following, don't panic. You can discover the current installation process from the videos located on the XAMPP website and from YouTube. When searching YouTube, be sure to include the XAMPP release number, such as "Installing XAMPP 8.1.1." Make sure to also check the creation date of the video to make sure it was created recently.

## Step 1: Download XAMPP

In this demonstration, we will install a Windows version of XAMPP. The process is similar for other operating systems. If you are confused on how to install XAMPP for your operating system, search YouTube for a related video.

Your first task is to obtain a copy of the XAMPP software. Head over to the XAMPP site (`www.apachefriends.org`). Then click "Download" on the menu. Select the newest stable version for your operating system by clicking the Download button to the right of the version. These steps and the examples in this book are created using version 8.1.1 for Windows.

***Figure 1-2.*** *XAMPP versions*

After clicking the button, you may be asked if you want to open or save the installation file. Select "save" as shown in Figure 1-3.

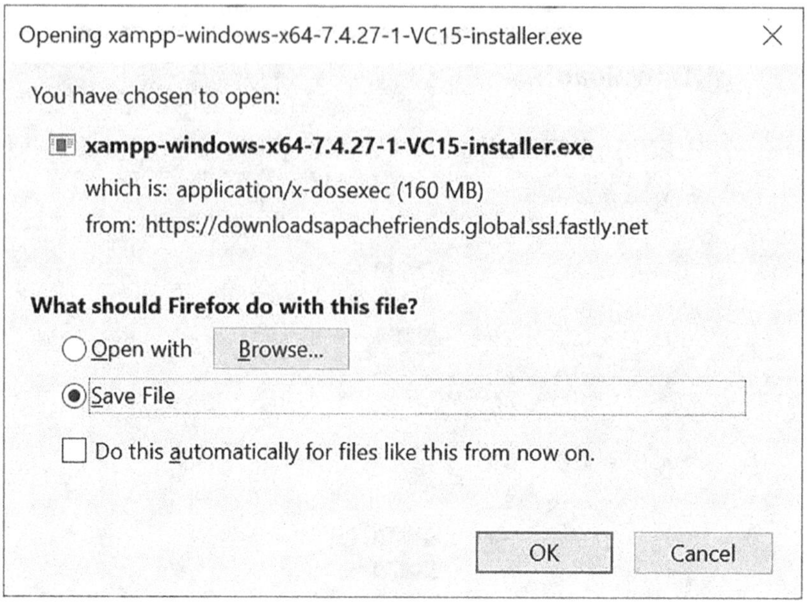

Opening xampp-windows-x64-7.4.27-1-VC15-installer.exe                                    ✕

You have chosen to open:

   ▣ **xampp-windows-x64-7.4.27-1-VC15-installer.exe**

      which is: application/x-dosexec (160 MB)
      from: https://downloadsapachefriends.global.ssl.fastly.net

   **What should Firefox do with this file?**
      ○ O̲pen with      B̲rowse...
      ◉ S̲ave File
      ☐ Do this a̲utomatically for files like this from now on.

                                          OK              Cancel

*Figure 1-3.* *Saving installation file*

After clicking the OK button, the installation program will be downloaded to your computer. Depending on the browser you are using, you will need to access the downloaded file. In Firefox, you can find the downloaded file by clicking the download arrow at the upper right corner of the browser. Once you find the installation file, click the file to begin the installation process.

## Step 2: Follow the Instructions

In the Windows environment, the operating system may ask if you want to allow this application to make changes. Answer "yes." You may also get a warning about an Active User Account Control (UAC) on your system. You can choose to turn off this security feature on your machine, or (better choice), as the warning states, install XAMPP in a different location, other than "Program Files."

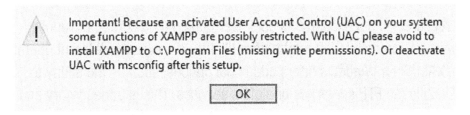

**Figure 1-4.** *UAC warning message*

After clicking OK for the warning message, or OK on the initial window, you should now see a screen similar to Figure 1-5.

**Figure 1-5.** *Initial setup screen*

**Note**   All screenshots used in this book were taken on a computer running Windows 10. Your installation might differ slightly, if you use a different operating system. XAMPP for Windows offers additional options, such as the ability to install FileZilla (an FTP server) as one of its services. This is unnecessary and will consume computer resources, even when they are not being used, so it's probably best to leave these services off. Additionally, Windows users should select to install XAMPP in the c:\xampp directory for the sake of following this book's examples more easily.

Click the Next button to move to the next screen (see Figure 1-6), to choose which components to install. Let's just go with the default selections to make life easier. This will install some tools we will not use in this book. However, they are very useful in program development. The XAMPP installer will guide you through the installation process.

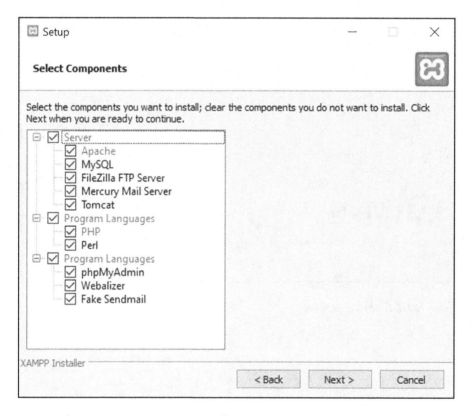

***Figure 1-6.***  *Select components to install*

Leave the default location, as shown in the following, for the creation of the XAMPP files. If you already have a previous version of XAMPP, you can change this location. Just remember that the examples in this book assume the files are located at C:\xampp.

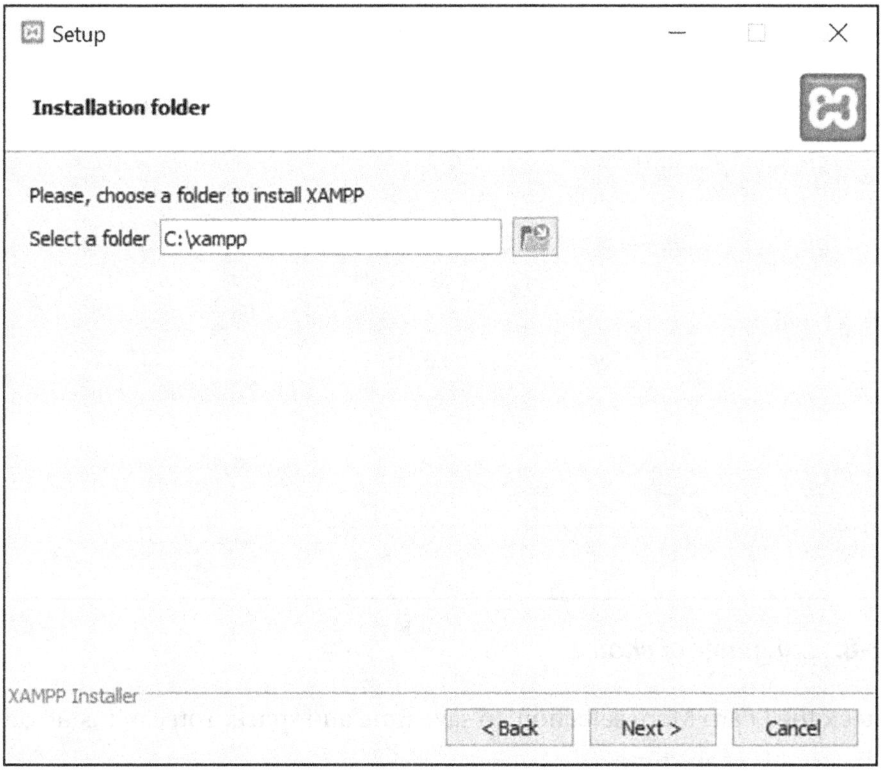

***Figure 1-7.*** *Installation folder*

Pick your language of choice.

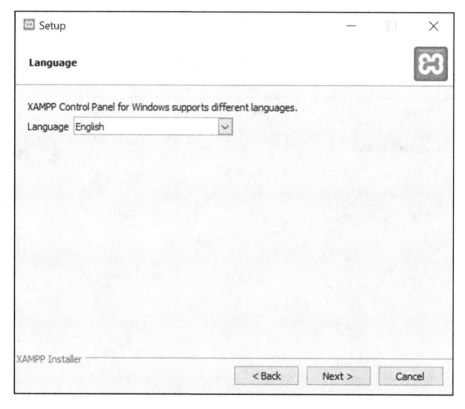

***Figure 1-8.*** *Language of choice*

**Uncheck** the Learn More selection, to save time and space. You can install one or more of these tools at any time.

***Figure 1-9.*** *Learn more about Bitnami*

Click next in the screen shown in Figure 1-10.

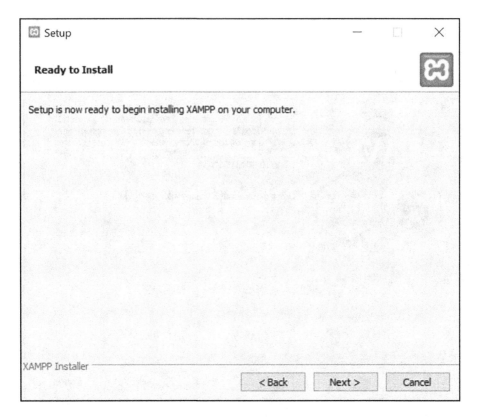

**Figure 1-10.** *Ready to install*

Finally, the installation begins!

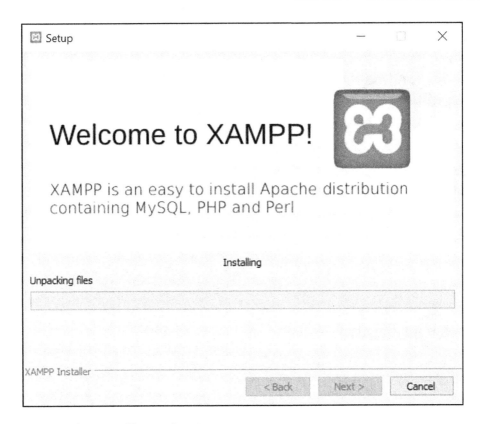

**Figure 1-11.** *The installation begins*

The installation is complete! Click finish.

***Figure 1-12.*** *Installation complete*

## Step 3: Test XAMPP to Ensure Proper Installation

So far, we've used the XAMPP wizard to install Apache, PHP, and MySQL. The next step is to activate Apache, so we can write some PHP.

## Open the XAMPP Control Panel

In Figure 1-12, we left the start control panel button checked. This will automatically show us the control panel (Figure 1-13). Whenever you need the panel, you can locate it in your start menu for your operating system. If you need to access it after it has started, click the XAMPP icon located in your system tray (the menu line at the bottom of your operating system window). This icon will only appear after the panel has initially been started.

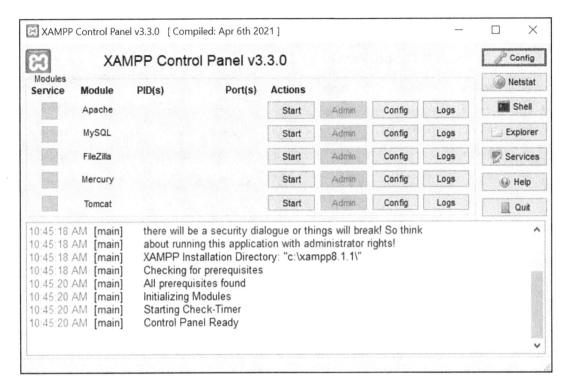

*Figure 1-13.* *Control panel*

---

**Note**  The author has stored the files in the folder xampp8.1.1 because other versions exist on the demo machine. Your message should indicate the files are stored in the folder xampp.

---

Activating Apache, PHP, and MySQL on your development machine is as simple as clicking the Start buttons next to Apache and MySQL in the XAMPP manager. You might be prompted to confirm that the server is allowed to run on your computer, and you might be required to enter your system password. After you do this, the Status should indicate that Apache is running, as shown in Figure 1-14.

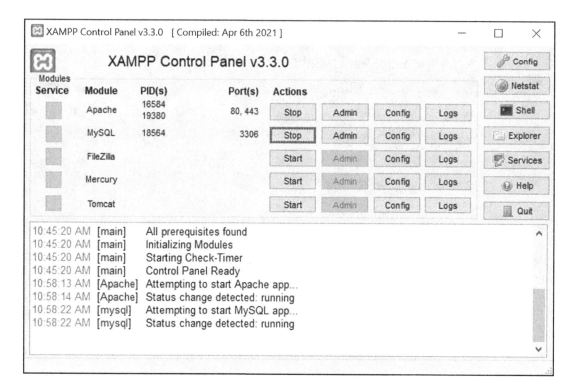

*Figure 1-14.  Apache and MySQL running successfully*

---

**Note**    There is an FTP FileZilla (file transfer protocol) option available in XAMPP. FTP provides a method for moving files between networks. The examples in this book don't require this option, so there is no need to activate it in the XAMPP control panel. Mercury and Tomcat also do not need to be activated. The first few chapters don't even require a MySQL database.

---

# What If Apache Isn't Running?

Sometimes, XAMPP Apache Server doesn't run, even if you try to start it. The most common problem is that it conflicts with some other service using the same *port* on your computer. Check if you have Skype or Messenger or some similar networking service running. Shut them completely down, and if you're lucky, your Apache can run. If you are brave, you can also click the config button in the control panel to change the port in which Apache (or MySQL) is running.

If it still doesn't run, you could turn to the Internet for help. The XAMPP online community is extremely helpful, and most installation issues have been addressed in the Apache Friends forum at `https://community.apachefriends.org/f/`. You could also check `http://stackoverflow.com/`. Remember the Internet is your friend; someone has run into the same problem. If you receive an error message, copy and paste it into the browser. You will discover suggested solutions to your problem. Don't ever pay for a solution. There are free sites and blogs that will provide the answers you are seeking.

## Verify That Apache and PHP Are Running

It's a simple matter to check whether Apache is running properly on your development machine. Simply open a browser and go to the following address: `http://localhost`. If everything has gone correctly, you should see a screen similar to Figure 1-15.

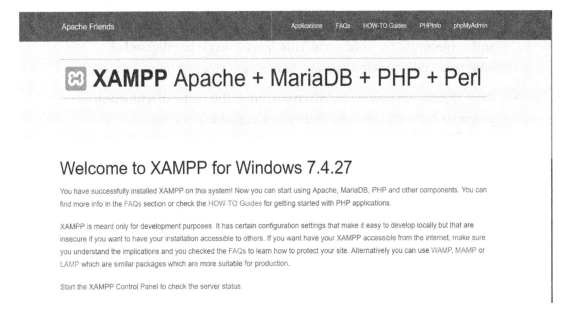

***Figure 1-15.***  *Apache works!*

If this screen loads, you've installed Apache and PHP on your development machine successfully! We have not checked the status of MySQL/MariaDB; we will check that status when we create programs using databases. The address `http://localhost` is an alias for the current computer you're working on. When using XAMPP, navigating to `http://localhost` in a browser tells the server to open the root web directory. This is the *htdocs* folder contained in the XAMPP install directory. Another way to use your server to access the root web directory on your local machine is to navigate to the *IP address* (a numerical identifier assigned to any device connected to a computer network) that serves as the "home" address for all HTTP servers: `http://127.0.0.1`.

# Choosing a PHP Editor

Your development machine is now running all the necessary programs for executing PHP. The next step is to decide how you're going to write your scripts. PHP scripts are text based, so you have a myriad of options, ranging from the simple `Notepad.exe` and text-edit programs to highly specialized *integrated development environments* (*IDEs*).

You can probably write PHP code using whichever program you have used for writing HTML and CSS. There are some features you should expect from a good editor:

- *Syntax highlighting*: This is the ability to recognize certain words in a programming language, such as variables, control structures, and various other special texts. This special text is highlighted or otherwise differentiated to make scanning your code much easier.

- *Built-in function references*: When you enter the name of a function or an object method, this feature displays available parameters, as well as the file that declares the function, a short description of what the function does, and a more in-depth breakdown of parameters and return values. This feature proves invaluable when dealing with large libraries, and it can save you trips to the PHP website to check the order of parameters or acceptable arguments for a function.

- *Auto-complete features*: This feature adds available PHP keywords to a drop-down list, allowing you to select the intended keyword from the list quickly and easily, saving you the effort of remembering and typing it out every time. When it comes to productivity, every second counts, and this feature is a great way to save time.

- *Code folding*: This feature lets you collapse snippets of code, making your workspace clutter-free and your code easy to navigate.

- *Auto-indent*: This automatically indents the code you write in a consistent manner. Such indented code is vastly easier to read for human readers, because indentation indicates relationships between code blocks.

- *Built-in FTP*: You need FTP to upload your PHP files to an online web server when you want to publish your project on the World Wide Web. You can use a stand-alone FTP program, but if it is built into your IDE, you can upload an entire project with a single click.

There are many good IDEs and editors to choose from. Beginners may find it easier to start with a simpler editor. The examples in this book were created with Notepad++ (notepadplusplus.com) to keep development simple. However, feel free to explore other options. The following list includes download links for four of the most popular free IDEs for PHP:

- *NetBeans* – `https://netbeans.org/`

- *Aptana* – `www.aptana.com/`

- *Eclipse* – `www.eclipse.org/`

- *Visual Studio* – `https://visualstudio.microsoft.com/`

There are also many PHP IDEs for purchase, some of which provide a 30-day free trial. We have chosen to promote those that don't charge us to use them.

**Exercise**: Explore your different options for editing PHP programs. Choose an editor or IDE that you feel most comfortable using. For assistance in installing your selection, go to YouTube and search for a video demonstrating the installation. Don't forget to include the version number in your search. In the next section, we will create our first program. Thus, we need an editor to do so.

As stated, previously, we will use Notepad++ for the examples in this book. You should have no difficulties following the examples with any other editor. If you decide to use an IDE, you will have to consult online documentation to learn how to set up a new project in your chosen IDE.

# Creating Your First PHP Program

With everything set up and running as it should, it is time to take the plunge and write our first PHP script.

As a server-side scripting language, PHP requires a web server such as Apache to run. You have just installed Apache on your local computer, so your system is ready. Apache will interpret any PHP files saved inside a folder called htdocs. You can find it inside your XAMPP installation in XAMPP/xamppfiles/htdocs.

You'll be making many PHP files soon, so it is a good idea to keep them organized. Create a new folder inside htdocs and call it ch1.

---

**Note**   To fully grasp and understand PHP programming, it is imperative that you attempt to program all examples provided in the book. While the completed code can be downloaded, you will only learn and remember by doing. It is worth the time and effort to create your own programs. As with all programming books, publishing errors might occur. If you are sure that you have created code as shown in the book and still are receiving errors, check the code files provided for the chapter. Each code file has been tested for accuracy and completeness.

---

Now open your editor or IDE of choice. Determine how to create a "new" file within your editor, so you can begin coding. Then enter the following program exactly as shown. If you have problems with this code, verify your code with the example provided in the code files (test.php) for Chapter 1, which can be downloaded using the directions provided in the preamble of this book.

***Listing 1-1.***  test.php

```php
<?php

echo "Hello from PHP";

?>
```

Make sure to save the file as test.php in the ch1 folder that you created under htdocs. Your editor may require you to either "save as" "all files" or "save as" "php." It is very important that you make sure the file ending is .php, not .txt or some other ending. PHP files will only execute if they have a .php file ending. This is a simple process that can be a "got ya" moment, if not saved properly.

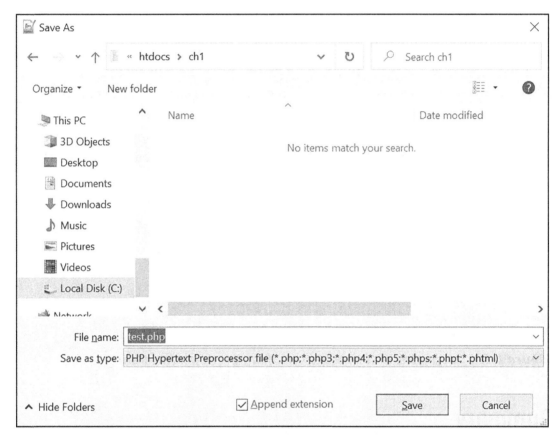

***Figure 1-16.***  *Saving test.php in Notepad++*

# Running Your First PHP Script

The next step is to get Apache to process your PHP script. That happens automatically, if you request the script through a browser. So, open a web browser and navigate to `http://localhost/ch1/test.php` and marvel at the PHP-generated output you should see in your browser (Figure 1-17). You have successfully created and executed your first PHP script!

Hello from PHP

**Figure 1-17.** *Seeing the output from* `test.php`

If you accidently save your file with a .txt ending, your code will not execute (Figure 1-18), and you will see a listing of your code. This will also occur if your code is not saved under the htdocs folder or Apache is not running. If this occurs, correct either the file ending, the location of your file, or turn on Apache, and attempt to run it again. Once you're successful, pat yourself on the back. You did it! You created your first PHP program (and made it to the end of the chapter).

```
<?php
echo "Hello from PHP";
?>
```

**Figure 1-18.** *Saving test and running it with an improper file ending*

## Summary

In this chapter, we learned about operating systems and their interactions with programs. We discovered how operating systems make our lives easier as program developers. We learned a little bit about PHP, MySQL, and Apache. We found out what they are and what role they play in the development of dynamic websites. We completed a quick and easy installation of a fully functional development environment on our local computer to create a safe and secure place to test programs.

In the next chapter, we'll learn a small but potent subset of PHP, including variables, objects, and some native language constructs and statements. Nearly everything you learn will be tested in your new development environment, so keep XAMPP's Apache Server open and running.

# Projects

1. Create a simple PHP program which displays your name, address, and paragraph of information about you using the echo instruction shown in this chapter.

2. Create a PHP program which displays HTML code within the echo instruction. How could this be useful for dynamic websites?

# CHAPTER 2

# Understanding PHP: Language Basics

## Objectives

After completing this chapter, you will be able to

- Embed PHP in web pages

- Add comments in code

- Create and use variables

- Decipher PHP errors

- Create an HTML5 template

- Create and use basic objects

- Concatenate strings

- Access URL variables with $_GET

- Declare a class

- Embed CSS

In the first chapter, we developed our very first PHP program. While it was basic, we were able to test the development environment and even display some information. As we stated, PHP is a powerful tool for creating dynamic web applications. With this in mind, we will, over the next several chapters, develop the skills to create a basic blog. The tools used to develop a blog can also be used to create other dynamic sites. One goal of this book is to "learn by doing." Thus, we will use our examples and projects to build our knowledge.

© Jason Lengstorf, Thomas Blom Hansen, Steve Prettyman 2022
J. Lengstorf et al., *PHP 8 for Absolute Beginners*, https://doi.org/10.1007/978-1-4842-8205-2_2

As a stepping stone to blog development, we first need to determine how to create a basic dynamic website. In this chapter, we will create a simple personal website with dynamic web pages. Along the way, we will learn how to create, store, manipulate, and display data using PHP.

---

**Note**   This chapter discusses basic aspects of the PHP language, but not in complete detail. Our goal is to develop skills which can help you be productive as quickly as possible. For clarification, more examples, or for concept reinforcement, you should visit the PHP manual at `www.php.net` and search for additional information. Alternatively, you can search YouTube for demonstration videos. Always check the PHP version discussed (PHP 8), as some PHP coding has changed over time. Don't forget to read the comments, because many of your fellow programmers offer insight, tips, and even additional functions in their commentary.

---

# Embedding PHP Scripts

In Chapter 1, we mentioned that web servers look for PHP only in files that end with the `.php` extension. But a `.php` file can contain elements that aren't part of our PHP script, and searching the entire file for potential scripts can be confusing and resource intensive. To solve this issue, all PHP scripts are provided between *PHP delimiters*. To begin a PHP script, we start with the opening delimiter `<?php`. To complete a PHP script, we add the closing delimiter `?>`. Anything outside of these delimiters will be treated as HTML, CSS, JavaScript, or plain text by the web server.

Let's look at some examples. First, we want to continue to keep our programs organized, so let's create a new folder, ch2, in `/xampp/htdocs/`. Using our favorite editor, we will create a new file, `test.php`. Let's enter the following code within the file.

***Listing 2-1.*** test.php

```
<p>Static Text</p>

<?php
        echo "<p>This text was generated by PHP!</p>";
?>

<p>This text was not.</p>
```

Save the file and then test it by navigating to `http://localhost/ch2/test.php` in a browser.

---

**Hint**    Most PHP code lines require a semicolon at the end to indicate where the line ends. Did you remember to include it at the end of the echo statement?

---

If we did not make any typing mistakes, our output should be similar to the following.

***Figure 2-1.*** *test.php output*

Even in this simple program, we can discover several aspects. First, the display included both the results of the browser parsing the HTML code and the results of the PHP code being interpreted. The results from the PHP code were even displayed in the same location (between the HTML results) as existed in the code itself. The code inside the PHP delimiters was handled as a PHP script, but the code outside was rendered as regular HTML. The PHP interpreter executed the PHP code, while the browser executed the remaining code.

# Program Design and Logic

There is no limit to how many blocks of PHP you can include in a web page. However, do not go overboard. All programmers should create clear organized code that is as easy as possible to maintain. As a programmer, you will constantly modify code. Make your experience easier by keeping the code clean and logical.

The following snippet is completely valid, but is it clean and logical?

***Listing 2-2.*** test2.php

```php
<?php
echo "<p>This is some text.</p>";
?>
<p>Some of this text is static, <?php echo "but this sure isn't!"; ?></p>
<?php echo "<p>"; ?>
This text is enclosed in paragraph tags that were generated by PHP.
<?php echo "</p>"; ?>
```

The preceding code snippet outputs the following to the browser.

This is some text.

Some of this text is static, but this sure isn't!

This text is enclosed in paragraph tags that were generated by PHP.

***Figure 2-2.*** *test2.php output*

# Program Design and Logic

When we write a PHP script that holds nothing but PHP, we don't have to end it with the PHP delimiter. However, should we? We can open the refrigerator door to get a snack without closing it. Mom will eventually come around and close it. But is that right? It only makes more logical sense that if we opened it, we should close it. For consistency and ease of debugging, a programmer should always use closing delimiters for each opening delimiter. It also makes debugging code easier as you trace down missing required delimiters.

# Using echo

Let's take an extra look at the use of echo in the preceding code examples. PHP's echo is a *language construct* (a basic syntactic unit of PHP code). Without much discussion, we have discovered that this statement will display a string of text that is placed between double quotes. The echo statement is probably the most common approach for outputting text from PHP to the browser. However, there are other constructs we can use to display information.

**Exercise**: Go to the php.net website and search for information on the *print* command. What is the difference in how echo and print are used?

Notice that echo outputs strings that are delimited with double quotes. The initial double quote indicates the beginning of a string of characters. The second double quote marks the end of the string to output. In PHP, we must delimit (use quotes) for any strings in our code. The *string delimiters* tell PHP when a string of characters begin and end, something PHP needs to know in order to process your code.

---

**Note**   *String* is a geeky word for "text." Because computers are not human, they don't really see texts, much less words. They see *strings* of characters, which to a computer is a lot of 1s and 0s.

---

# What Is a Variable?

In Chapter 1, we introduced the concept of *variables*. We discovered that a variable acts as an identifier for a value stored in a system's memory. This is useful, because it allows us to write programs that will perform a set of actions on a variable value, without being concerned about how and where the variable is stored in memory. The program can change output simply by changing what is stored in the variable, rather than changing the program code itself. Variables help us begin to create dynamic coding!

## Storing Values in a Variable

It is quite straightforward to store a value in a variable. In PHP, with one single line of code, we can declare a new variable and assign a value to it.

***Listing 2-3.*** test3.php

```php
<?php
$myName = "Thomas";
$friendsName = "Brennan";
echo "<p>I am $myName and I have a friend called $friendsName.</p>";
?>
```

The result of executing the code in Listing 2-3 within a browser is shown in Figure 2-3.

I am Thomas and I have a friend called Brennan.

***Figure 2-3.*** *test3.php output*

As mentioned in Chapter 1, the equal sign is an *assignment operator*. It tells the interpreter to take whatever is on the right-hand side, a string in these examples, and place it into the variable on the left-hand side. In many languages, we also need to tell the system what type of information will be stored, such as a string, number, or single character. PHP allows us to optionally declare *data types*.

The operating system needs the data type to determine what set of bits to use to represent the data in memory. If a data type is not declared, PHP will look at the information first stored in the variable, strings in this example, to inform the operating system of the type of data being stored.

## A Variable Is a Placeholder

Variables are used extensively in programming. They provide programs the flexibility to temporarily store data while the program is running and to change the data used whenever necessary. Let's look at more details from the previous listing.

```
echo "<p>I am $myName and I have a friend called $friendsName.</p>";
```

When the program was executed, the variable $friendsName displayed Brennan and the variable $myName displayed Thomas. The information displayed replaced each corresponding PHP variable in the original string.

Did you notice that we had some HTML code within the string? Remember that the results of the execution of PHP code are sent to the browser. The completed string, including the <p> tags, is sent to the browser to be interpreted. If we view the source code within the browser, we will see that the <p> tags exist and have been interpreted. We can pass any HTML, CSS, or even JavaScript code to the browser to be interpreted by including it in an echo string. We will soon see great benefits to using this technique.

In some other programming languages, a variable cannot be contained within a string. The string has to be broken apart, as shown in the following line.

```
echo "<p>I am $myName and I have a friend called " . $friendsName" .
".</p>";
```

The period is a *string concatenator* character, which allows us to connect multiple strings together. We can replace our previous code line with this example, and it will produce the same result. However, hopefully, you can see that it becomes much more of a problem to keep up with all the periods and quotes. Debugging becomes more difficult. Thank you, PHP developers, for making our job easier!

## Valid PHP Variable Names

In PHP, all variables must begin with a dollar sign character ($). Variable names are case sensitive. Variables can also contain underscores (_). Usually, when we create a variable, we start with an alphabetic character. However, some special variables begin with underscores.

## Program Design and Logic

When creating variable names, be consistent. Each programmer has their own style in designing names; the key is to use the same style throughout your program. You may prefer camel hump ($myName), underscores ($my_name), a combination ($my_Name), or a different technique. All are acceptable. Some programmers will also include the type of data stored within the name ($stringMyName) to allow easier debugging. For readability, we suggest using names that are meaningful. As you note in our simple examples, so far, we did not name our variables $name1 or $name2. We provided some meaning to the variable by using $myName and $friendsName. This allows anyone reviewing our code some understanding of what type of data will be stored. Remember, when creating larger programs, this will be important in helping to determine which variable relates to what areas of a program.

---

**Note**   You can actually use numbers in variable names but not in initial positions. So, $1a is an invalid variable name, whereas $a1 is perfectly valid.

---

# Displaying PHP Errors

On your journey toward learning PHP, you will produce code errors. It is easy to think that you have done something bad when you have written some erroneous PHP. In a sense, it is, of course, bad. You would probably prefer to write perfect PHP from the very start, but even experts sometimes make coding mistakes.

In another sense, errors are a very good thing. Many such errors present a learning opportunity. If you understand the cause of an error, you are less likely to repeat it, and even if you do repeat it, you can easily correct the error if you recognize it.

PHP error messages are not always displayed; it depends on your environment. Why are errors not always displayed? The simple answer is in a live environment, we don't want to display errors to our users. This shows both poor programming on our part and might even cause a security breach.

# Secure Programming

Error messages can sometimes display some of our code in an attempt to help us determine how to fix a syntax problem. For example, the error might show the locations or even userids and passwords to access our databases. A user is more likely to come back to our site if a "temporarily unavailable" message is displayed instead of an error indicating the system crashed.

**Note**   By default, the setup file for PHP sets the display of all errors to on. In a live environment, we would need to turn this parameter off by modifying its setting in the *php.ini* configuration file.

If you are creating programs in an environment in which you do not have access to the php.ini file, the display of errors might be turned off. In this situation, you can include the following two lines of PHP at the beginning of your scripts to display all error messages.

```
error_reporting( E_ALL );
ini_set( "display_errors", 1 );
```

All example programs shown in this book will not include these statements, as we are assuming you are creating code in a test environment in which all errors can be displayed.

**Hint**   Learn the location of the *log files* created in your LAMP, WAMP, or MAMP stack. On occasion, some errors that are not directly related to your program code may be listed in these files. If your program does not execute and seems to also not produce an error, the actual error might be in a log file.

Let's produce an error.

***Listing 2-4.*** test4.php

```
<?php

//here comes the error
echo "This string never ends;
?>
```

Do you see the error? PHP might not display the error, but there is a problem. There is only one string delimiter (double quote). To write valid PHP, we must wrap our strings in string delimiters. In the preceding example, since the end delimiter is missing, PHP cannot see where the output ends. If we run the code, we might see the following error message in our browser.

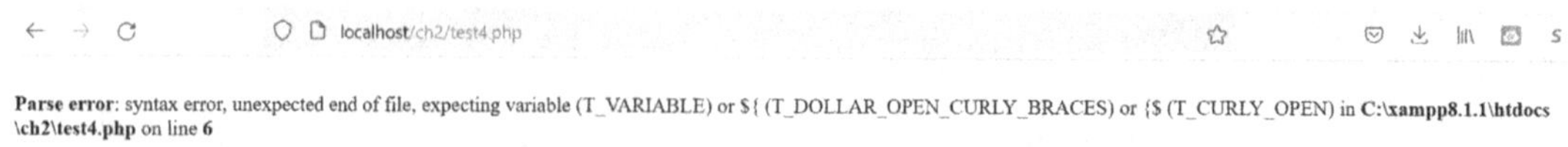

← → C          ○ ⅅ localhost/ch2/test4.php                                  ☆         ☺ ⤓ ⍟ ⬚ s

**Parse error**: syntax error, unexpected end of file, expecting variable (T_VARIABLE) or ${ (T_DOLLAR_OPEN_CURLY_BRACES) or {$ (T_CURLY_OPEN) in **C:\xampp8.1.1\htdocs \ch2\test4.php** on line **6**

***Figure 2-4.***  *test4.php error*

Error messages are friendly but not always as precise as you might prefer. When PHP is unable to process code, an error is triggered. The previous message clearly does not point out that a double quote is missing in the code. PHP will make an educated guess about what the problem might be. In the example, PHP has encountered an "unexpected end of file" on line 6. But wait, the error was on line 4, not line 6! Why did it miss the correct line? Remember that the starting delimiter indicates the start of a string; the interpreter will assume everything after the double quote is a string until it finds another one. However, it never finds another double quote. It is assuming that the rest of the code, including ?>, is part of the string. Thus, it complains about the program ending too soon before the string was complete.

---

**Hint**    When working with error messages, if you do not see an error in the line indicated by the message, check one or more lines above the line indicated. You probably forgot to include a double quote or a semicolon.

---

**Exercise**: Return to the example programs we have covered previously in this chapter. Adjust the programs to remove or change code to cause errors. Run the programs to discover what error messages will display. You might want to even keep a list of error messages and possible problems in a text file, for reference, while you are learning PHP. Being familiar with the most common errors and possible solutions will greatly increase your time used to debug programs.

If you encounter an error message you don't understand, search the Internet for an explanation. A site such as `www.stackoverflow.com` is very likely to have an explanation for your particular error message. Someone in this world has had the same error as your program produced. There are many free sites and blogs that will help you determine a solution.

# Creating an HTML5 Page with PHP

PHP is a wonderful language for creating dynamic HTML pages. With a tiny bit of PHP, we can create a valid HTML5 page with variable content in memory and have PHP output the created page to the browser.

## HTML Review

HTML requires a few tags to be properly formatted. Additional tags are available in html5 to organize the information in a more logical design.

```
<!DOCTYPE html>
<html>
<head>
<title>Page Title</title>
<meta http-equiv='Content-Type' content='text/html;charset=utf-8'/>
</head>
<body>
<p> The page body </p>
</body>
</html>
```

All HTML must exist between the opening (<html>) and closing (</html>) tags. After the opening tag, a head section (<head></head>) should be included to provide the title of the page (<title></title>) and other page information. The actual HTML tags used to display contents of a web page are placed between the body tags (<body></body>). The <p></p> tags will display the string in paragraph form.

For additional details on these HTML tags, visit one of the free online tutorial sites, such as w3schools.com.

We will use this basic HTML structure to create a bare-bones skeleton for a personal portfolio site. Let's create index.php with the code shown in Listing 2-5.

***Listing 2-5.*** index.php

```
<?php

$title = "Test title";
$content = "<h1>Hello World</h1>";
```

```php
$page = "
<!DOCTYPE html>
<html>
<head>
<title>$title</title>
<meta http-equiv='Content-Type' content='text/html;charset=utf-8'/>
</head>
<body>
$content
</body>
</html>";

echo $page;
?>
```

This index.php program includes three variables: $title, $content, and $page. The first two set information within the HTML provided in $page. The only actual instruction that sends information to the browser is the final echo statement. This statement sends all the HTML tags within $page to be interpreted, producing the output shown in Figure 2-5a.

# Hello World

***Figure 2-5a.*** *index.php output*

```
←   →   C                    🔒  view-source:http://localhost/ch2/index.php

 1
 2  <!DOCTYPE html>
 3  <html>
 4  <head>
 5  <title>Test title</title>
 6  <meta http-equiv='Content-Type' content='text/html;charset=utf-8'/>
 7  </head>
 8  <body>
 9  <h1>Hello World</h1>
10  </body>
11  </html>
```

***Figure 2-5b.*** *index.php source code*

When we view the *source code* produced in the browser (Figure 2-5b), we discover a well-formed HTML5 page with a title and a heading. It's a good habit to inspect the source code of your PHP-generated HTML pages. Any HTML errors are usually highlighted by the browser in the source view.

# Including a Simple Page Template

Creating a valid HTML5 page with PHP is a very, very common task. Let's try to create the same output in a way that's easier to reuse in other projects. If you can reuse your code in other projects, you can develop solutions faster and more efficiently. We will keep the HTML5 page template in a separate file.

We will create a new folder called `templates` in our existing PHP project. The PHP file `page.php` will be placed in the templates folder, containing the code shown in Listing 2-6.

***Listing 2-6.*** page.php

```php
<?php
$page=
 "<!DOCTYPE html>
<html>
<head>
<title>$title</title>
<meta http-equiv='Content-Type' content='text/html;charset=utf-8'/>
```

51

```
</head>
<body>
$content
</body>
</html>";
?>
```

The page.php file contains only the $page variable seen in Listing 2-6. The other two variables and the echo statement will exist in the newindex.php file.

# Including the Template

Our template is our first entry into our library. A *library* is a set of existing code that can be reused in other programs. To use the template in the newindex.php file, we will need to pull it into the program. PHP provides four instructions that can access information from a library.

> *include*: This instruction attempts to insert the code from a library file from within the calling program. If the library file does not exist, the command will not raise an error. If an attempt to insert the same library file occurs more than once in the program, the instruction will not raise an error.

> *include_once*: This instruction will attempt to insert the library file code. If the library file does not exist, it will not raise an error. However, if the same program attempts to insert the same library file more than once, it will not include it again.

> *require*: When an attempt is made to include a nonexisting library file, this instruction will raise an error. However, if more than one attempt is made in the same program to include the same library file, it will not raise an error.

> *require_once*: Attempting to use a nonexisting library file or attempting to use an existing library file more than once in the same program, it will not include it again.

Our program will not work properly if the page.php file does not exist. Logically, we will use either the require or require_once instruction because the contents are required. Since our program is short, we don't need to be concerned about an attempt to use the page.php file more than once. It would be harmless, anyway, because the library file would just reset the $page variable to the same contents we are already using. We can safely use the require command.

# Secure Programming

As we are learning the basics of PHP, we should always attempt to create *secure programs*. The programmer should take the time to select the most secure option when including library files. There is always a chance that the file might be missing. Will a missing library file make the program inoperable? If so, use one of the require instructions. Otherwise, use one of the include instructions. If including the library file more than once in a program will cause potential harm to the outcome of the program, use one of the commands with the once option. Currently, with our programming skills, any error raised will be displayed in the browser. This example would not be considered safe for a live site. We will learn how to handle errors in a more professional manner in a later chapter.

Why not just use require_once or require for every attempt to pull in a library file?

The answer is efficiency. Using require_once causes multiple checking for an existing file and for the use of the file used more than once. If this is not required, we are adding unnecessary commands into our program. Always keep an eye out for efficiency, as we want to develop programs that execute correctly as quickly as possible.

*Listing 2-7.* newindex.php

```php
<?php
//complete code for index.php
$title = "Test title";
$content = "<h1>Hello World</h1>";
//indicate the relative path to the file to include
require "templates/page.php";
echo $page;
?>
```

The newindex.php file is now a very short program. The program now sets the $title and $content variables, pulls in the code from the page.php file, and echoes out its contents. The output of the preceding code will be identical to that from the previous program. There are no functional changes, but there are some aesthetic changes in code architecture. A reusable *page template* is now kept in a separate file. We're really splitting different parts of the code into different files. The result is that more of the code becomes readily reusable in other projects. This process of separating different parts is also known as *separation of concerns.*

# Commenting Your Code

You should always place *comments* (nonexecutable text) in your programs. Such comments should remind you what the code does and why. In the real world, you will be creating hundreds of programs. If changes need to be made to an existing program, comments can help the programmer quickly determine the logical design. Even if you created the program years ago, you would appreciate the reminder of how the program is designed. Many companies also require comments which include a description of what the program will accomplish, a list of the inputs and outputs, the creator, and information on any changes to the program since its first release.

---

**Note**    We are using a limited number of comments in this book to reduce the number of printed pages. This is not to be construed as an indication that comments are not important. They are very important!

---

## Block and Single-Line Comments

In PHP, we must clearly delimit comments, so PHP will not try to interpret comments as if they were actual production code. Let's look at two ways of writing code comments in PHP: *block* and *single-line comments.*

```php
<?php
//this is a single-line comment
/*
This is a comment block
It may span across
```

```
several lines
*/
?>
```

Single-line comments begin with //. The comments exist in just one line. Of course, we can include additional // to add several lines of comments. However, the block format allows you to use an opening delimiter, /*, and a closing delimiter, */. With the block format, several lines of comments can be included without repeating // on each line.

## Avoiding Naming Conflicts

Programs can contain hundreds of lines of code. These programs will use many variables, and each one must be named uniquely and meaningfully. It is easy to make the mistake of accidentally reusing a variable in PHP. Since variables are created and updated using similar instructions, a program could replace data existing within a variable by mistake. We need to avoid potential name conflicts, so this does not occur.

---

**Note**    In languages that declare variables before they can be used, an error would be raised if there is another attempt to declare the variable. PHP does not require variables to be declared and does not raise an error if the variable is reused by accident. However, efficient programs can reuse variables, by design, rather than using unnecessary memory to create additional variables.

---

```php
<?php
$title = "Welcome to my blog";
/*
hundreds lines of code later
*/
$title = "Web developer";
```

Do you see a problem with the preceding code? Initially, a variable named $title is used to indicate the value of an HTML page's <title> element. Much later in the same program, a variable also named $title is used to store a job title. This can especially occur when importing library files into an existing program. The library file might

55

contain variable names that are the same as used in the calling program. The *namespace* instruction can be used to separate portions of a program to avoid a potential conflict. This is especially useful for programs using many libraries.

**Exercise**: Go to the php.net website and search for information on namespaces. You can also view videos on YouTube covering PHP namespaces. How can we adjust the example programs shown to use namespaces instead of an object?

We can also avoid a naming conflict by creating an *object*. In *object-oriented programming*, an object can include multiple variables (*properties*) and functions (*methods* – blocks of code). For example, an object can contain information about where we live and the ability to generate directions to drive to the location. A *class*, which declares the contents of the object, is similar to a blueprint for a house. The blueprint provides many details about the house, but it is not an actual house. The actual house must be built following the blueprints. Then the house exists. For an object to exist in programming, it must be declared (using a class) and then an instance must be created (using the new keyword). The instance of a class is the object. The object exists within memory (with its own variables and blocks of code) for the calling program to use. When the object is no longer needed, it can be released within the program itself. All existing objects will automatically be released when a program ends.

```php
<?php
$pageData = new StdClass();
$pageData->title = "Welcome to my blog";
/*
hundreds lines of code later
*/

$jobData = new StdClass();
$jobData->title = "Web developer";
?>
```

Without digging too deep into object-oriented programming, after all this is only Chapter 2, we can easily create an object to hold multiple values. We will use PHP's native *StdClass* class to do so. In the preceding code example, we see two different objects, each with a title property. The new keyword is used to create the objects from the existing class. In this example, $pageData and $jobData are created from the

StdClass. Each object then creates a title variable (property) within itself. `$pageData->title` creates its own separate title property. Later in this program, the instruction `$jobData->title` creates a different title property for $jobData.

The object provides a context, and that will make it easier for us to use the right title in the right place in our code. We can use objects to organize our code into meaningful units that belong together. We could say that an object and its properties are much like a folder and the files inside.

---

**Note**   For developing a quick list of variables (properties) which are associated with a specific name (object), stdClass is useful. However, it is not as efficient as arrays, because it creates unnecessary object code for this type of task. It also does not allow the creation of set and get routines which can increase the objects data security and reliability. Later in the chapter, we will create our own class and object which will allow us more control over the data, its accessibility, and its reliability. Using objects in your code is a de facto standard for dealing with complexity in systems, without introducing unnecessary complexity in your code. We will learn much more about programming with objects throughout the book.

---

## The Object Operator

To get values from an object property, we must specify two things: which object and which of its properties to get. To that end, we can use PHP's *object operator*. The general syntax is as follows:

```
$objectName->propertyName;
```

PHP's object operator looks like an arrow. It indicates that you are using a particular property (indicated on the right side) from inside a specific object (indicated on the left side). We can alternatively use *dot notation*. As stated before, be consistent, pick a style that you are comfortable using, and use the same style throughout your program.

**Exercise**: Go to php.net and research the use of dot notation in PHP. Adjust our previous coding example to use dot notation instead of the object operator. Which style do you prefer? Why?

# Using a StdClass Object for Page Data

Let's refactor newindex.php and the page template with an object to prevent annoying naming conflicts. Here is the newerindex.php file.

***Listing 2-8.*** newerindex.php

```php
<?php
//complete code for index.php
$pageData = new stdClass();
$pageData->title = "New, object-oriented test title";
$pageData->content = "<h1>Hello from an object</h1>";
require "templates/newerpage.php";
echo $page;
?>
```

We will also need to update page.php, so it uses the newly created object and its properties in the right places. We will now call it newerpage.php.

***Listing 2-9.*** newerpage.php

```php
<?php
$page = "<!DOCTYPE html>
<html>
<head>
<title>$pageData->title</title>
<meta http-equiv='Content-Type' content='text/html;charset=utf-8' />
</head>
<body>
$pageData->content
</body>
</html>";
?>
```

Load newerindex.php in your browser. You should expect to see the changed values in the <title> and <body> elements. However, all other display and source code is unchanged.

# Page Views

A personal portfolio site is likely to have a few different pages. Perhaps one page about skills and educational background, and another page with links to examples of work.

Because we are making a dynamic website, we will use our template to display pages for the portfolio. We actually are not creating multiple pages; we are creating multiple *page views*. A page view is something that looks like an individual page. One page view may be composed of several smaller views. We could think of a page view as a Lego house and a view as a Lego brick: the smaller parts are combined to build something bigger. Where did I put that Lego pirate ship anyway?

Remember, one key to successful programming is to stay organized. With that in mind, we will keep all views in one folder. Let's create a new folder called `views` inside the existing project folder. We will also create a new file, skills.php, saved in the views folder, with the contents shown in Listing 2-10.

***Listing 2-10.*** skills.php

```php
<?php
$info= "<h1>Skills and educational background</h1>
<p>Read all about my skills and my formal training</p>
";
?>
```

We only need to include any information we want displayed in the file. The template will do all the other work. The complete file is a quite small view at this point. It is often a good idea to begin small when you are developing code. Any error that might creep in will be easier to spot in fewer lines of code. Let's also create another small view (file) containing project information.

***Listing 2-11.*** projects.php

```php
<?php
$info= "<h1>Projects I have worked on</h1>
<ul>
<li>Ahem, this will soon be updated</li>
</ul>";
?>
```

# HTML Review

In Listing 2-10, the HTML tag <h1> is introduced. This tag, along with other similar tags, displays header text for logically dividing information in a web page. Figure 2-6 provides a display of some of the most popular header tag sizes.

# This is an h1 heading

## This is an h2 heading

### This is an h3 heading

#### This is an h4 heading

*Figure 2-6.*  *headers.php output*

In Listing 2-11, the <ul> tag creates an unordered list (not numbered). The <li> tag is used to create the individual list items. Listing 2-12 provides an additional example of an unordered list.

*Listing 2-12.*  unorderedlist.php

```
<html>
<head>
<title>An unordered list</title>
</head>
<body>
<ul>
Food I like To Eat
<li>Pizza</li>
<li>Snails</li>
<li>Lizards</li>
</ul>
</body>
</html>
```

The results of executing this HTML will produce the display shown in Figure 2-7.

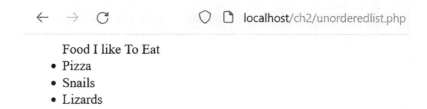

**Figure 2-7.** *unorderedlist.php output*

There are many additional options for both the header tags and lists. For more information, visit a free tutorial website, such as w3schools.com.

## Making a Dynamic Site Navigation

We must display the correct view at the right time. We can make a global, *persistent site navigation*, i.e., a navigation that will be the same on every page of the website, with just a few lines of code. Because PHP can include files, we can store the code for the navigation in one file and include it in every script that needs it. An advantage to saving it as a separate file is the ability to change the navigation in that one file, and the change automatically be reflected on every site page, however many pages exist. Let's create our new file, navigation.php, in the views folder, with the code shown in Listing 2-13.

**Listing 2-13.** navigation.php

```php
<?php
$nav= "
<nav>
    <a href='newindexnav.php?page=skills'>My skills and background</a>
    <a href='newindexnav.php?page=projects'>Some projects</a>
</nav>
";
?>
```

The entire navigation string is delimited with double quotes. We use single quotes to delimit the href attribute values. Double quotes (or even single quotes) cannot be placed within other double quotes (or single quotes). This would confuse the interpreter. It would be unable to determine where a string begins and ends. Attempting to do so will cause an error.

# HTML Review

The HTML <nav> tag is used to identify any navigation within a page. The <a href> tag will create a hyperlink within a page. The page to be displayed is included after the equal sign, within the quotes. The text to click is placed between the actual tags. Additional information can be passed to the page being called using the *HTTP GET* method discussed in the following.

We now need to add the navigation to the newerindex.php file. We will rename this file indexnav.php.

***Listing 2-14.***  indexnav.php

```php
<?php
//complete code for index.php
include_once "views/navigation.php";
$pageData = new stdClass();
$pageData->title = "Thomas Blom Hansen: Portfolio site";
$pageData->content = $nav;
require "templates/newerpage.php";
echo $page;
?>
```

We are using include_once because while the navigation would make our page completely functional, if the navigation is missing, we could still display valuable information. Using the once option ensures that our navigation only appears once on the page, even if we mistakenly try to include the navigation file again. Let's save and run the code. We should see a page with a navigation. Don't expect to see any of the views just yet.

# Passing Information with PHP

The ability to pass data is what separates dynamic web pages from static ones. By customizing an experience based on the user's choices, we are able to add an entirely new level of value to a website.

We have two choices we can use to pass information: HTTP GET and HTTP POST.

*HTTP GET*: Information is passed by creating URL variables in the actual URL line. This does not require additional server memory but does expose the information passed to all users of the website.

*HTTP POST*: Information is passed to the server memory. The information can then be retrieved by the PHP program from memory. While we don't want to say that this information is more secure than HTTP variables, it is not displayed for every user to see. However, since this process uses server memory, for high-traffic websites, if possible, HTTP GET might be a better choice. For example, Google uses HTTP GET to pass search information as this is not secure information which in turn does not need to use server memory.

Since our information does not require high security measures, we will pass it to PHP through *URL variables* using the HTTP GET method. In Listing 2-13, we saw two URL variables in the navigation. Let's take a closer look at the href attributes in the navigation <a> elements.

```
newindexnav.php?page=skills
newindexnav.php?page=projects
```

The href indicates that clicking the navigation item will load newindexnav.php (this page will be created soon) and place the word skills or projects into a *URL variable* named page. If you click one link, the URL variable named page will get a value of skills. If you click the other link, page will get the value of projects.

Our PHP program can access the URL variable and use it to determine the right page view at the right time. URL variables are the lifeblood of dynamic sites.

# Accessing URL Variables

To access URL variables, we use the *$_GET superglobal array*. Here's how we will use it in our new program, newindexnav.php.

***Listing 2-15.*** newindexnav.php

```php
<?php
//complete code for index.php
include_once "views/navigation.php";
$pageData = new stdClass();
$pageData->title = "Thomas Blom Hansen: Portfolio site";
$pageData->content = $nav;
//changes begin here
$navigationIsClicked = isset($_GET['page']);
if ($navigationIsClicked ) {
    $fileToLoad = $_GET['page'];
    $pageData->content .= "<p>Will soon load $fileToLoad.php</p>";
}
//end of changes
require "templates/newerpage.php";
echo $page;
?>
```

The few lines added to the code actually accomplish quite a lot! We are using HTTP GET to access our URL variables. To access the value of the URL variable named page, we use the PHP instruction $_GET['page']. The value contained in page (skills or projects) is then saved into the variable $fileToLoad. Remember, this value is set depending on if the user clicked the link requesting the skills or projects. There will be a URL variable named page only when a user has clicked one of the navigation items.

# Using isset( ) to Test If a Variable Is Set

If we attempt to use a variable that does not exist, we will trigger a PHP error. So, before we try to access a variable, we should be sure that the variable is set. PHP has a language construct (isset()) to that end. We have already seen it in action.

# Secure Programming

It is easy to fall into the habit of assuming that everything is going to work properly in a program. Whenever a program is dependent on files that exist outside of a program, the program becomes vulnerable. The files (such as our library files) might be corrupted or might not exist. We need to program with the view that everything might not all fall into place and work properly. We need to check for missing or corrupted files and determine how to handle the situation. Depending on the program, it may require shutting the program down and asking the user to come back later or, if it's minor, allowing the user to continue with what does work in the program. Remember that programs also depend on users to do the right thing. In our program, we expect the user to click on a navigation link, which will load information into our URL variable, soon causing the proper information to be displayed. However, what happens if the user plays around with the URL line and attempts to load a different page or create a different URL variable? We must prepare for this possibility. Not all attempts to change what is expected are caused by a hackers attempt to change data but sometimes others do too. Expect the unexpected and prepare for it.

```
$navigationIsClicked = isset($_GET['page']);
```

The *isset()* function will return TRUE if the item inside the parentheses (page) is set. If a user has done what is expected and clicked a navigation item, $navigationIsClicked will be TRUE; if not, it will be FALSE.

---

**Note**    The item passed into $_GET does not include a dollar sign since it is not a PHP variable. It is a URL variable, which does not require a dollar sign.

---

```
if ($navigationIsClicked ) {
```

A *conditional statement* (*if statement*) will determine if the information contained in the parentheses is TRUE or FALSE. If $navigationIsClicked is TRUE, the if statement will execute any code contained within the curly brackets ({}).

```
$fileToLoad = $_GET['page'];
```

If True, the program will declare a PHP variable named $fileToLoad to store the value of the URL variable named page. Next, it will add a string to the $pageData->content property to display the value of the URL variable named page. Save and run the code. Once loaded in the browser, click the "My skills" navigation item. This action should produce the following output.

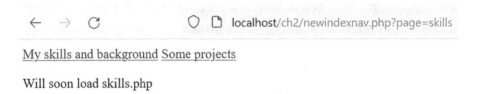

*Figure 2-8.*   *newindexnav.php output after skills link selected*

Click the other navigation item to see the output change. We are seeing that output changes dynamically, *according to how the user interacts* with the site.

What happens if the user does not click on a link or passes a different URL variable?

Nothing. The page remains unchanged. Even though our program is small, it still is able to handle these possible situations.

**Exercise**: Try to break the newindexnav.php program. A skilled programmer will continuously feed unexpected information into their program to try and catch all possible vulnerabilities. Once these weaknesses are identified, we can fix them. Did you find any in the program? If you did, then use your current knowledge to strengthen this example.

# $_GET, a Superglobal Array

PHP can access URL variables through a superglobal array called $_GET. PHP also includes other superglobal arrays for other uses. With $_GET, we can access URL variables by their name. In the navigation program, we have two <a> elements. Clicking either one will encode a unique value for a URL variable named page.

We can see a URL variable in the browser's address bar in Figure 2-8. Notice how the value of the URL variable page is represented in the output.

```
$pageData->content .= "<p>Will soon load $fileToLoad.php</p>";
```

To use the value of the URL variable in the information displayed on the page, we placed $fileToLoad in our string and added it to the content variable. You may not have noticed that there is a period right before the equal sign. The .= is a concatenation symbol which tells the interpreter to append the string to whatever is already in the variable content, which already contains some other information. When we echo the contents of $page, this appended information will be included in our output, as we have seen in Figure 2-8.

# Including Page Views Dynamically

The dynamic site navigation is nearly complete. It works perfectly, except that page views are not loaded when navigation items are clicked. Let's change that, by placing our updated code in newestindexnav.php.

***Listing 2-16.*** newestindexnav.php

```php
<?php
//complete code for index.php
include_once "views/newestnavigation.php";
$pageData = new stdClass();
$pageData->title = "Thomas Blom Hansen: Portfolio site";
$pageData->content = $nav;
//changes begin here
$navigationIsClicked = isset($_GET['page']);
if ($navigationIsClicked ) {
    $fileToLoad = $_GET['page'];
    include_once "views/$fileToLoad.php";
    $pageData->content .= $info;
}
//end of changes
require "templates/newerpage.php";
echo $page;
?>
```

---

**Note**   newestnavigation.php has been updated to link to the current version of the program.

---

Only two other changes have occurred in the newestindexnav.php program.

```
include_once "views/$fileToLoad.php";
$pageData->content .= $info;
```

The include statement loads the contents of the selected view (which populates the $info variable). The $info information is appended to the contents of $pageData.

My skills and background Some projects

# Skills and educational background

Read all about my skills and my formal training

*Figure 2-9.   newestindexnav.php after skills selected*

It works! This is a basic, dynamic site with a persistent, global navigation. Congratulations, together, we have accomplished a lot!

## Strict Naming Convention

It is great to see our first dynamic site working, isn't it? It depends on a *strict naming convention*. The navigation items encode different values for a URL variable named page. The corresponding page view file must be named identically and be saved inside the views folder. As long as we follow this convention, we can add additional pages with relative ease.

| Href | URL variable | view file |
| --- | --- | --- |
| newestindexnav.php?page=**skills** | page=**skills** | views/**skills.php** |
| newestindexnav.php?page=**projects** | page=**projects** | views/**projects.php** |

# Displaying a Default Page

The dynamic navigation works wonderfully, but it has one flaw: there is no default page view displayed when a user navigates to newestindexnav.php, in which case the URL variable named page does not have a value. It is easy to change this; we simply have to change the if statement a tiny bit.

***Listing 2-17.***  updatedindexnav.php – partial

```
//partial code for index.php
if ($navigationIsClicked ) {
    $fileToLoad = $_GET['page'];
} else {
    $fileToLoad = "skills";
}
    include_once "views/$fileToLoad.php";
    $pageData->content .= $info;
```

The program now includes an *if/else statement*. The code within the else statement is executed if the value checked in the if statement is FALSE. Thus, if a navigation link was not clicked by the user, the line of code contained in the else section would execute instead of the line in the if section. This allows the program to load a value into $fileToLoad from the URL variable page if that is set. If page is not set, $fileToLoad will have a default value of skills. Once $fileToLoad has a value, we can use it to load either the page view requested by a user or the default page view about "My skills."

# Securing the Program

We will make one more update to our PHP code to provide a more secure and stable program. The program depends on the existence of variables from our library files. $nav, $page, and $info are all populated with contents from various files. However, what if those variables do not exist?

***Listing 2-18.***  secureindexnav.php

```
<?php
//complete code for index.php
string $nav = "";
```

```php
string $info = "";
include_once "views/securenavigation.php";
$pageData = new stdClass();
$pageData->title = "Thomas Blom Hansen: Portfolio site";
$pageData->content = $nav;
//changes begin here
$navigationIsClicked = isset($_GET['page']);
if ($navigationIsClicked ) {
    $fileToLoad = $_GET['page'];
} else {
    $fileToLoad = "skills";
}
include_once "views/$fileToLoad.php";
$pageData->content .= $info;
require "templates/newerpage.php";
echo $page;
?>
```

---

**Note**    securenavigation.php has been updated to link to the current version of the program.

---

You might have thought that we would again use isset to check on the existence of the variables; we could. However, an easier way is to provide *default values* for $nav and $info. Both are created with a string data type and set to "" in Listing 2-18 to provide a holder for future information. $page was already given a default value earlier. Now our program can handle situations in which these variables might be missing due to corruption or missing information. A more stable program for sure.

# Validating Your HTML

The process of generating HTML pages is a bit abstract. It is easy to assume that everything is perfect if the right page view is displayed at the right time. If you see the right action, your PHP script works perfectly. But that does not mean your HTML is perfectly valid. Remember that any contents within the echo text strings are treated as a nonexecutable string by the PHP interpreter. Thus, the interpreter does not check the validity of any code (HTML) within the string.

How can we check our HTML contents?

Remember, dynamic web pages should conform to web standards, just as static HTML pages should.

---

**Note**   You could load a dynamic page in your browser and view the generated HTML source code through your browser. When you see the generated HTML source code, you can select it all, copy it, and paste it into an online HTML validation service, such as `http://validator.w3.org/`, to determine if the code is valid.

---

# Styling the Site with CSS

When the HTML of all page views validates, we can start styling our site with CSS. We add CSS exactly as we would normally style a static HTML site: create an external style sheet with style rules for the visual design of our site. Using an external page will allow us to attach the CSS to all pages within the website, providing a consistent feel and look. To do that for the portfolio site, we will create a new folder called `css` in our project folder. Then we will create a new file called `layout.css` in the `css` folder.

***Listing 2-19.*** layout.css

```
nav {
    background-color: #CCCCDE;
    padding-top: 10px;
}
nav a{
    display:inline-block;
    text-decoration:none;
    color: #000;
    margin-left: 10px;
}
nav a:hover{text-decoration: underline;}
```

# CSS Review

The CSS nav tags define the area of navigation as defined by the <nav> HTML tags in our pages. The background color displays a light gray. The padding setting provides a small amount of space padding above the navigation menu. "Nav a" defines the look and feel of the link itself. It translates the display into an inline block, which creates a block (box) for the links, instead of the original text links. The text itself is unchanged (text-decoration: none). The color is set to black (#000). Space is provided between each link as specified with the margin-left setting.

For more information on CSS, review the free tutorials on the Web, such as www.w3schools.com, or a free video series on YouTube.

You can change or add any style rules you prefer. The preceding css is just to get us started. We will style all our dynamic HTML pages, so let's build this functionality into the page template. We will add one new placeholder for <link> elements pointing to external style sheets.

***Listing 2-20.*** pagewithcss.php

```php
<?php
$page= "<!DOCTYPE html>
<html>
<head>
<title>$pageData->title</title>
<meta http-equiv='Content-Type' content='text/html;charset=utf-8' />
$pageData->css
</head>
<body>
$pageData->content
</body>
</html>";
?>
```

The new property css is used as placeholder for <link> elements referencing external style sheets. To use the updated page template, we must update our index file and declare a value for the new property.

***Listing 2-21.*** indexwithcss.php

```php
<?php
//complete code for index.php
string $nav = "";
string $info = "";
include_once "views/cssnavigation.php";
$pageData = new stdClass();
$pageData->title = "Thomas Blom Hansen: Portfolio site";
$pageData->css = "<link href='css/layout.css' rel='stylesheet' />";
$pageData->content = $nav;
$navigationIsClicked = isset($_GET['page']);
if ($navigationIsClicked ) {
    $fileToLoad = $_GET['page'];
} else {
    $fileToLoad = "skills";
}
include_once "views/$fileToLoad.php";
$pageData->content .= $info;
require "templates/pagewithcss.php";
echo $page;
?>
```

---

**Note**    cssnavigation.php has been updated to link to the current version of the program.

---

**$pageData->css = "<link href='css/layout.css' rel='stylesheet' />";**

The css variable in $pageData is set to a link which will attach the external style sheet. The output is shown in Figure 2-10.

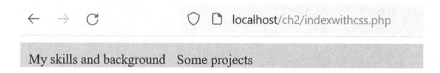

**Skills and educational background**

Read all about my skills and my formal training

***Figure 2-10.*** *indexwithcss.php output*

**Exercise**: Adjust the CSS file to create a better-looking navigation bar which is more pleasing to the user.

# Declaring a Page_Data Class

Sometimes, it can be quite useful to use internal CSS to supplement external style sheets. We can easily update the page template with a placeholder for a `<style>` element.

***Listing 2-22.*** pagewithstyle.php

```php
<?php
$page= "<!DOCTYPE html>
<html>
<head>
<title>$pageData->title</title>
<meta http-equiv='Content-Type' content='text/html;charset=utf-8' />
$pageData->css
$pageData->embeddedStyle
</head>
<body>
$pageData->content
</body>
</html>";
?>
```

We can declare a property value from `indexwithcss.php`, but let's do something different. The problem is that sometimes you don't need any embedded `<style>` element and sometimes you do.

Now that our template has a placeholder for embedded CSS, that property must always have a value. We don't want to waste time declaring a value for a redundant `<style>` element, so let's make a more intelligent solution. Let's take the next step toward object-oriented programming and create a *custom class* for page data. We will create a new folder called `classes` in our project folder. Then let's create a new file called `Page_Data.class.php` in this folder.

***Listing 2-23.***  Page_Data.class.php

```php
<?php
class Page_Data {
    public string $title = "";
    public string $content = "";
    public string $css = "";
    public string $embeddedStyle = "";
}
 ?>
```

# Program Design and Logic

We have saved the class information in a file with the ending class.php. There is nothing magical about this file ending. However, by including the class name in the file ending, it makes it more apparent that a stand-alone class is contained in the file. Also note that the file name begins with a capital letter. This is also a common style to indicate that it is a class file. PHP does not care what file name is used. However, it is a good programming technique to use common practices that the industry uses for identification.

The class structure is defined with the lowercase word class. The class name (Page_Data) is an exact match for the file name containing the class. Class names should match file names. Variables (properties) and methods used by the class are created between the curly brackets. We created this class with predefined empty string values for those properties required by the page template. We have declared each string with the string data type. This declaration will help increase security within our program by only allowing strings to be saved. In later chapters, we will increase the security of our classes by setting access to private and use get and set methods to update values. The use of declared class within our program, rather than using stdClass, provides us the ability to protect the data we are storing.

# Classes Make Objects

We can use the new class definition in the index file. It will require a tiny change.

***Listing 2-24.*** indexwithclass.php

```php
<?php
//complete code for index.php
string $nav = "";
string $info = "";
include_once "views/classnavigation.php";
include_once "classes/Page_Data.class.php";
$pageData = new Page_Data();
$pageData->title = "Thomas Blom Hansen: Portfolio site";
$pageData->css = "<link href='css/layout.css' rel='stylesheet' />";
$pageData->content = $nav;
$navigationIsClicked = isset($_GET['page']);
if ($navigationIsClicked ) {
    $fileToLoad = $_GET['page'];
} else {
    $fileToLoad = "skills";
}
include_once "views/$fileToLoad.php";
$pageData->content .= $info;
require "templates/pagewithcss.php";
echo $page;
?>
```

The stdClass has been removed and replaced with the Page_Data class. If we load indexwithclass.php into our browser, we will discover that the outcome is the same as we discovered in Figure 2-10. The results are the same, but the program has become more secure.

The Page_Data class enables us to keep a placeholder for embedded styles in the page template and only assign an actual value to that property whenever we need a page with an embedded <style> element.

## Highlighting Current Navigation Item with a Dynamic Style Rule

We have created a page template and a Page_Data object, each with embedded styles. We kept common styles used throughout a web page in an external style sheet. But there are a few cases in which dynamic styles on individual pages are quite powerful.

**Exercise**: We could use a dynamic style rule to highlight the current navigation item. Review your CSS skills and adjust the indexwithclass program to include a dynamic internal style sheet which highlights the current navigation selected on the menu, and use the embeddedStyle property to save and interpret the new CSS code.

## Summary

We have discovered how to use a little basic PHP to build a very dynamic site. Your learning process will probably benefit from a bit of experimenting at this point. Try attempting some of the project suggestions at the end of this chapter. In the next chapter, we will learn about HTML forms, PHP functions, and more details on conditional statements.

## Projects

1. Complete the personal portfolio site from this chapter. Add however many page views you see fit and update your navigation accordingly.

2. Create some more comprehensive, detailed page views. In the process, you should gradually become more comfortable with the dynamic site structure and how page views are returned to be displayed in the index file.

3.  Use your existing CSS skills to develop a consistent website design
    for the portfolio. It will be a very good exercise to use your existing
    HTML and CSS skills in this new context of dynamic sites. It is a
    good idea to do this exercise while the site you are working on
    is simple.

# CHAPTER 3

# Form Management

## Objectives

After completing this chapter, you will be able to

- Create and use HTML forms

- Use superglobal arrays

- Encode URL variables with HTML forms using the GET method

- Encode URL variables with HTML forms using the POST method

- Create a dynamic PHP quiz program

- Use if-else conditional statements

- Create and use named functions

- Create secure classes and objects using constructors, setters, and getters

- Understand how an American western film can teach you about clean code

- Discover why code really is poetry

In Chapter 2, we built a dynamic, personal portfolio site. In the process, we saw how to encode URL variables with <a> elements and how to access such URL variables using the $_GET superglobal. Passing data is what separates dynamic web pages from static ones. By customizing an experience based on the user's choices, we are able to add an entirely new level of value to a website.

© Jason Lengstorf, Thomas Blom Hansen, Steve Prettyman 2022
J. Lengstorf et al., *PHP 8 for Absolute Beginners*, https://doi.org/10.1007/978-1-4842-8205-2_3

Now that we have seen a little PHP and written a basic dynamic site, we are ready to go deeper into URL variables. HTML `<form>` elements are commonly used to create interfaces that allow users to interact with a dynamic site. If you have spent any time on the Web, you have used an HTML form to submit information. To create an interactive website, we need to learn how to create and use these HTML forms.

# What Are Forms?

HTML forms allow visitors to interact and provide information on a website. Figure 3-1 shows Google's search form. When a user visits `www.google.com`, types a search term into the text input field, and then clicks Google Search, Google will perform the requested search.

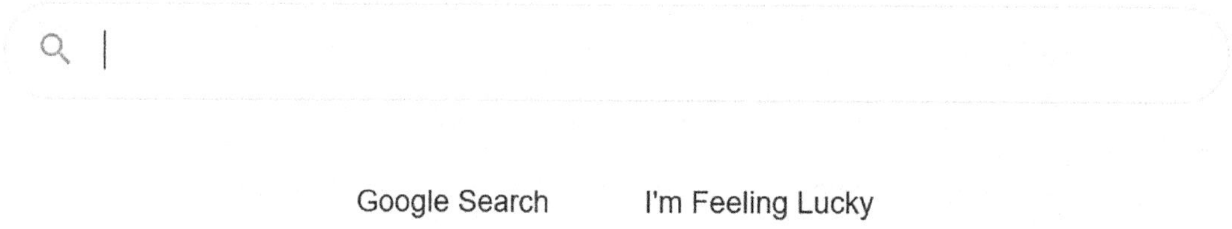

Google Search          I'm Feeling Lucky

*Figure 3-1.* *Search form from* `www.google.com`

Another kind of form you probably have come across is a login form, through which registered users can log in and enter a restricted area. You may have seen such forms when you log in to your Facebook account, your bank account, or your Gmail account. The login in Figure 3-2 is from Facebook.

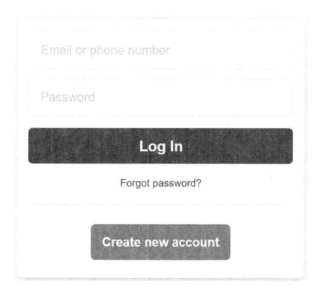

***Figure 3-2.***  *Login form from* www.facebook.com

A final familiar example could be the star rating system. You may have come across a star rating system when you bought a book from an online bookstore. Figure 3-3 shows the star rating form from Amazon.

**Overall rating**

**Add a headline**

What's most important to know?

**Add a photo or video**

Shoppers find images and videos more helpful than text alone.

***Figure 3-3.***  *Star rating form from* www.amazon.com

If you are going to work as a web developer or web designer, you will develop and design usable, functional forms. Web forms are the interface between a system and its users; developing and designing web forms is extremely important.

# Setting Up a New PHP Project

Let's create a new project folder called ch3 in the XAMPP/htdocs folder to hold all the work we will accomplish in this chapter. Inside ch3, we will need copies of the templates and classes folders, and the PHP scripts, from Chapter 2. We can copy these from our Chapter 2 folder or by downloading them from the publisher's website. We also need to create an empty folder called views.

Let's add a basic PHP template for the index.php file. Notice that we are reusing classes/Page_Data.class.php and templates/page.php, from Chapter 2, without changing a single line of code inside either script. Efficient and effective programmers reuse library files within their programs. Whether the files were provided by PHP or created by the programmer (or someone else in a corporation), stable and secure programs can be developed with more efficiency and speed by reusing code that is known to be reliable. Just solve it once; don't reinvent the wheel over and over again!

***Listing 3-1.*** index.php

```php
<?php
//complete code for index.php
include_once "classes/Page_Data.class.php";
$pageData = new Page_Data();
$pageData->title = "Building and processing HTML forms with PHP";;
$pageData->content = "<nav>will soon show a navigation...</nav>";
$pageData->content .= "<div>...and a form here</div>";
require "templates/pagewithcss.php";
echo $page;
?>
```

# Seeing for Yourself

To check if everything has been entered correctly, save the index.php and navigate using a browser to http://localhost/ch3/index.php. The expected output is shown in Figure 3-4.

will soon show a navigation...
...and a form here

***Figure 3-4.*** *Output of index.php*

**Exercise**: There is no Zen master to prod you with a stick but see if you can answer these questions. Your answers will indicate what you have learned so far. If you're in doubt, you can consult Chapter 2 for explanations.

- What does `include_once` do?

- How can `$pageData->title` change the `<title>` of the generated HTML page?

- What does `.=` mean? What is the technical name for it?

- What happens when we `echo $page`?

# Creating a Dynamic Navigation

We will be creating two different forms. Thus, we will require a site menu to navigate between these forms. Let's create a new file, `ch3/views/navigation.php`, with the following code.

***Listing 3-2.*** navigation.php

```php
<?php
$nav= "
<nav>
    <a href='index.php?page=search'>Search on bing</a>
    <a href='index.php?page=quiz'>Dynamic quiz</a>
</nav>
";
?>
```

Notice that the code we are using for navigation is very similar to the code used in Chapter 2. We only changed the pages and the strings to be displayed in the navigation. Now let's add the code required to display this navigation in the index file.

***Listing 3-3.*** indexwithnavigation.php

```php
<?php
//complete code for index.php
include_once "views/navigation.php";
include_once "classes/Page_Data.class.php";
$pageData = new Page_Data();
$pageData->title = "Building and processing HTML forms with PHP";
$pageData->content = $nav;
$pageData->content .= "<div>...and a form here</div>";
require "templates/pagewithcss.php";
echo $page;
?>
```

The output is not pretty, yet. But we are making progress. We now have a new index page with navigation by using similar code to what we learned in Chapter 2.

***Figure 3-5.*** *Output from indexwithnavigation.php*

# Creating Page Views for the Form

We can follow the naming convention from Chapter 2, because it provides a solid code architecture for dynamic websites. This way of organizing and naming page views can give us a mental framework for building dynamic sites. When we have the framework internalized, we'll know which files we need to develop for the site. We don't need to reinvent a good dynamic architecture every time we make a new site.

The navigation described in the preceding section has links to pages called *search* and *quiz*. So, we will have to create two new PHP files in the views folder.

| Href | url variable | view file |
|---|---|---|
| index.php?page = **search** | page = **search** | views/**search**.php |
| index.php?page = **quiz** | page = **quiz** | views/**quiz**.php |

Let's create the two new files as follows.

***Listing 3-4.*** search.php

```php
<?php
$info= "will soon show the search form";
?>
```

***Listing 3-5.*** quiz.php

```php
<?php
$info= "quiz will go here";
?>
```

Very simple code. But enough to help us start testing our navigation.

## Displaying Page Views on the Index Page

To display these page views when requested, we have to write a few extra lines of code almost identical to those we wrote in the index file for Chapter 2. The only changes from the Chapter 2 project are the use of the quiz and search views. Professional programmers develop a style of coding and stick with that style to increase reliability, security, and code development time.

***Listing 3-6.*** indexwithclass.php

```php
<?php
//complete code for index.php
$nav = "";
$info = "";
include_once "views/classnavigation.php";
include_once "classes/Page_Data.class.php";
$pageData = new Page_Data();
```

```php
$pageData->title = "Building and processing HTML forms with PHP";
$pageData->content = $nav;
$pageData->content .= "<div>...and a form here</div>";
$navigationIsClicked = isset($_GET['page']);
if ($navigationIsClicked ) {
    $fileToLoad = $_GET['page'];
} else {
    $fileToLoad = "search";
}
include_once "views/$fileToLoad.php";
$pageData->content .= $info;
require "templates/pagewithcss.php";
echo $page;
?>
```

The page will now load any view requested by a user. If no navigation item is clicked, it will display views/search.php. We can test our code by loading http://localhost/ch3/indexwithclass.php in a browser.

***Figure 3-6.***  *Output from indexwithclass.php*

# Program Design and Logic

Reusing code is a good idea, because this allows the programmer to develop solutions much faster, more reliable, and more secure. If you have scripts that work in one project that has been well tested, you can trust them to do the same in other projects. Hence, code reuse decreases debugging time and speeds up development time.

There will always be parts you can't easily reuse, such as the navigation. But if you get into the habit of creating dynamic navigations in much the same way across different projects, you'll be able to develop new dynamic navigations quickly and painlessly. So, when you can't reuse code as is, you can still reuse the principles underpinning the code that is already tested and reliable.

# A Simple Search Form

HTML forms are created with the `<form>` element. There are a number of other HTML elements that are made specifically for forms. Perhaps the most essential one is the `<input>` element to accept values from the user. Let's create a short form as follows.

*Listing 3-7.* simplesearch.php

```php
<?php
$info= "<form method='get' action='http://www.bing.com/search'>
<input type='text' name='q' />
<input type='submit' value='search on bing' />
</form>";
?>
```

**Note**   The navigation (simplenavigation.php) and index (simpleindex.php) files were also updated to use the simple search form. Take some time to view the changes to these files.

Let's test our new search form by calling it from simpleindex.php.

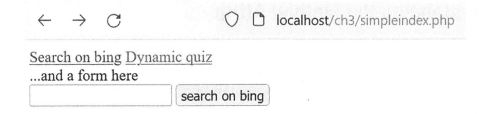

*Figure 3-7.* *Output from simpleindex.php*

We can type a search string in the text field and click the button. The browser will load `bing.com` because the action setting in the form tag will pass the information via the get command to the Bing search engine. Bing will perform a search for whatever we enter. If we type *cats* and click the search button, then "cats" is passed to Bing. After passing "cats," the URL for Bing will contain `www.bing.com/search?q=cats`.

As we have stated previously, search engines accept information via the get method to avoid using extra server memory when completing searches. Thus, Bing was expecting a URL variable and we provided it. Notice that Bing uses the variable q for the search information. Listing 3-7 shows that this variable is created with the text box from the simple search form.

---

**Note**    When using a form, clicking the Submit button will cause any GET or POST variables to be sent to the application on the web server listed in the action parameter. The application can then retrieve that information for its use. The application will execute within the web server, and the results of that execution will be sent to the user's browser to be displayed. In our example, the browser will display the results of Bing's search for cats.

---

# The <input> Element and Some Common Types

Did you notice that `<input type='text' />` displays as a single-line text field and that `<input type='submit'/>` displays as a Submit button? There are many possible values for the input `type` attribute. In this book, we will see a small handful of input types. Once you can work with those, you should have no problems learning how to use the remaining input types.

# Understanding the Method Attribute

So far, we have only seen variables that could be seen in the URL, in the browser's address bar. This kind of URL variable is encoded using the HTTP method `GET`. We have used such variables to create a dynamic navigation and a form that can perform a search at `www.bing.com`.

Any URL variable encoded with GET is limited to relatively few characters. The exact number varies from browser to browser. Because GET variables are evident from the URL, pages can be bookmarked and linked. Therefore, GET variables are perfectly suited for site navigation or in any situation in which server memory usage must be limited, such as websites with a lot of traffic. Too much dependence on the use of server memory can cause the server to quickly run out of memory and shut down. Not something you want to happen when your site is busy!

# Named PHP Functions

Perhaps one of the most powerful features of a programming language is the ability to define and execute functions. A *function* is a named block of code we declare within our scripts that we can call at any time.

# Program Design and Logic

Many new programmers assume that program code is executed from the top of the program, one instruction after the other, to the bottom of the program. However, this is not the case. Programs have many instructions that cause the flow to go a different path. For example, the if statement that we introduced in Chapter 2 will make a choice whether to execute the code within the first set of brackets or execute the code after an else statement. We say that the code jumps to the else structure or jumps over the else structure depending on whether the conditional statement was true or false.

The page object we have been using in our examples resides within its own location in memory. The program jumps to the page object whenever we use it and jumps back to the next instruction in the main code afterward. Functions cause a similar flow change. The program jumps to the function when called, executes the code within the function, and then returns to the main code afterward. We will soon discover other instructions that change our program flow.

# The Basic Syntax for Named Functions

Let's take a first look into the basics of named functions in PHP.

```
function functionName () {
```

```
    //function body
}
```

The syntax format of a function requires that we first declare the function using the function keyword and then create a function name to uniquely identify the function. Function names can contain any alphanumeric characters and underscores, but they must not start with a number. The function name is followed with a set of parentheses and a code block delimited by curly braces.

# Program Design and Logic

While we have the freedom to create function names in almost any format we choose, the goal is to create a program that is easy to read and understand. With this in mind, one standard way to declare function names is to use an action verb and a subject, such as getFirstName. By declaring functions using this standard, it is clear that this function will bring back the first name, without us having to look at the actual code. It is also common to use camel hump (first word lowercase, all other words uppercase). Some programmers will separate the words with an underscore, such as get_First_Name. Determine your own style and use it consistently throughout your programs.

Let's create a new PHP file which contains a function within our ch3 folder.

***Listing 3-8.*** testfunction.php

```php
<?php
function getParagraph(){
    echo "<p>This paragraph came from a function</p>";
}
?>
```

If we load http://localhost/ch3/testfunction.php into our browser, we will see no output. Many beginners would expect to see an output from the preceding code. But functions don't always behave as beginners assume. The code inside the function body will not be executed until the function name is explicitly *called*. We can add a function call in the new file testfunction.php to execute the code as follows.

90

***Listing 3-9.*** calltestfunction.php

```php
<?php
function getParagraph(){
    echo "<p>This paragraph came from a function</p>";
}
getParagraph();
?>
```

If we run this new file in a browser, we will see the expected output.

This paragraph came from a function

***Figure 3-8.***  *Output of calltestfunction.php*

A really interesting feature of functions is that they can be reused very easily. Simply call a function twice, and it runs twice. Let's do it.

***Listing 3-10.*** calltwicetestfunction.php

```php
<?php
function getParagraph(){
    echo "<p>This paragraph came from a function</p>";
}
getParagraph();
getParagraph();
?>
```

You can probably correctly guess that the code will output two `<p>` elements, each with the same text: `This paragraph came from a function`. What is more important is that we can see the difference between *function declarations* and *function calls*. The example has two distinct function calls.

This function isn't very flexible. It can only do one thing, i.e., output that one string. When we create functions, we should consider all possible uses for the function. Instead of making a beginning programmer's mistake of using echo to output the string within the function, a better choice is to "return" the string and allow the code that called the function the decision on how to use the string returned. Let's adjust our example.

***Listing 3-11.*** returntestfunction.php

```php
<?php
function getParagraph(){
    return "<p>This paragraph came from a function</p>";
}
$output = getParagraph();
$output .= "<h1>Just some heading</h1>";
$output .= getParagraph();
echo $output;
echo getParagraph();
?>
```

Let's look at the output when we run this.

This paragraph came from a function

# Just some heading

This paragraph came from a function

This paragraph came from a function

***Figure 3-9.*** *Output from returntestfunction.php*

Now this is much, much better! Why? Let's take a look.

```php
return "<p>This paragraph came from a function</p>";
```

The function return statement passes the string provided back to the instruction that called the function. This then allows that instruction to determine how to use the string.

```php
$output = getParagraph();
```

We can create a variable to hold the string.

```php
$output .= getParagraph();
```

We can append the string passed to the existing contents of a string variable.

```php
echo getParagraph();
```

Or we can simply echo out the string to the user. We have a lot more flexibility!

## Program Design and Logic

Experienced programmers rarely echo out information (strings) directly in a function. It is much better to use a `return` statement. This provides a much more useful function that can be used in many ways, as seen earlier. Useful functions can be placed in libraries. This allows the function to be used by other programs. These programs can use the function in the manner that works best for their needs.

**Exercise**: Adjust the previous example by placing the function into a library file. Then import the function into the original program. Keep the original code for the $output string. Run the program. The output should be the same as Figure 3-9. However, now you have a function that can be used in any program!

## Using Function Arguments for Increased Flexibility

This function is still not as flexible as it could be. So, let's improve the `function` getParagraph() with a *function argument*.

***Listing 3-12.*** argumenttestfunction.php

```php
<?php
function getParagraph( string $content ) : string {
    return "<p>$content</p>";
}
$output = getParagraph( "I want this text in my first paragraph" );
```

```
$output .= "<h1>Just some heading</h1>";
$output .= getParagraph("...and this in my last paragraph." );
echo $output;
echo getParagraph("But I want to finish it with this paragraph");
?>
```

The output of each function call now displays whatever we pass into the function.

I want this text in my first paragraph

# Just some heading

...and this in my last paragraph.

But I want to finish it with this paragraph

***Figure 3-10.*** *Output of argumenttextfunction.php*

We made some changes to the function header.

```
function getParagraph( string $content ) : string {
```

The argument (string $content) now restricts all input into the function to allow strings only. But it allows any string passed by the instruction that calls the function. The return statement in the function is also restricted (:string) to returning only strings.

```
    return "<p>$content</p>";
```

The return statement now uses the argument (whatever was passed into the function) to build the paragraph string and then passes that string back to the instruction that called it. We could have also declared $output as a string. However, since the return statement already restricts the output to be a string, it's not necessary.

PHP provides four scalar data hints (types) for our use in functions.

*int*: An integer (whole number) which can be used in calculations.

*string*: A series of characters that will not be used in a calculation.

*float*: A number with decimal places, such as 32.23, which can be used in calculations.

*bool*: Boolean. The value is true or false only.

Let's look at other possible uses.

```php
function getParagraph( ?string $content ) : string {
```

If we include a question mark, as shown in the preceding code, with our data type hint, the function will also allow null values (empty values) to be passed. If no value is passed, it will raise an error. We can also include the question mark to allow the function to return a null value or string.

```php
function getParagraph( ?string $content ) : ?string {
```

We can even allow different data types to be passed back to the calling instruction by using the pipe symbol.

```php
function getParagraph( ?string $content ) : int | string {
```

---

**Note**    For more information on data type hints and functions, visit www.php.net.

---

Function arguments are extremely cool, because they allow us to write one function that can be reused with many different values. We will get to see many more examples of functions with parameters later in the book. Next, Let's write a dynamic quiz using functions.

# Creating a Form for the Quiz

Let's create a new PHP file called quizform.php in the views folder.

*Listing 3-13.* quizform.php

```php
<?php
//complete code for views/quizform.php
$info = "<form method='post' action='index.php?page=quiz'>
        <p>Is it hard fun to learn PHP?</p>
        <select name='answer'>
```

```
        <option value='yes'>Yes, it is</option>
        <option value='no'>No, not really</option>
    </select>
    <input type='submit' name='quiz-submitted' value='post' />
</form>";
?>
```

We have seen a similar form tag before that includes the call to an index file and the passing of a page URL variable. However, we are including some new HTML statements.

# HTML Review

Let's look deeper at our HTML strings.

```
<select name='answer'>
```

The select tag creates a variable (answer) that can be passed to another program using Get or Post. It also indicates that we are creating a drop-down list.

```
<option value='yes'>Yes, it is</option>
<option value='no'>No, not really</option>
```

The option tags provide the user a choice of "Yes, it is" or "No, not really." However, the values 'yes' and 'no' are what is set in the variable answer.

```
<input type='submit' name='quiz-submitted' value='post' />
```

We have seen a submit input type before. The submit button must be included in order for the answer variable to pass to the program indicated in the form tag. Did you notice we are passing the variable using POST? We will soon discover how to accept this value into the program.

---

**Hint**    It is common for beginning programmers to forget that the HTML drop-down list box only sets the variable; it does not pass it on to other programs. We must include an input submit tag along with the list to pass the set information to another program.

---

## Showing the Quiz Form

To show the quiz form, we need to make a couple of minor changes to our index and navigation files. In the index file, we will change our include statement for the navigation to call an updated version.

```
include_once "views/quiznavigation.php";
```

---

**Note**   In the new navigation file (quiznavigation.php), we will call the quizform program instead of the quiz program.

---

```
<a href='indexquiz.php?page=quizform'>Dynamic quiz</a>
```

Review the indexquiz.php and navigationquiz.php files to note these changes.

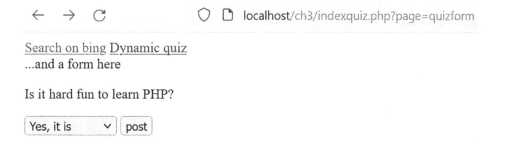

*Figure 3-11.* *Output from indexquiz.php using navigationquiz.php*

Try running this program and determine the results, after selecting a value in the drop-down list box. What did you discover? We are not, yet, using the value passed. We will soon fix this problem.

## The POST Method

The first form used the GET method, but it is not the only possible HTTP method. There is another method called POST. The POST method has no defined maximum of characters – in fact, the POST method is not even limited to text. When using the HTTP POST method, it is even possible to upload files through a form.

HTTP POST variables are not visible in the URL. They are sent hidden from view. This makes HTTP POST the perfect candidate for forms that have to deal with larger amounts of content and forms with sensitive information.

# Secure Programming

Don't confuse the hiding of sensitive information with the idea that the data is secure. POST does hide the information. However, it does not encrypt the information. Hackers can still gain access to the information passed. POST does, however, eliminate the user's ability to bookmark a page that has URL variables. With the POST method, the variables are no longer contained in the URL string.

## Using the $_POST Superglobal

Let's use the superglobal called $_POST to process the form when it is submitted. Let's update the quiz program to display our response.

***Listing 3-14.*** newquiz.php

```php
<?php
//add a new variable and an if statement
$quizIsSubmitted = isset( $_POST['quiz-submitted'] );
if ( $quizIsSubmitted ){
    $answer = $_POST['answer'];
    $info = showQuizResponse( $answer );
} else {
    include_once "views/newquizform.php";
}
//declare a new function
function showQuizResponse( string $answer ) : string {
    $response = "<p>You clicked $answer</p>";
    $response .= "<p>
        <a href='indexnewquiz.php?page=newquiz'>Try quiz again?</a>
    </p>";
    return $response;
}
?>
```

```
$quizIsSubmitted = isset( $_POST['quiz-submitted'] );
```

Using the isset PHP function, the program first will determine if the user submitted the quiz. They have to click the submit button in the quiz form for the true part of the if statement to be executed.

# Program Design and Logic

Programs should allow users to change their minds when selecting from a list of choices, especially if it is a quiz! By requiring the user to click a submit button after decisions have been made, the user can double-check their selections before committing their answers. Otherwise, the program would only go with their first choice.

```
if ( $quizIsSubmitted ){
    $answer = $_POST['answer'];
    $info = showQuizResponse( $answer );
} else {
    include_once "views/newquizform.php";
}
```

If the user did click the submit button, the answer will be placed in $answer using $_POST. Then the value is passed into a function called showQuizResponse. If the user did not click the submit button, the program will display the form, until they click the submit button, or navigate somewhere else.

```
function showQuizResponse( string $answer ) : string {
    $response = "<p>You clicked $answer</p>";
    $response .= "<p>
        <a href='indexnewquiz.php?page=newquiz'>Try quiz again?</a>
    </p>";
    return $response;
}
```

If the submit button was clicked, the function accepts the response (located in $answer) and builds a string ($response) which includes the answer selected and a link asking the user if they want to try the quiz again. This string is returned by the function.

```
$info = showQuizResponse( $answer );
```

The returned string is placed into $info. The index program (indexnewquiz.php) will then display the contents of $info.

---

**Note**    Minor changes have been made to indexnewquiz.php, newquiznavigation. php, and newquizform.php to call the new versions of these programs. However, no logic changes have taken place.

---

Search on bing Dynamic quiz
...and a form here

You clicked yes

Try quiz again?

*Figure 3-12.   Results from clicking yes*

**Exercise**: Adjust the newquizform.php program to ask more than one question. Adjust the indexnewquiz.php program to display the responses to all the questions asked.

# $_POST Is an Array

We stated that $_GET is a superglobal array. $_POST is another superglobal array. But what is an array really? Basically, an *array* can hold multiple items. Each item is stored under an index. In PHP, the index can be numeric, or it can be a string. Arrays with string indexes are called *associate arrays*. $_POST and $_GET create associative arrays to hold the values that are passed from one program to another. When we retrieve the values, we are accessing them from the associative array that PHP created in memory.

We can create our own associative arrays. Let's look at an example.

*Listing 3-15.*  testAssocArray.php

```php
<?php
//complete code for ch3/testAssocArray.php
$my['name'] = "Thomas";
```

```
$my['year-of-birth'] = 1972;
$my['height'] = "193cm";

$out = "My name is " . $my['name'];
echo $out;
?>
```

If we run this program in our browser, we will see "My name is Thomas." In this example, $my is an associate array. We can see that it holds a collection of data stored in the same name ($my) but with different indexes (name, year-of-birth, height). In order to retrieve data from an array, we must use the array name with an index. "Thomas" is stored in array $my under the index ['name'].

PHP allows the storage of different types of data within the same array. In our example, two strings and an integer are stored. Remember, PHP usually determines data types when the first values are stored. Thus, the data types are actually determined after the array has already been initially created. In many other programming languages, arrays are restricted to one data type which must be declared when the array is created.

It can often be handy to inspect all items in an array. PHP has a function to do just that. It is called print_r(). Here's one way to use it.

***Listing 3-16.*** printAssocArray.php

```
<?php
//complete code for ch3/printAssocArray.php
$my['name'] = "Thomas";
$my['year-of-birth'] = 1972;
$my['height'] = "193cm";

$out = "<pre>";
$out .=print_r($my, true);
$out .= "</pre>";
echo $out;
```

If we run this code, we will see every index of $my and its corresponding value.

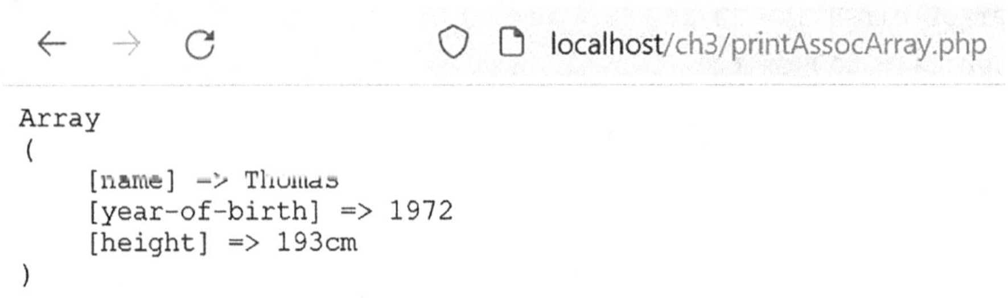

```
←   →   C                    ○   🗋  localhost/ch3/printAssocArray.php
```

```
Array
(
    [name]  => Thomas
    [year-of-birth]  => 1972
    [height]  => 193cm
)
```

***Figure 3-13.*** *Output from printAssocArray.php*

Arrays can be very helpful, because they allow us to group items together. The $_GET and $_POST arrays are provided by PHP to give us easy access to all data encoded with the HTTP methods GET and POST. Let's update our quiz program to look at the associate array that is created.

***Listing 3-17.*** printnewquiz.php

```php
<?php
//add a new variable and an if statement
$quizIsSubmitted = isset( $_POST['quiz-submitted'] );
if ( $quizIsSubmitted ){
    $answer = $_POST['answer'];
    $info = showQuizResponse( $answer );
    $answer = $_POST['answer'];
    $info = showQuizResponse( $answer );
    //inspect the $_POST superglobal array
    $info .= "<pre>";
    $info .= print_r($_POST, true);
    $info .= "</pre>";
} else {
    include_once "views/printnewquizform.php";
}
//declare a new function
function showQuizResponse( string $answer ) : string {
    $response = "<p>You clicked $answer</p>";
    $response .= "<p>
        <a href='indexprintnewquiz.php?page=printnewquiz'>Try quiz
again?</a>
```

```
    </p>";
    return $response;
}
?>
```

---

**Note**    The following files have also been changed to use the new version of printnewquiz.php

indexprintnewquiz.php, printnewquizform.php

---

A print_r statement has been added to printnewquiz.php to display the contents of the array.

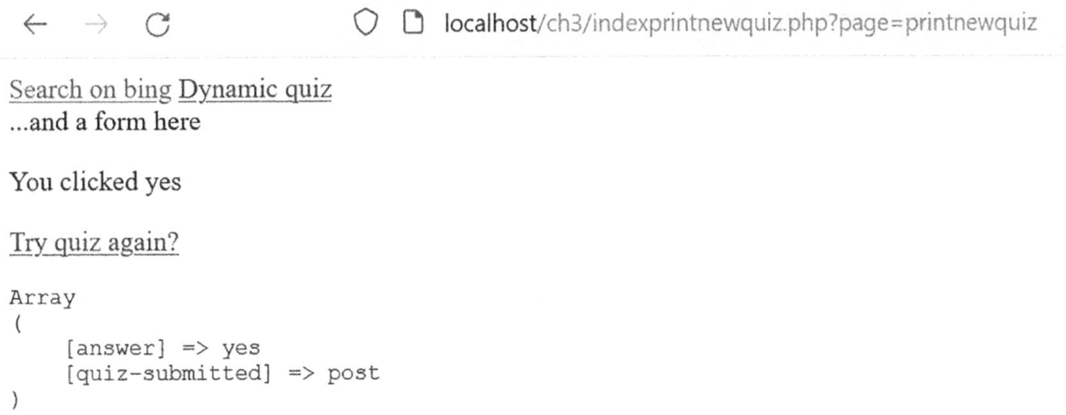

---

←  →  C                         ○  🗋  localhost/ch3/indexprintnewquiz.php?page=printnewquiz
Search on bing Dynamic quiz
...and a form here

You clicked yes

Try quiz again?

```
Array
(
    [answer] => yes
    [quiz-submitted] => post
)
```

**Figure 3-14.**  *Output of quiz results with array*

We can see from the output that both answer and quiz-submitted indexes are created. The answer index has a value of yes because the user answered the question with this selection. The value stored in quiz-submitted gives us an indication that the array was created via the POST method. The use of print_r can be a great debugging tool that allows us to see what is being passed from one program to another.

## Secure Programming

Don't expose information to the user that they don't need to know. In a live environment, we would not use print_r to display information to the user because it will show them all information we are passing between the programs. This might cause a major security problem with the data we are using in the program.

# Curly's Law: Do One Thing

Have you ever seen the 1991 movie *City Slickers*? Yes, that feel-good western comedy featuring Billy Crystal. Jack Palance played Curly, a rugged, old cowboy who knew the secret of life and reluctantly shared it with Crystal's character, Mitch:

> *Curly*: Do you know what the secret of life is?
>
> *(Holds up one finger)*
>
> *Curly*: This!
>
> *Mitch*: Your finger?
>
> *Curly*: One thing. Just one thing. You stick to that, and the rest don't mean shit.
>
> *Mitch*: But what is the "one thing"?
>
> *Curly*: (*smiles*) That's what *you* have to find out.

We can probably rest assured that Curly wasn't talking about principles of clean code. But incidentally, he formulated a principle we can use to write clean functions. Every function should do one thing. Just one thing.

---

**Note**    Jeff Atwood wrote a funny and interesting blog entry about applying Curly's law to clean code. Read it at `http://blog.codinghorror.com/curlys-law-do-one-thing/`.

---

## Program Design and Logic

Clean code is code that is easier to understand. If functions do just one thing, they normally will be short. Short code is easier to read and understand than long code. A function should almost never be more than a screen's worth of instructions. If you discover that your functions become long, reevaluate the logic of your design. Can the function be broken down into multiple simpler functions? If we can read and understand our code, it becomes much easier to find errors – and we *will* make errors! Don't be surprised if you spend 50% of your development time chasing errors in your code.

In the earlier code examples, we saw two clean functions, each doing just one thing. One function shows the quiz; the other function shows a response.

## Code Is Poetry

Strive for expressive, beautiful code. Strive for code that is easy to read. When you develop new solutions with code, you will spend a very significant part of your time reading your own code. Code is like poetry. You write it once but read it many times. So, write your code as if you were writing poetry: choose your words carefully.

Before we finish with our coding examples, let's make some changes to the Page Data Class to tighten down security.

# OOP: Using Constructors, Getters, and Setters

It has been a while since we updated the Page Data Class. In case you forgot its current structure, see the following code.

***Listing 3-18.***  Page_Data.class.php

```php
<?php
class Page_Data {
    public string $title = "";
    public string $content = "";
    public string $css = "";
    public string $embeddedStyle = "";
}
?>
```

As we can see, the class name and file name are the same. It is standard practice in object-oriented languages to have this relationship. We initially created our strings within the class itself and set them to empty strings. However, classes include a unique method (function) called a *constructor*, whose main purpose is to initiate properties (variables). We can provide default values within the constructor for each of our strings. The constructor is automatically called when an object is created from the class, using the *new keyword*.

```php
function __construct() {
        print "In constructor";
   }
```

For PHP classes, two underscore symbols (__) and the word *construct* identify the constructor. In this example, we are simply printing out a message. However, we will soon provide some meaningful information.

Let's look a little deeper at object-oriented programming to understand why the use of constructors is important.

A true object-oriented program must provide three methodologies. These include

*Encapsulation*: Protecting all parts of the program by forming a shield (capsule) around the code, using classes, objects, and other object-oriented techniques.

*Polymorphism*: The ability to call and use items (such as methods/functions) with the same name but accepting and producing different results. For example, the ability to have two functions called adder. One function adds two integers, and one adds two floating-point numbers.

How does the program know which to use?

By what is passed into the function (integers or floating point) and what is returned by the function, commonly called the function header information.

*Inheritance*: The ability for one object to inherit the characteristics of another object. The same as us inheriting the characteristics of our parents, but still keeping some uniqueness about ourselves.

Let's provide some improved encapsulation of our class while, at the same time, increasing both the reliability, integrity, and security of our program.

***Listing 3-19.*** Construct_Page_Data.class.php

```php
<?php
class Page_Data {
```

```php
    public string $title = "";
    public string $content = "";
    public string $css = "";
    public string $embeddedStyle = "";
        function __construct() {
            $title = "Title Goes Here";
            $content = "Page Content Goes Here";
            $css = "CSS Goes Here";
            $embeddedStyle = "Embedded CSS Goes Here";
        }
}
 ?>
```

In the preceding example, we are declaring (creating) each property at the beginning of the class. Then the constructor is called to give each property an initial value in case whatever program uses this class does not use the property. However, we still have a potential problem that almost anything can be loaded into the properties by any program. This could cause harm to the display of the web page, or even worse, when we discuss databases, open up the ability for a hacker to attempt to access our information. Let's add a little better security and reliability by rejecting content submitted that does not meet our requirements. To accomplish this, we will create *setter* and *getter* methods.

***Listing 3-20.*** Partial Listing of Private_Page_Data.class.php

```php
<?php
class Page_Data {
    private string $title = "";
    private string $content = "";
    private string $css = "";
    private string $embeddedStyle = "";
        function __construct() {
                $this->title = "Title Goes Here";
                $this->content = "Page Content Goes Here";
                $this->css = "CSS Goes Here";
                $this->embeddedStyle = "Embedded CSS Goes Here";
        }
        public function getTitle() : string {
```

```
            return $this->title;
    }
    public function setTitle(string $value) {
            if (strpos($value, '^')) {
                    $this->title = $value;
            }
    }
    public function getContent() : string {
            return $this->content;
    }
    public function setContent(string $value) {
            if (strpos($value, '<')) {
                    $this->content = $value;
            }
    }
    public function appendContent(string $value) {
            if (strpos($value, '<')) {
                    $this->content .= $value;
            }
    }
}
```

Listing 3-20 is a partial listing of the code changes for the Page Data Class. For a complete listing, review the code in Private_Page_data.class.php.

```
private string $title = "";
```

The first change to the program is the change in the *access modifier* for each property from public to private. The *public* modifier allows open access to any program. A public variable is vulnerable while the program is residing in memory (executing). A *private* variable can only be accessed by the class that creates it. A *protected* variable can be accessed by the class itself and any inheriting classes or parent classes. By setting our variables to private, we can control any changes to the contents of the variables.

```
$this->title = "Title Goes Here";
```

The use of the property has been changed from $title to $this->title. This is a direct result of changing the variable to private. *$this* is a special PHP pointer that provides access to items that are not declared as public within an object. In our example, $this indicates that we are accessing the private variable $title and placing the provided string within it.

```php
public function getTitle() : string {
        return $this->title;
    }
```

To allow programs outside of the class access to our private variables, we create getter and setter methods. Think of this as providing read and write access to the variable. A *get method* provides read access. A *set method* provides write access. We can actually create variables that are only readable by just providing a get method. We can also create variables that are just writable by only providing a set method. Most get methods are simple methods, as shown in the example; they just return the value requested to the calling program.

```php
public function setTitle(string $value) {
        if (strpos($value, '^')) {
                $this->title = $value;
        }
    }
```

The goal of a set method is to protect the data (encapsulation). Set methods should check the validity of the information before making any changes to the variable. In the example, an if statement uses the PHP function *strpos* to determine if the variable $value (the information passed into the function) contains a carrot (^) symbol. If it does, it allows the title variable to be updated with the information passed. This example will actually fail because our title string does not contain a carrot. If you run the program, you will discover that the default value is used for the title.

# Secure Programming

A secure and reliable program will reject attempts to update information with invalid data without causing the program to raise errors and/or crash. In this example, an invalid string has been submitted to update the title variable. The program merely rejects the invalid data and keeps the default value. The user of the program will only see that the title is set to the default, which does not affect what the user is attempting to accomplish. Thus, the program is more secure and more reliable than using public variables. If the program could not continue due to invalid data, an informative message should be provided to the user, which does not raise errors or cause the program to crash.

```php
public function appendContent(string $value) {
        if (strpos($value, '<')) {
                $this->content .= $value;
        }
    }
}
```

In the code example, the content variable has an additional method which appends the information, instead of replacing (setting) the information. Our index program sets and appends information to the content variable. Thus, the additional method is necessary for this operation.

*Should we always use setters and getters?*

The answer is no. If there is no reason to protect the data, then the data can remain public. Many textbooks demonstrate the user of setters and getters but do not emphasize that a set routine which does not do any validation is just a waste of efficiency. If validation is not required, just set the variable to public access. However, with the amount of hacking that occurs in the program environment, the programmer should think long and hard about leaving any variable as a wide-open public variable.

---

**Note**   The strpos method searches a string to determine if the value checked exists within the string. If it does, it returns the location of the value within the string. String positions are numbered starting with a 0 for the first position. If the value is not within the string, the function returns a -1. A TRUE result is determined by any value greater than or equal to 1. A FALSE value is any value less than or equal to zero. Thus, the if statement will be TRUE whenever the value is discovered and become FALSE if the value is not found. For more information on strpos, visit `www.php.net/manual/en/function.strpos`.

---

**Listing 3-21.** Privateindex.php

```php
<?php
//complete code for index.php
$nav = "";
$info = "";
include_once "views/printnewquiznavigation.php";
include_once "classes/Private_Page_Data.class.php";
$pageData = new Page_Data();
$pageData->setTitle("Building and processing HTML forms with PHP");
$pageData->setContent($nav);
$pageData->appendContent("<div>...and a form here</div>");
$navigationIsClicked = isset($_GET['page']);
if ($navigationIsClicked ) {
    $fileToLoad = $_GET['page'];
} else {
    $fileToLoad = "search";
}
include_once "views/$fileToLoad.php";
$pageData->appendContent($info);
require "templates/privatepage.php";
echo $page;
?>
```

Since we can no longer directly place values into the variables in the class, we need to make some adjustments to our index file.

```php
$pageData->setTitle("Building and processing HTML forms with PHP");
$pageData->setContent($nav);
$pageData->appendContent("<div>...and a form here</div>");
```

The instructions to pass strings into our variables have now been replaced with calls to the set and append methods within the class.

**Listing 3-22.** privatepage.php

```php
<?php
$page= "<!DOCTYPE html><html><head><title>";
```

```
$page .= $pageData->getTitle();
$page .= "</title>
<meta http-equiv='Content-Type' content='text/html;charset=utf-8' />";
$page .= $pageData->getCss();
$page .= "</head><body>";
$page .= $pageData->getContent();
$page .="</body></html>";
?>
```

Adjustments have also been made to the page program to read the information in the variables.

```
$page .= $pageData->getTitle();
```

The getter methods are now called to retrieve the information. The updating of the $page variable was also broken down into multiple lines to allow for better readability of the process taking place.

**Exercise**: The strings checked by the strpos function in the Private_Page_Data.class. php have intentionally been set to information that does not make logical sense. Scan over the files used in this chapter and determine what content would make logical sense to check for existence. Make the required updates and run the program to verify that it works properly. After adjusting, go back to the program and change the strings to check for something not expected to be placed in the variables. Run the program and look at the results. What occurred? The program should display the default results, but not cause any errors to be raised.

We now have a more secure and reliable program. A great place to complete our discussion for this chapter.

# Summary

We covered a lot of ground in this chapter. We learned how to write HTML forms. HTML forms can encode URL variables when they are submitted. URL variables are passed from the browser to the web server with a GET HTTP request. We also learned that we could pass variables using the POST HTTP request which passes the variables to the server memory. Actually, the request creates an array that contains the information passed. We learned how to retrieve the information passed into our PHP programs by using $_GET or $_POST. We discovered how to organize our code and control the flow of our program with named functions. We dug deeper into object-oriented programming by securing our information stored in a class with the private access modifier, and the use of a constructor, and getter and setter methods. But most important, we learned how Curly's law can be applied to enhance the logic and efficiency of our code.

# Exercises

1. If you are familiar with CSS, create an external style sheet to control the look and design of the pages we have created. Link the style sheet to the index page (see Chapter 2 for hints). Make any additional adjustments needed. Don't forget to test your pages in more than one browser. Sometimes, CSS can behave differently in different browsers.

2. Redesign the dynamic quiz. Add additional questions and additional question formats. How would we create multiple-choice questions, True/False questions, or short answer questions? This will require some research to determine the use of other HTML form input objects. If you are unfamiliar with them, you can find additional information on www.w3schools. com or on YouTube.com. Adjust the output that is produced from the quiz results to be more meaningful.

3. Create another HTML form that can calculate a person's body mass index (BMI), based on the person's height and weight. The formula for calculating BMI follows. The task is to create a form, on which users can input height and weight, and to write some PHP code to calculate BMI based on the input. There are examples on the Web to help guide you. But attempt to complete it yourself before looking for possible solutions.

```
//metric
bmi = kg/ (2 * m)
//for UK and US readers
bmi = ( lb/(2 * in) ) * 703
```

4.   Create a form that converts money from one currency to another. If you want it to be really advanced, you could have a `<select>` element with a list of possible currencies to convert. Again, there are example programs on the Web, but first, attempt it yourself before looking at these examples.

# CHAPTER 4

# Building a Dynamic Image Gallery

## Objectives

After completing this chapter, you will be able to

- Set up a dynamic site

- Create named functions

- Use $_GET and $_POST superglobal arrays

- Create and iterate with a foreach loop

- Use PHP's glob to limit access to specific file types

- Write custom object methods

- Upload files with PHP's $_FILES superglobal array

We now know how to make a simple dynamic website. We also know how to create a dynamic form. We learned how to access URL variables with $_GET or $_POST. It is time to put our new knowledge to good use. Let us build a dynamic image gallery with a form to allow users to upload new images to the gallery. Along the way, we will discover how to upload files, use loops, and improve our ability to create dynamic websites.

© Jason Lengstorf, Thomas Blom Hansen, Steve Prettyman 2022
J. Lengstorf et al., *PHP 8 for Absolute Beginners*, https://doi.org/10.1007/978-1-4842-8205-2_4

# Setting Up a Dynamic Site

Let us make a new project folder called ch4. We can then copy the folders and the PHP files from the publisher's website into these locations. Of course, you can also create the files as you move through the chapter. Practice makes perfect. If you choose to do so, you will need to create several folders: classes, views, templates, and imgs.

# Prerequisites: A Folder with Some Images

Our image gallery needs some images. We will restrict this image gallery to use JPEG images only. Let us prepare a small handful of JPEG images for the gallery. These images will reside in the img folder.

# Copyright Laws

As a developer, we must be aware of the *copyright laws* for any country in which our site might be used. We must respect and abide by these laws. In the United States, images very often are copyrighted, which means we must ask permission of the owner to use the image. There are some exceptions, including educational purposes. However, we should not get in the habit of just grabbing whatever image we like.

How can we tell if an image is copyrighted?

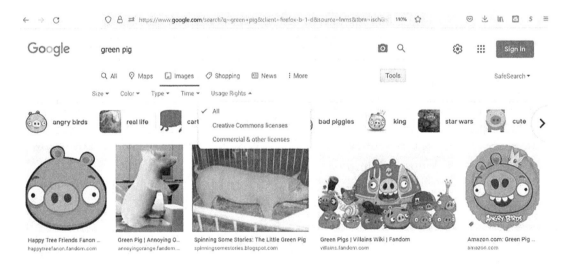

***Figure 4-1.*** *Google Search for green pig*

In Google, the Tools menu selection allows you to narrow down your image search related to the type of restrictions for their use. However, this is not a perfect method (even Google agrees). Once you have discovered an image that might not be copyrighted, visit the website that contains the image. Find the copyright information on the site. If you still are unsure, email the owner of the website to obtain permission to use the image. Once you get a response (if you do), save that email. It can keep you out of hot water later.

The safest method to obtain noncopyright images is to search for noncopyright image sites on the Web. There are lots of sites out there. Some are free and some charge a small fee. The fee is well worth the money to avoid any future problems!

**Exercise**: Search the Web for copyright laws in the country, region, and/or state in which you live. How are these different from other areas? Remember, you must follow all the copyright laws for countries that may use your website. Search the Web and find a handful of noncopyrighted images for use in the photo gallery we are about to create.

By the way, we are sticking to a site architecture that was used in the previous chapters. This will make it easier to reuse code from previous projects. Reusing existing code will help develop reliable solutions faster. Let us get started!

# Creating a Navigation

This site will have two main page views: one for displaying the gallery and one to show a form to allow users to upload new images. Because we know we will need these two page views, we can prepare a site navigation with two navigation items. Let us create a new file in the views folder and call it navigation.php.

*Listing 4-1.* navigation.php

```php
<?php
$nav = "
<nav>
    <a href='index.php?page=gallery'>Gallery</a>
    <a href='index.php?page=upload'>Upload new image</a>
</nav>
";
?>
```

# Creating Two Dummy Page View Files

It is always a clever idea to start small when coding something new. Let us prepare two separate page views: one for the gallery and one for the upload form. Each page view will be generated and returned from separate files. So, we create two files inside the views folder.

***Listing 4-2.*** gallery.php

```php
<?php
//complete source code for views/gallery.php
$info =  "<h1>Images Gallery</h1>";
?>
```

***Listing 4-3.*** upload.php

```php
<?php
//complete source code for views/upload.php
$info =  "<h1>Upload New Images</h1>";
?>
```

# Creating the Index File

As mentioned earlier, every site has an index page. This is the default page that is displayed in a browser when the user enters a URL (such as www.google.com). As the main door to the site, it is important that the page be clean, clear, reliable, and attractive. Our first version of the index page will display a functional, dynamic navigation linking to two quite simple page views.

***Listing 4-4.*** index.php

```php
<?php
//complete code for index.php
$nav = "";
$info = "";
include_once "views/navigation.php";
include_once "classes/Page_Data.class.php";
$pageData = new Page_Data();
```

```php
$pageData->setTitle("Dynamic image gallery");
$pageData->setContent($nav);
$navigationIsClicked = isset($_GET['page']);
if ( $navigationIsClicked ) {
    $fileToLoad = $_GET['page'];
} else {
    $fileToLoad = "gallery";
}
include_once "views/$fileToLoad.php";
$pageData->appendContent($info);
require "templates/page.php";
echo $page;
?>
```

As we can see, the index page is similar to the last version in Chapter 3. Reusing code speeds creation time and increases reliability at the same time. The Page_Data class and the page file are not shown because, at this point, we have made no changes from the previous versions.

## Time to Test

All code so far has been just like that we have been working on in the first few chapters. In total, we have very few lines of code, but this code is enough to perform an initial test. When we are working with code, it is recommended that we write a little code, test it, and then write a little more.

While frequently testing progress, we will be able to identify errors in their infancy. An error is much easier to find in fewer lines of code. It only takes a few moments to test our progress. Let us make it a habit to test often and catch errors as early as possible.

As mentioned before, a good programmer plans for the unexpected to occur. When testing programs, make a valid attempt to try and break the code. See if you can cause the code to produce errors. If errors are produced, adjust the code so it will gracefully handle the unexpected. Let us test the code and look at the results.

Gallery Upload new image

# Images Gallery

**Figure 4-2.** *Default view for index.php*

Gallery Upload new image

# Upload New Images

**Figure 4-3.** *index.php view after clicking Upload new image*

**Exercise**: Try to break the current code. Make changes to the Page Data class which will cause the upload pages to not display properly. Hint: Change the values checked within the if statements. At least one if statement currently needs to be adjusted to allow all information to be properly displayed. Can you find it? Remember the class is designed to display default values if it does not validate information passed.

## Preparing a Function for Displaying Images

Let us update the gallery file to declare a short function that simply returns an HTML string including a `<ul>` with one `<li>`. This change is a step toward the site's ability to display all images that are contained within a given folder (directory).

**Listing 4-5.** showgallery.php

```php
<?php
//complete source code for views/gallery.php
//function definition
function showImages() : string{
    $out = "<h1>Image Gallery</h1>";
    $out .= "<ul id='images'>";
```

```php
    $out .= "<li>I will soon list all images</li>";
    $out .= "</ul>";
    return $out;
}
//function call
$info = showImages();
?>
```

See how the variable $out inside the function showImages() gradually gets increased content over several lines of code, using *incremental concatenation*. In the end, when the HTML string is complete, the content of the variable $out is returned to the line of code that calls the function.

```php
$info = showImages();
```

The generated string is returned to index.php, via the $info variable, where it will be added to the $pageData object, merged with the page template, and echoed to the browser.

# Iteration

Hopefully, function, variables, and incremental concatenation are slowly beginning to make sense. Since we will be using multiple images, we need to take some time to understand iteration: repeating the use of the same code several times.

# While Loop

Let us begin with *while loops*. while loops will repeat the same code block, as long as a condition is true. The basic syntax is

```php
while ( $condition ) {
    //repeat code here
}
```

A while loop is syntactically quite similar to an if statement. If the condition holds true, the code in the subsequent code block will repeat until the condition becomes false. Here is an example to illustrate the concept.

***Listing 4-6.*** whileloop.php

```php
<?php
$number = 1;
while ( $number < 5 ) {
    echo "the while loop has concluded $number loops<br />";
    $number = $number + 1;
}
?>

while ( $number < 5 ) {
```

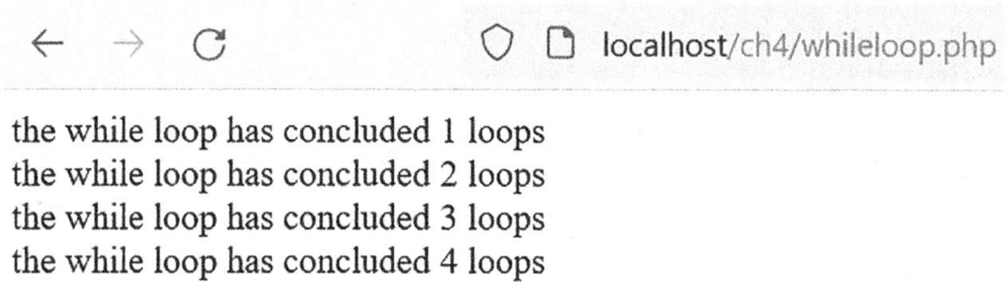

| ← → C | ○ ◻ localhost/ch4/whileloop.php |
| --- | --- |

the while loop has concluded 1 loops
the while loop has concluded 2 loops
the while loop has concluded 3 loops
the while loop has concluded 4 loops

***Figure 4-4.*** *Output from whileloop.php*

The code block is repeated four times. That is because of the condition declared inside the parentheses of the while statement. It looks at $number to determine if it is smaller than five. The first time the loop executes, the $number is set to one.

```php
$number = $number + 1;
```

Every time the code block runs, $number is increased by one. The *counting variable* $number has a value of 5 when the while loop has repeated four times. Because five is not smaller than five, the while loop terminates, and a fifth line is never echoed.

---

**Note**    What happens if the programmer forgets to increment the variable used to count loops? If the variable is not incremented, it does not change. The loop would continue to evaluate the expression as true, because the value of one does not change and it still is less than five. This creates an *infinite loop*. This is a common mistake, especially for beginning programmers. Always double-check that you remembered to include incrementing the counting variable.

---

# For Loop

As a new programmer, we want to be reminded, as much as possible, of any code required to successfully create iterations. While loops are a great general loop for any time, we need to iterate until a condition changes. However, a *for loop* is designed specifically for situations in which we know how many times we want to loop.

*Listing 4-7.* forloop.php

```php
<?php
for ( $number = 1; $number < 5 ; $number++) {
    echo "the for loop has concluded $number loops<br />";
}
?>
```

As we can see, the for loop takes less lines of code than the while loop to accomplish the same result.

```php
for ( $number = 1; $number < 5 ; $number++) {
```

The counting variable $number is initialized to one, compared to the number five, and incremented in the same program statement. Actually, for loops automatically execute statements in the first position (before the first semicolon) once at the beginning of the loop. They then execute the code in the second position (between the semicolons) whenever they reach the top of the loop (including the first time entering the loop). The code in the third position (between the last semicolon and the parentheses) is executed whenever they reach the bottom of the loop. In other words, the for loop produces the same result as the while loop. However, it helps remind us to create a counting variable, to give it an initial value, to compare it, and most importantly to increment it every time.

Before we move on, one change we did add to the previous example was another way to increment a value. In the for statement $number is incremented using ++, instead of $number = $number + 1. There are actually several ways we can increment values.

```php
$number = $number + 1;
$number++;
$number += 1;
```

All the preceding statements increment the variable by one. Each increments the value after it has been used. What?

```
$number = 1;
echo $number++;
echo $number;
```

The preceding statements will display the value of 1 with the first echo and 2 with the second echo. The value is increased, using $number++, after it has been echoed the first time.

```
$number = 1;
echo ++$number;
echo $number;
```

If we move the ++ symbols to the left, the variable will be incremented before it is used. Thus, the first echo statement will display two and the second will display three.

We could have switched our incrementation to occur before use in the for statement. Since we are not actually using the value (such as displaying it with an echo), it will not actually change any result with this for-loop example. Most of the time, it does not matter if you increment before or after, but, as we just discovered, we should be careful that we produce the results we expect.

```
$number = 2;
echo $number--;
echo --$number;
```

We can also decrement variables using --. The process is the same; if it is on the right side, it will decrement after use. If it is on the left side, it will decrement before use. In this example. The first echo will display two and the second zero. Zero? Did you think it was one? The value is decremented with the first echo to one. Then it is decremented again to zero before the second echo displays the results.

**Exercise**: Adjust the for-loop example to loop ten times. Then adjust the loop to only display odd numbers. Hint: Change the incrementation to add two each time. Finally look up the use of the *continue* and *break* statements at www.php.net. How can we skip the value of four, but continue the loop? How can we exit the loop early if the counting variable holds the value of six?

Let us get back to creating our images gallery.

# Using glob to Find Files in a Folder

The PHP *glob* method can be used to find pathnames that match a pattern. It can quickly scan a directory and create an array which contains all items that match the pattern. We could use the for loop to retrieve the results, because we do not know how many results will be returned. We could discover this information with the length property of the array. However, there is an even better option, the *foreach loop*. This loop was specifically created to iterate arrays and other lists.

# For Each Loop

```
foreach ($arrayname as $value) {
    statement
}
```

The foreach syntax requires an array (or list) name and a variable to hold the current item being viewed. For example:

```
<?php
$cars = array("ford", "chevy", "honda", "kia");

foreach ($cars as $value) {
  echo "$value <br>";
}
?>
```

In this example, an array of cars has been declared. The foreach loop will increment through the array and place each value (car) in the variable $value. It then displays the value. The loop continues until there are no more cars. We do not need to worry about the size of the array and can easily change the array without having to change the loop!

# Showing All Images

Let us use the foreach loop to retrieve images for our gallery.

***Listing 4-8.*** listgallery.php

```php
<?php
//complete source code for views/gallery.php
//edit existing function
function showImages() : string{
        $out = "<h1>Images Gallery</h1>";
        $out .= "<ul id='images'>";

        $dir_name = "imgs";
        chdir($dir_name);
        $images = glob("*.jpg");

        foreach($images as $image) {
        $out .= '<li><img src="'.$dir_name. '/' .$image.'" /></li>';
        }
        $out .= "</ul>";
        return $out;
}
$info = showImages();

?>}
```

The first few lines of the function pass HTML code to the $out variable to format the display of the images. We will clean up this display in another example.

```php
$dir_name = "imgs";
```

The $dir_name variable holds the directory that contains the images. Since the directory is located within our ch4 folder, no additional path is necessary. Although we can include a path if needed.

```php
chdir($dir_name);
```

The *chdir* command will change our current location from the ch4 directory to the imgs directory in preparation for searching the directory for images.

```php
$images = glob("*.jpg");
```

This is a very powerful statement. *Glob* will filter out all values within the current folder which do not have the file ending shown. It will then create an array in a format similar to the following.

```
Array ( [0] => image4-1.jpg [1] => image4-2.jpg [2] => image4-3.jpg [3] =>
image4-4.jpg )
```

Since we placed the results into $images, glob automatically formatted $images as an array holding the file names for any JPEG images in the directory. If we want to include more than one type of image, we can separate them with commas as shown in the following.

```
$images = glob("*.{jpg,jpeg,png,gif,JPG,JPEG,PNG,GIF}");
```

The foreach loop displays the images.

```
foreach($images as $image) {
    $out .= '<li><img src="'.$dir_name. '/' .$image.'" /></li>';
    }
    $out .= "</ul>";
```

Each image is placed into the list with the directory name because the index program runs from the ch4 folder, while the images are in the imgs folder.

---

**Note**   Minor changes have been made to the navigation and the index programs to use the listgallery.php program. To test the current version, run the listindex.php program in the browser.

---

## Secure Programming

Let us make some changes to the gallery code to reduce the chances of overloading the system with files that are too large, or a total file size that is not reasonable.

**Note**    *Denial-of-service (DOS) attacks* are common attempts by hackers to cause websites and servers to crash. All programmers should be aware that hackers will, at some point, attempt to bring down a web page and/or server. Anytime files are being retrieved from another location or uploaded from the user, file limits should be set to stop these attempts.

***Listing 4-9.*** securelistgallery.php

```php
<?php
//complete source code for views/gallery.php
//edit existing function
function showImages() : string{
    $out = "<h1>Images Gallery</h1>";
    $out .= "<ul id='images'
        style='
        list-style-type:none;
        width: 550px;
        border: 5px solid black;
        padding: 50px;
        margin: 20px;'
        ><li>";
    $totalSize = 0;
    $numberOfImages = 0;
    $dir_name = "imgs";
    chdir($dir_name);
        $images = glob("*.jpg");

        foreach($images as $image) {
            if((filesize($image) < 500000) and ($totalSize < 2500000)) {
                $out .= '<img src="'.$dir_name. '/' .$image.'"
                style="
                    height: 200px;
                    width: 250px;
                    border: 2px solid black;
```

```
                        padding: 5px;
                        margin: 5px;
                "/>';
                $totalSize += filesize($image);
                $numberOfImages++;
          }
          if (($numberOfImages % 2) == 0) {
                $out .= "</li><li>";
          }
      }
      $out .= "</li></ul>";
      return $out;
}
$info = showImages();
?>
```

---

**Note**    Minor changes occurred in the index and navigation files to use
securelistgallery.php. To test this version, use securelistindex.php.

---

At first, this version looks a lot more complicated than the previous version.
However, most of the added code was CSS to format the display of the images.

# CSS Review

```
style='
      list-style-type:none;
      width: 550px;
      border: 5px solid black;
      padding: 50px;
      margin: 20px;'
```

*List-style-type* allows flexibility in the type of images (circle, dot) that are displayed
in an unordered list. In this example, the value is set to none to not display any images
next to the pictures. The width is set to 550 pixels to allow enough room for two pictures,

each with a width of 250 pixels. *Padding* (50px) is the amount of space within the box between the images and the border. The *border* is set to five pixels with a color of black. The *margin* (20px) is the amount of space outside the box (border).

```
if(((filesize($image) < 500000) and ($totalSize < 2500000)) {
```

The *filesize* method returns the size of the file in bytes. Thus, a size of 500000 is equivalent to 500KB (kilobytes). $totalSize will keep track of the total of all the pictures being displayed. In this example, the total will not exceed 2500 KB. This simple if statement increases the security of our program.

```
$totalSize += filesize($image);
$numberOfImages++;
```

Do not forget to add the file size of each image to $totalSize and increment the number of images. Why are we keeping track of the number of images?

```
    if (($numberOfImages % 2) == 0) {
            $out .= "</li><li>";
    }
```

We have set up our display to allow two images per row. Thus, we can use an if statement to determine if we need to go to the next row, by closing the list element (</li>) and opening a new list element (<li>). The % operator is a *modulus operator*. It looks at the remainder of a division. If there is no remainder, then the number of images is divisible by two – which indicates we have a multiple of two images (0, 2, 4, ...), which would be the time to start a new row.

We now have a good-looking secure gallery.

## Images Gallery

***Figure 4-5.***  *Output from securelistgallery.php via securelistindex.php*

**Exercise**: Adjust the settings in the securelistgallery.php program to not display some of the images provided. Does it handle the removal of these pictures well? Add your own images to the folder and adjust the file size and total size allowed to display your images. How would we add captions below the images? How would we add an Alt parameter for each image? Add each. Remember, to provide the best experience for visually impaired viewers, we must include Alt parameters.

# Creating a Form View

Let us create an HTML form to upload new images to the gallery. We will create a file in the views folder and name it uploadForm.php.

***Listing 4-10.*** uploadForm.php

```php
<?php
$info = "
<h1>Upload New jpg Images</h1>
<form method='post' action='index.php?page=upload' enctype='multipart/
form-data' >
    <label>Find a jpg image to upload</label>
    <input type='file' name='image-data' accept='image/jpeg'/>
    <input type='submit' value='upload' name='new-image' />
 </form>";
?>
```

Some of the preceding code should look familiar. We have an HTML form with method and action attributes. But this form does have some differences from the previous forms we have written.

```
<form method='post' action='index.php?page=upload' enctype='multipart/
form-data' >
```

Did you notice the *enctype* attribute declared for the form? The default encoding used by forms will not allow file uploads. We must specifically declare that this particular form should use *multipart/form-data* as *content-type*, because this is required to upload files through HTTP. This information is attached to the http get command that is created by the browser to request information from the server.

```
<input type='file' name='image-data' accept='image/jpeg'/>
```

Another notable difference is the new input *type='file'* attribute. It will create a *file upload control* to allow users to browse their own hard drives for image files to upload. Notice the *accept* attribute on the same <input> element. It sets the default file format to a *content-type* of *image/jpeg*.

Declaring an `accept` attribute is quite helpful for end users. When it is declared, it will narrow down which files users can see through the form. Users are directed to select a file with an appropriate file type.

---

**Note**   The `accept` attribute can be used with any *Internet media type.* An Internet media type is a standard way of identifying a file type. See more about Internet media types at `http://en.wikipedia.org/wiki/Internet_media_type`. Remember, hackers can change the restrictions set by the HTML code. Also, the file upload window still allows the user to change the file type to "all files." We will also need to restrict the file type using PHP to ensure that no unapproved file types sneak through.

---

## Showing a Form for Uploading Images

Let us change the upload program to use this form when the user clicks the "Upload new image" selection in the navigation.

*Listing 4-11.* imageUpload.php

```php
<?php
//complete source code for views/upload.php
include_once "views/imageuploadForm.php";
?>
```

There is not much to the imageUpload.php file. However, we will add more to it soon.

*Figure 4-6.* *Output from imageUpload.php*

**Note**    Minor changes have been made to the navigation and index programs to call the new imageUpload.php program. To test this program, load imagelistindex. php in the browser. At this point, the image will still not be uploaded. But we will fix this soon.

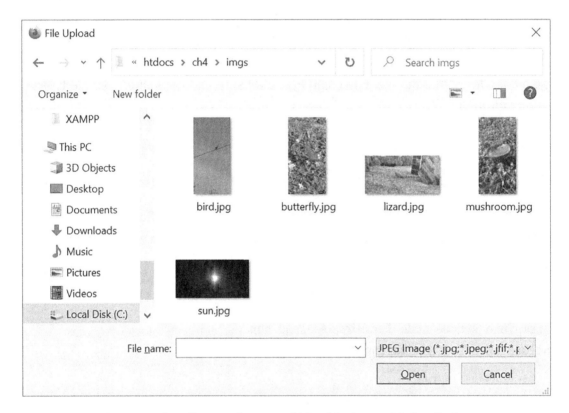

***Figure 4-7.*** *Output when browse button clicked in imageUpload.php*

Notice that when the user clicks the browse button, the HTML retrieves a familiar file upload window. This window is actually called using a hidden *API (application programming interface) call* to the user's operating system. This keeps consistency in the user experience. Also, the limitation to only allow JPEG images is passed as a parameter through the API call, which is set to the default display of the files available to only JPEG images.

# php.ini

There are several settings we need to check or adjust within the *php.ini file* to allow and limit file uploads. The php.ini file contains all initialization settings that are accessed whenever a PHP program is interpreted. Depending on the Apache/PHP/MySQL package you have chosen to install, the location of this file will vary. However, it is located in the same location as other PHP files. If you installed XAMPP, it is located in the PHP folder under the XAMPP folder. You can view and edit this file with any text editor (such as Notepad or Notepad++). However, if you do make changes, first make a backup copy, in case you make a mistake. In order for the changes to take effect, the Apache server must be stopped and restarted again.

---

**Note**    The php function *php_ini_loaded_file()* can be displayed (echoed) within a simple PHP program to discover the location of the php.ini file.

---

```
;;;;;;;;;;;;;;;;
; File Uploads ;
;;;;;;;;;;;;;;;;

; Whether to allow HTTP file uploads.
; http://php.net/file-uploads
file_uploads=On

; Temporary directory for HTTP uploaded files (will use system
default if not
; specified).
; http://php.net/upload-tmp-dir
upload_tmp_dir="C:\xampp8.1.1\tmp"

; Maximum allowed size for uploaded files.
; http://php.net/upload-max-filesize
upload_max_filesize=40M

; Maximum number of files that can be uploaded via a single request
max_file_uploads=20
```

Within the php.ini file, we need to make sure that file_upload is set to On. We can also specify a different location to temporarily hold our upload files (if we choose). We can adjust the maximum file size to be uploaded and the maximum number of files that can be uploaded in a single request. Careful thought should be given to what limits should be used. We should always assume that someone will attempt to bring down our server by attempting to flood it with a massive amount of file uploads.

# $_FILES

When files are uploaded into PHP, the metadata associated with the file are stored into an associative array. This superglobal array is named *$_FILES*. The array contains several important aspects about the file uploaded.

```
Array (
        [image-data] => Array (
        [name] => alberte-lea.jpg
        [type] => image/jpeg
        [tmp_name] => /Applications/XAMPP/xamppfiles/temp/phpYPcBjK
        [error] => 0
        [size] => 119090
    )
  )
```

The name and type are self-explanatory. The *tmp_name* is the temporary name of the file after it has been uploaded. If the file size is too big (according to the settings in php.ini), then this will be set to "none." An error code of 0 or UPLOAD_ERR_OK indicates that the file was uploaded successfully. The file size is the number of bytes. Additional possible error messages are listed in the following.

```
UPLOAD_ERR_OK = File uploaded successfully
UPLOAD_ERR_INI_SIZE = File is too big to upload
UPLOAD_ERR_FORM_SIZE = File is too big to upload
UPLOAD_ERR_PARTIAL = File was only partially uploaded
UPLOAD_ERR_NO_FILE = No file was uploaded
UPLOAD_ERR_NO_TMP_DIR = Missing a temporary directory on the server
UPLOAD_ERR_CANT_WRITE = File cannot be saved to disk
UPLOAD_ERR_EXTENSION = Invalid file extension
```

# Secure Programming

Hackers can manipulate the contents of the $_File associate array. The one exception is that the *tmp_name* cannot be changed. Thus, when using the information from this array, we need to validate it.

We can create a function to validate the file and its size before we move it.

***Listing 4-12.***  checkFile.php

```php
<?php
function checkFile($tmpName, $variableName) {

$valid_File_Types =  array('image/jpeg' => 'jpg');

$max_Size  = 40 * 1024 * 1024;
//  40MB must be the same size or less than the setting in php.ini

$errorStatus = false;

if(!isset($_FILES[$variableName]) ) {
        // error $_FILE does not exist
        $errorStatus = true;
} else {
         $info = finfo_open(FILEINFO_MIME_TYPE);
         if (!$info) {
                // error Can't open finfo using mime type
                $errorStatus = true;
         } else {
                $mime_type = finfo_file($info, $tmpName);
                if (!in_array($mime_type, array_keys($valid_File_
                Types))) {
                        // error invalid file type
                        $errorStatus = true;
                } else {
                        if (filesize($_FILES[$variableName]
                        ['tmp_name']) > $max_Size) {
                            // error file size too big
                            $errorStatus = true;
                        }
                }
```

```php
                                finfo_close($info);
            }
    }
}
return $errorStatus;
}
// Code below used for testing only
$variableName ='image-data';
$tmp = $_FILES['image-data']['tmp_name'];
if ( !checkFile($tmp, $variableName))
        { echo "File is valid";}
else { echo "Invalid File"; }
?>
```

Wow. A lot of new code. But let's break it down one part at a time to see what is happening.

```php
$valid_File_Types =  array('image/jpeg' => 'jpg');

$max_Size  = 40 * 1024 * 1024;
//  40MB must be the same size or less than the setting in php.ini

$errorStatus = false;
```

$valid_File_Types is an array of our acceptable file types. Currently, there is only one entry, but we can easily add additional file types. $max_Size is our allowable maximum size for an individual file. This must be the same or less than the value stored in the php.ini file. $errorStatus is set to false, which, by default, indicates there are no problems with the file we are uploading.

```php
if(!isset($_FILES[$variableName]) ) {
        // error $_FILE does not exist
        $errorStatus = true;
```

If the variable name (image_data) passed from the HTML form does not exist in the $_FILE array, we set the error status to true. This would be a possible indication that someone corrupted the array.

```
$info = finfo_open(FILEINFO_MIME_TYPE);
    if (!$info) {
            // error Can't open finfo using mime type
            $errorStatus = true;
```

If $info is not set, something happened when we attempted to create the ability to look at mime types using finfo. This is not an indication of a problem with our uploaded file but is an indication we have some other problem.

```
$mime_type = finfo_file($info, $tmpName);
        if (!in_array($mime_type, array_keys($valid_File_
        Types))) {
                // error invalid file type
                $errorStatus = true;
```

If the *mime type* (file ending) does not match one in our $valid_File_Types array, then we set the error status to true.

```
if (filesize($_FILES[$variableName]['tmp_name']) >
$max_Size) {
                // error file size too big
                $errorStatus = true;
```

If the file size of the temporary file uploaded is larger than the maximum we are allowing, the error status is set to true.

```
return $errorStatus;
}
$variableName ='image-data';
$tmp = $_FILES['image-data']['tmp_name'];
if ( !checkFile($tmp, $variableName))
    { echo "File is valid";}
else { echo "Invalid File"; }
```

---

**Note**   You can run this program using testUploadForm.php available under the views folder under the ch4 folder.

---

The error status is returned to whatever program called it. In this test, we called it right below the function and set the variable name and gathered the temporary name of the file from the $_FILES array created when the file was uploaded from the HTML form. This information was then passed into the function. If the function returns false, everything is OK. If it returns true, we have a problem.

Now that we have an ability to validate our uploaded file, we can finish the process by moving the file from the temporary location.

# Uploading Files with PHP

When the file is initially uploaded, it is placed in a temporary directory on the server with a temporary name as shown in the tmp_name value in the array. Remember that this location is determined in the php.ini file and can be changed by updating the php.ini and restarting Apache. To permanently store the file, we must move it from the temporary location to a permanent one.

```
move_uploaded_file( $fileName, $destination );
```

The function *move_uploaded_files* will accomplish this task. It takes two arguments. The first, $fileName, should hold the valid temporary file name (located in tmp_name in the $_File associate array). The second, $destination, is the folder to store the file permanently. This location must be writable and already exist. The function move_uploaded_file() will return TRUE, if the file was saved successfully, and FALSE, if something went wrong.

# Planning an Uploader Class

You will write code to upload files many times in your life as a PHP or full stack developer. It would be a clever idea to write some code for uploading in such a way that you can easily reuse it in later projects. Objects are easily reused, so let us plan a class we can reuse anytime we want to upload files.

## UML

*UML* provides a simple diagram for planning how to organize a class. The basic design is shown in the following.

```
Class Name
------------------
property1
property2
------------------
method1()
medthod2()
```

***Figure 4-8.*** *Basic UML diagram*

Remember, class names always begin the first name with an uppercase letter. If the class name is a compound word, we can uppercase the first letter for each additional word. We can also choose to separate each with an underscore. If the class is in a separate file from the main program, the file name which contains the class should be the same name as the class itself.

---

**Note**    UML is an acronym for "Unified Modeling Language." The language provides a standard syntax for documenting code. There is more to UML than just class diagrams. For more information on UML, visit `www.uml.org`.

---

## Uploader Class Requirements

As we discovered, we will need to save file data received from a form by moving it from the temporary directory to a permanent location. Thus, the class needs a property for storing the file metadata and a method for saving the file. The method will need a file name, so let us create a $filename property. We also need to save it someplace, so let us create a property to remember the location called $destination and a method to save it. We can now begin to plan our new class definition.

***Figure 4-9.*** *UML diagram of the Uploader class*

With a plan and a UML class diagram, it is easy to get started writing the class definition. Let us create a new file, `classes/Uploader.class.php`, as follows:

***Listing 4-13.*** Uploader.class.php

```php
<?php
class Uploader {
    private $filename;
    private $fileData;
    private $destination;

    public function saveIn( $folder ) {
        $this->destination = $folder;
    }

    public function save(){
        //no code here yet
    }
}
?>
```

The preceding code declares a class with a class name and class code block delimited with curly braces. Inside the class, there are three properties and two methods declared. It makes it much easier to create a class when we have already created a UML class diagram.

The property `destination` will get its value whenever the method `saveIn` is called. The properties `filename` and `fileData` do not currently have any values. We can retrieve both `filename` and `fileData` values from the superglobal array `$_FILES`. It would be nice if they got values whenever a new `Uploader` object was created, so their values reflect whatever file we wanted to upload at that point.

# The Magic Method __construct()

It just so happens that we can use the *__construct() constructor method* to accomplish our task. It will run only once, whenever a new `Uploader` object is created, using the new keyword. Remember there are *two underscore characters* before the method name. Let us declare a constructor method for the `Uploader`, so `filename` and `fileData` properties can get their values from `$_FILES` whenever a new `Uploader` object is created.

***Listing 4-14.*** ImageUploader.class.php

```php
<?php
//complete code for classes/Uploader.class.php
class ImageUploader {
    private $filename;
    private $fileData;
    private $destination;

    //declare a constructor method
    public function __construct( $key ) {
        $this->filename = $_FILES[$key]['name'];
        $this->fileData = $_FILES[$key]['tmp_name'];
    }

    public function saveIn( $folder ) {
        $this->destination = $folder;
    }

    public function save(){
        //no code here yet
    }
}
?>
```

Remember, we must know the name attribute of the <input type='file'> element used to upload a file. As we discovered earlier, we need the name attribute to access all file data in $_FILES. In the preceding code, the constructor method uses $key as an argument. The $key value will be used to pass the name attribute value into the constructor. With that in place, the constructor method can access all the metadata for the uploaded file.

## Saving the Uploaded File

The Uploader class is getting close to completion. We need to complete the method for saving the new file and verify that the file we are attempting to upload is valid. Remember to always prepare for the unexpected. There is one frequent problem we are likely to come across while performing file uploads: the destination folder might not be writable. We can prepare for it in our code.

**Listing 4-15.** ImagesUploader.class.php

```php
<?php
//complete code for classes/Uploader.class.php
require_once "views/checkImageFile.php";
class ImagesUploader {
    private $filename;
    private $fileData;
    private $destination;
      private $keyValue;

    //declare a constructor method
    public function __construct( string $key ) {
            $this->keyValue = $key;
        $this->filename = $_FILES[$key]['name'];
        $this->fileData = $_FILES[$key]['tmp_name'];
    }

    public function saveIn( $folder ) {
        $this->destination = $folder;
    }

    public function save(){
        $variableName = $this->keyValue;
        $tmp = $_FILES[$this->keyValue]['tmp_name'];
            $folderIsWriteAble = is_writable( $this->destination );
        $notValid = checkImageFile($tmp, $variableName);
        if( !$notValid and $folderIsWriteAble) {
            $name = "$this->destination/$this->filename";
            $success = move_uploaded_file( $this->fileData, $name );
        } else {
            $success = false;
    }
    return $success;
    }
}
?>
```

Let's look at the changes.

```
require_once "views/checkImageFile.php";
```

The previous function to check the validity of the image has been slightly modified by removing the call to the function, which will now occur in the save method in the ImagesUploader class. The new name of the file containing the verify method is checkImageFile.php.

```
$variableName = $this->keyValue;
$tmp = $_FILES[$this->keyValue]['tmp_name'];
$folderIsWriteAble = is_writable( $this->destination );
$notValid = checkImageFile($tmp, $variableName);
if( !$notValid and $folderIsWriteAble) {
      $name = "$this->destination/$this->filename";
      $success = move_uploaded_file( $this->fileData, $name );
```

The $variableName and $tmp variables are set within the save method, with the same values as they were previously set in the original check file method. Also, the PHP is_writable function is used to determine if the directory in which the file will be moved is writable. If the file passes verification and the directory is writable, the if statement produces a true result and the file is moved to the permanent location.

```
      } else {
             $success = false;
      }
  return $success;

}
```

If there is a problem, the else part of the if statement is executed. We have set $success to false, which indicates there is a problem, and have passed the value in $success (true or false) back to the calling program.

## Using the Uploader Class

We can now put the Uploader class to effective use and upload a file. It does not take a lot of code because most code is written inside the Uploader class.

*Listing 4-16.* imagesUpload.php

```php
<?php
//complete source code for views/upload.php
function upload(){
    include_once "classes/ImagesUploader.class.php";
    //image-data is the name attribute used in <input type='file' />
    $uploader = new ImagesUploader( "image-data" );
    $uploader->saveIn("imgs");
    $fileUploaded = $uploader->save();
    if ( $fileUploaded ) {
        $out = "New file uploaded to Images Gallery";
    } else {
        $out = "Something went wrong";
    }
    return $out;
}
$info = upload();
?>
```

---

**Note**   Minor adjustments have occurred in the following files to access
the current versions: ImagesUploader.class.php, imageslistnavigation.php,
imageslistindex.php, imagesUploadForm.php. Take the time to view these changes
from the files provided by the publisher.

---

The upload function pulls in the uploader class. It then creates an instance of the uploader (object $uploader) and passes the property name which holds the image information. This name was set in the HTML upload form. The permanent file location (imgs) is also passed into saveIn which stores it in the object. Then the save function is called from $uploader, which validates the image and checks to make sure the folder (imgs) is writable. If the file does get moved, $out is set to "New file uploaded to Images Gallery." If it does not get moved due to invalidation or the folder not being writable, the message "Something went wrong file not uploaded to Images Gallery" is passed into $out. $out is returned and set to $info, which will cause it to be displayed on the page.

Test the program using imageslistindex.php. The program should allow the upload of any JPEG files that don't exceed the size requirements.

**Exercise**: What can be added to these final programs to make them more secure? Scan each of the programs and use the knowledge you have gained so far to provide more secure programs. How can we limit the total size of all files to be uploaded into the final destination? Add code to provide this limitation. This will also help reduce the chance of successful DOS attacks. Also, go to `www.php.net` and discover how to create constants. Constants cannot be changed once they are initially created. Edit the programs and change any variables that do not change after being given an initial value to constants. Constants do add another tool in creating secure programs.

How cool is that? We have a completely dynamic image gallery, and users can upload their own images through the website. It is not quite `flickr.com` yet, but we hope you will agree that you are really starting to use PHP to create something fun and useful.

## The Single Responsibility Principle

We hope you marvel at the beauty of the `Uploader` class definition. It is planned and written with a single focus: It wants to upload files. It has properties and methods used to accomplish only one task. The properties are all about the file to be uploaded, and the methods are about uploading a valid file.

The *single responsibility principle* is a common principle used in object-oriented programming. The single responsibility principle states that a class should be written for a single purpose. All properties and methods of the class should relate directly to that single purpose. The class should only have a single reason to change.

For example: The `Uploader` has only one reason to change. It will change if you want to use it for uploading a different file. The single responsibility principle is a beautiful ideal to strive for in code. It is really Curly's law again, only this time, applied to object-oriented programming.

---

**Note**   You can read more about the single responsibility principle at `http://en.wikipedia.org/wiki/Single_responsibility_principle`.

---

# Summary

In this chapter, we have seen how we can make a dynamic image gallery, using objects and object methods. We also declared a custom class definition with properties and methods. We learned about the several types of loops and discovered that the `foreach` loop is designed to access information within an array, especially arrays in which we might not know the actual size.

We now have written two class definitions: the `Uploader` and the `Page_Data`. We are just starting to learn about classes and objects. We will get to work with many more classes and objects throughout the rest of this book. There are plenty of examples and explanations waiting for you in the pages to come, so hang in there. Learning takes time, and we are just getting started.

# Projects

1. Explore examples on the Web about uploading multiple files using HTML and PHP. Adjust the examples in this chapter to upload multiple files at the same time. Discover and use the HTML setting which limits the size of upload to the same size contained in the php.ini file. However, be aware that a hacker can change the HTML and avoid this limitation. To plan for this possibility, add code to the PHP uploader class to limit the multi-file upload to the value in php.ini. Also, add code to the HTML form to limit the number of files uploaded at the same time to the value set in the php.ini file. Add PHP code in the uploader class to also limit the number of files to be uploaded.

2. Add PHP code that will determine the number of files in the imgs folder before the images are displayed. Only display the number of images to the value set in the php.ini file.

3.  Explore examples on the Web to restrict access to the HTML
    upload form to specific users by requiring a userid and password
    be entered before the file(s) is uploaded. Again, expect that a
    hacker might try to bypass this restriction. Use PHP code to check
    the userid and password before calling the uploader program.
    If you want a challenge, how can we hash the password and
    verify it when hashed? Check `www.php.net` for the most current
    techniques to secure passwords.

4.  Change the program examples to upload documents (such as
    pdfs) instead of images. Instead of displaying the images, display
    HTML links to the documents.

# CHAPTER 5

# Reviewing PHP 8 Basic Syntax

## Objectives

After completing this chapter, you will be able to

- Understand the use and value of conditional statements

- Understand the use and value of for, while, and foreach loops

- Understand the use and value of functions

- Understand the use and value of arrays

Now that we have successfully created our first usable project, let us take a minute to review the basic PHP syntax. We will review some topics already covered and explore additional new topics in this chapter. After gathering the knowledge from this chapter and the previous chapters, we will be ready to explore the use of databases and other external files and tackle a much larger project: a blogging system. Take the time to enter in the code from the examples in this chapter and alter it to challenge yourself to become a better programmer. The more you work with code, the more you will get comfortable with quick efficient code development.

## From the Beginning

```php
<?php
    // code goes here
?>
```

© Jason Lengstorf, Thomas Blom Hansen, Steve Prettyman 2022
J. Lengstorf et al., *PHP 8 for Absolute Beginners*, https://doi.org/10.1007/978-1-4842-8205-2_5

As stated earlier, all PHP code must be placed between the <?php and ?> tags. The web server first looks at the file ending (.php) for an indication of the existence of PHP code. Once it determines its existence, it uses the tags to indicate the location of the code.

```
<h1> I love Green Tomatoes</h1>
<?php
    echo "The greener the better!";
?>
<h2> My partner hates Green Tomatoes</h2>
<?php
    echo "Yes I do!";
?>
```

As shown in the preceding, PHP code can be scattered into different areas of the file (web page) by simply using the opening and closing tags. However, each time this occurs, it requires sending the code to the PHP interpreter for processing. So, do not get too carried away with the thrill of doing so. You want code that is easy to read and understand. You reduce the chances of creating logical errors when the flow of the code is easy to follow.

## Comments

Comments can be created using // or /*. Remember, comments are not executed. However, they are very important. Good programmers provide comments so others can understand any complicated code. Gone are the days in which only one person maintains a program. Anyone that supports the code you created will really appreciate the effort you put forth in providing comments.

```
<?php
    // Description: This program produces a monthly departmental
       sales report
    /* Inputs:  Department ID (DID), Department Name (DN) : DepartTBL
                     Department ID (DID), Sales Date (Date), Sales
                     Amount (SA): SaleTBL
                         from widgetTools database (mySQL 8) */
```

```php
// Outputs: Monthly Widget Sales Report (widgetsales.html)
// Updates: (02/12/2022) : Adjust output format, Sexton Jones:
    Programmer
?>
```

Many organizations keep track of change management within a program by providing details on who created the program, when it was created, and any changes that have occurred. Comments can also provide a list of the inputs and outputs of the program and a description of the program itself. Additionally, similar descriptions are provided for functions (methods or procedures) which have been created within the program.

# PHP Functions

```php
<?php
        echo "Hello World";
?>
```

All executable code must include a semicolon at the end of the statement. As a standard, adopt the policy that any text strings (such as the preceding Hello World) should be included in double quotes. PHP does allow some exceptions to the rule (such as using single quotes in some instances), but you will seldom run into a problem if you are consistent in providing them. The use of echo demonstrates the ability to use a PHP function.

PHP provides a large number of other functions (blocks of code), besides the echo statement shown in the preceding. The functions contain well-tested efficient secure code. Whenever possible, a smart programmer will use existing functions to save time and to reduce programming errors and possible security vulnerabilities.

When creating your own PHP functions, they should begin with a lowercase letter. Additional words can be started with an uppercase letter, such as myFunction. Some programmers also use underscores between the words. In the following example, the string "Hello World" is passed into a function named "myFunction." We will explore a lot of PHP functions throughout this book. Later in this chapter, we will see additional examples on how a programmer can create their own functions.

```php
<?php
        myFunction("Hello World");
?>
```

# Variables

Variables temporarily store information in memory. As we have seen, PHP does not require you to declare a data type when using a variable. However, when the opportunity is available, you should consider defining the data type, as this will increase security by restricting the type of information that can be stored.

---

**Note**   A data type describes the data that you plan on storing, such as strings (text), integers (whole numbers), or floating-point numbers (decimals). This information is used by the operating system to determine the amount of space required to store the information.

---

We have the option to declare data types in many situations. It is a good idea to declare data types when we want to limit the type of data to be stored in memory. Remember, PHP will do *data type conversion* (such as converting a string "10" to a numeric 10) unless you stop it. Let us look at the standard way to declare variables in PHP.

In PHP, we usually do not need to declare a variable separately before using it. When declaring variables or functions, the developer can use many styles. The most common is the camel case. In camel case, the first word is lowercase, and the remaining words have a capitalized first letter, such as addIt. However, other styles are acceptable, such as

```
$first_number = 0;

$second_Number = 1;

$number1 = 12;
```

The key is to be consistent within your code with whatever style you choose. There is really no advantage as to which format is better. Although plenty of programmers will be happy to tell you their opinion! In my opinion, you should use meaningful names such as "total_Sales." Some also include the data type in the name, such as "int_Total_Sales." In large programs, it will be much easier to keep track of variable usage with a good naming convention.

> **Note**    Variables must always include the $ as the first character and other alphanumeric characters to complete the name. You can also include the underscore (_). However, no other special symbols or spaces are allowed.

In the following example, a variable ($result) will hold whatever is returned by a function called addIt. Since we have not declared a data type, this variable could hold a numerical result, a string result, or some other possible format. As a programmer, we might want this flexibility. For example, if the function is able to produce a result, we return the result. If it is not able to return a result, we can return a string ("Invalid Result") or we could pass back *NULL* (which indicates no result, different from passing a zero).

Since this function accepts two parameters (12, 13), we assume it will add the numbers together and return the result. The echo statement will then display whatever is contained in the variable.

```php
<?php

    $result = addIt(12, 13);
    echo $result;

?>
```

If we have not declared data types to limit what is passed into the function (see in the following), then it is possible that the following examples will also produce good results with other types of information passed. However, there could be something within the function that will not properly execute when information that is not expected is passed. A good programmer always creates code that avoids any possible error situation caused by invalid data being saved or passed into a function. Every situation must be considered, even once the programmer may consider as illogical or next to impossible.

```php
<?php
    $result = addIt(12.1, 13.3);
    echo $result;
?>
```

```php
<?php
```

```
    $result = addIt(12, "13");
    echo $result;
?>
```

If we want to restrict what information to accept or use, we could declare data types. We will explore a few examples soon. For now, by default, remember, the data type of a variable is determined the first time a variable is used.

V-1: The data type is string (characters).

```
    $myValue = "Help";
```

V-2: The data type is set to an integer (whole numbers).

```
    $myValue = 123;
```

V-3: Two integers added together produce an integer which is then stored into the variable.

```
    $myValue = 123 + 456;
```

```
    Result: $myValue now contains 579
```

V-4: Two *floating-point numbers* added together produce a floating-point number stored in the variable.

```
    $myValue = 123.123 + 123.456;
```

```
    Result: $myValue now contains 246.579
```

V-5: A floating-point number added to an integer will produce a floating-point number.

```
    $myValue = 123.233 + 12;
```

```
    Result: $myValue now contains 135.233
```

V-6: An attempt to add a number to a string number will be successful, if the string can be converted to a number. Adding the values together will produce results similar to the preceding examples.

```
    $myValue = 123 + "456";
```

```
    Result: $myValue now contains 579
```

The *string concatenation character* (.) can be used to merge the two strings together. The result then can be placed in the variable (which you guessed it now contains a string). In the following example, the existing two strings are merged together to create a new string stored in $myValue.

```
$myValue = "Help" . " me!";

Result: $myValue now contains "Help me!"
```

C-1: When merging a string and integer, PHP will convert the integer to a string (123) to allow it to be concatenated with the other string (Help ) to produce a string "Help 123" which will be placed into the variable.

```
$myValue = "Help " . 123;

Result: $myValue now contains "Help 123"
```

C-2: When a merger is attempted with a string and two values (which in this case are to be added together), PHP will first do the calculation and then convert the result to a string.

```
    $num1 = 1;
$num2 = 2;
$myValue = "Help " . $num1 + $num2;

Result: $myValue now contains "Help 3"
```

Let's take a look at restricting our data types with data type hints.

```
<?php
    function myFunction(bool $value = null) : bool {}
?>
```

In the preceding example, the function limits $value to only contain Boolean (true/false) type values. It also limits the value returned to be Boolean.

```
<?php
    $value = myFunction();
    $value = myFunction(true);
?>
```

---

**Note**   true is not a string, it is a Boolean value. Thus, it does not require quotes.

---

Both of the preceding statements could be valid when calling the myFunction function. If there is no value passed, then the variable $value is set to the *default value*, which is null. Null indicates that the variable is empty. However, we could also pass a Boolean value (true) which would be used instead of null.

Arithmetic operations work in a similar way to mathematics. The exception is that the calculation is done on the right side of the assignment operator (right side of the = sign) and the result is placed into the variable, function, or other object on the left side of the expression. PHP already includes many functions to produce results seen on a calculator.

---

**Note**   For more information on available math functions, visit `www.php.net/manual/en/ref.math.php`.

---

PHP allows you to use parentheses () to change the order in which values are calculated. Otherwise, for numerical values, the language usually follows a mathematical *order of operations*. This order is similar to normal mathematics but does have a few differences. We will see some of these as we explore the remainder of the book.

---

**Note**   For more information on order of operations, visit `www.php.net/manual/en/language.operators.precedence.php`.

---

Let us look at some examples.

The assignment operator (=) will take the value from the right side of the expression (1) and place it into the variable ($my_num) on the left side of the expression. If the variable does not exist, it will be created in memory.

```
$my_num = 1;
```

Both the following statements add the value on the right side of the expression ($my_num) to the content that exists in the variable ($value) on the left side of the expression. If the variable has not existed before, zero will be added to the value on the right side and the result is placed into the variable ($value). If a string exists in the variable, an attempt will be made to convert it to a number before adding it.

```
$value += $my_num;
$value = $value + $my_num;
```

The following example is similar to the previous example, except the value on the right side is subtracted from the value contained in the variable. If the variable did not previously exist, the value on the right side ($my_num) is subtracted from 0. If a string exists in the variable, an attempt will be made to convert it to a number.

```
$value -= $my_num;
$value = $value - $my_num;
```

The following example is similar to the previous example, except the value is multiplied instead of subtracted. If the variable did not previously exist, the value on the right side ($my_num) is multiplied by 0. If a string exists in the variable, an attempt will be made to convert it to a number.

```
$value *= $my_num;
$value = $value * $my_num;
```

The following example is similar to the previous example, except the value from the right side ($my_num) is divided into the value contained in the variable. The division will return a floating-point number, unless both values were integers and divided evenly (without any decimal places). If a string exists in the variable, an attempt will be made to convert it to a number.

---

**Note**   If the variable $my_num does not exist, it will be set to 0. This would cause the throwing of an exception because you cannot divide by zero! The function *fdiv()* will return INF (infinity), -INF (negative infinity), or NAN (not a number), instead of throwing an exception, when dividing by zero.

---

```
$value  /= $my_num;
$value = $value / $my_num;
```

The following example is similar to the previous one, except the remainder of the division is placed into the variable. If a string exists in the variable, an attempt will be made to convert it to a number.

```
$value %= $my_num;
$value = $value % $my_num;
```

The following statement will raise $value to the power contained in $my_num and place the result back into $value.

```
$value = $value ** $my_num;
```

Variables can be incremented/decremented before they are used (++$num, --$num) or after they are used ($num++, $num--).

(Assume *$num = 1 before each statement is executed.*)

```
$value = $num++ - 5; // $value is -4, $num is 2
$value = $num-- + 5; // $value is 6, $num is 0
$value = ++$num - 5; // $value is -3, $num is 2
$value = --$num + 5; // $value is 5, $num is 0
```

**Exercise**: Create a program that sets two numerical values to two different variables. Then calculate the values when adding, subtracting, dividing, and multiplying the numbers. After each calculation, display the results in a sentence, such as "The sum of 1 and 2 is 3."

---

**Hint**    In most cases, PHP allows you to place variable names inside of strings. For example, "The sum of $firstNumber and $secondNumber is $sum" could produce the requested results.

---

# Conditional Statements

*Conditional statements* determine if a comparison is "true" or "false." If the statement is true, then the code right after the if statement is executed. If the statement is false, the code after the else statement (if there is one) is executed. Unlike the assignment operator (=), shown in the previous section, comparing two values to determine if they are equal requires two (==) or three (===) equal signs. Two signs ignore the case or data type. An "A" and "a" would be equal. Also, a 5 and a 5.0 would be equal. Three signs require an exact match. Both of the examples would not be considered equal with three signs.

**Note**   If the programmer mistakenly only uses one equal sign, the program will not produce an error. It will assume a "true" state and the conditional statement might produce invalid results.

```
if(statement to compare) {
    // Executed if the comparison is true
}
// Code after the if statement is executed whether the result is true
    or false

if(statement to compare) {
    // Executed if the comparison is true
}
else {
    // Executed if the comparison is false
}
// Code after the if/else statement executed whether the result is
    true or false
```

The basic structure of a conditional statement is shown in the preceding. In the first example, the code inside the if statement is only executed if the statement is true. No additional code is executed if the statement is false. In the second example, code is provided after the else statement to be executed if the statement is false. Embedded if/else statements can also be used.

Let us look at some examples using conditional statements with comparison operators.

I-1:

```
<?php
            $a = 25; $b = 36;

            if( $a == $b) {
                    echo "$b equals $a";
            }

            else {
```

```php
                echo "$b and $a are not equal";
        }
?>
```

Output: 36 and 25 are not equal.

Why: The value in $a (25) and $b (36) are not the same. Thus, the code in the else section will be executed.

I-2:

```php
<?php
    $a = "a";  $b = "A";

    if( $a === $b) {
            echo "$b equals $a";
    }

    else {
            echo "$b and $a are not equal";
    }
?>
```

Output: A and a are not equal.

Why: Using three equal signs (===) also compares cases. In this example, the comparison is false due to the case. If you remove one of the equal signs, the result will become true.

---

**Note**   In this example, double quotes are used which creates a string. Since each of these is only one character, single quotes could also have been used.

---

I-3:

```php
<?php
    $a = 25; $b = 36;

    if( $a != $b) {
            echo "$b and $a are not equal";
    }
```

```php
    else {
            echo "$b and $a are equal";
    }
?>
```

Output: 36 and 25 are not equal.

Why: The not operator (!) works in reverse of the results of the equals operator (see #1). The condition is reversed from a false state to a true state. The code right after the if expression is executed.

I-4:

```php
<?php
    $a = "A"; $b = "a";

    if( $a !== $b) {
        echo "$b and $a are not equal";
    }
    else {
        echo "$b and $a are equal";
    }
?>
```

Output: a and A are not equal.

Why: The *not case operator* (!==) works in reverse of the case operator (see #2). The comparison becomes true. The code right after the if statement is executed.

I-5:

```php
<?php
    $a = 25.1; $b = 36;

    if( $a < $b) {
            echo "$a is less than $b";
    }
    else {
            echo "$b is greater than $a";
    }
?>
```

Output: 25.1 is less than 36.

Why: Less than returns true if the value on the left is less than the value on the right. We can mix floating-point (decimal) and whole number (integer) comparisons. In this example, 36 will be converted to 36.0 before they are compared.

I-6:

```php
<?php
        $a = 36; $b = 36;

        if( $a <= $b) {
                echo "$a is less than or equal to $b";
        }
        else {
                echo "$b is greater than $a";
        }
?>
```

Output: 36 is less than or equal to 36.

Why: The less than or equal to comparison works similar to #5. However, if the values are equal, then it returns true.

I-7:

```php
<?php
        $a = 25; $b = 36;

        if( $a > $b) {
                echo "$a is greater than $b";
        }
        else {
                echo "$b is greater than $a";
        }
?>
```

Output: 36 is greater than 25.

Why: The greater than comparison returns true if the left value is greater than the right value. In this example, 25 is less than 36. The else portion of the code is executed.

I-8:

```php
<?php

    $a = 36; $b = 36;

    if( $a >= $b) {
        echo "$a is greater than or equal to $b";
    }
    else {
        echo "$b is greater than $a";
    }

?>
```

Output: 36 is greater than or equal to 36.

Why: The greater than or equal to comparison works similar to #7. However, if the two values are equal, it returns true.

I-9:

```php
<?php

    $a = 36; $b = 36;

    $result = $a <=> $b;

    if( $result === 0) {
        print "Both are equal";
    } else if( $result === 1) {
        echo "$a is greater than $b";
    } else {
        echo "$b is greater than $a";
    }

?>
```

Output: Both are equal.

Why: The *rocket ship operator* returns -1 if $a < b, returns 0 if $a equals $b, or returns 1 if $a > $b. The if statement shown determines that status returned by the rocket ship operator and displays the appropriate result. The use of the if/else/elseif structure is shown here to determine a range of possible values.

# Logical Operators

*Logical operators* allow you to ask more than one question in a conditional statement.

Let us look at some examples.

L-1:

```php
<?php

    $a = 25; $b = 25; $c = 25; $d = 35;

    If ( $a == $b or $c == $d ) {
        echo "Some or all of us are equal!";
    } else {
        echo "We are not equal";

    }

?>
```

Output: Some or all of us are equal.

Why: Both sides of the or statement evaluate to true. If either or both sides of an *or operator* are true, then the complete expression is true.

---

**Note**   The symbols || can also be used instead of or.

---

L-2:

```php
<?php

    $a = 25; $b = 25; $c = 35; $d = 35;

    If ( $a == $b and $c == $d ) {
        echo "All of us are equal!";
```

```
    } else {
        echo "No one is equal";
    }
```

?>

Output: All of us are equal.

Why: Both sides of the expression must be true for complete expression to be true when using an **and operator**. In this example, both sides are true.

---

**Note**    The symbols && can also be used instead of and.

---

L-3:

```
<?php

        $a = 25; $b = 25; $c = 25; $d = 25;

        If ( $a == $b xor $c == $d ) {
                echo "Everyone is equal!";
        } else {
                echo "Someone is not equal";
        }
```

?>

Output: Someone is not equal.

Why: With *exclusive or* (xor), only one side of the expression can be true. In this example, both sides were true, so it evaluates to false. If this were an or statement, it would have been evaluated to be true.

L-4:

```
<?php

        $a = 25; $b = 25; $c = 25; $d = 25;

        If ( ! ($a == $b xor $c == $d ) ) {
            echo "Everyone is equal!";
        } else {
```

```
        echo "Someone is not equal";
    }
?>
```

Output: Everyone is equal.

Why: The not expression (!) reverses the result. This exclusive or (xor) returned false because both sides are true. However, the not reversed.

The *? operator* is a short coding version of a conditional if-then-else statement.

```
<?php
        $a = 36; $b = 36;
        echo $a == $b ? "They are equal" : "They are not equal";
?>
```

Output: They are equal.

Why: The statement placed between the ? and : is executed if the comparison is true. The statement between the : and ; is executed if the statement is false. Since a print command is to the left of the comparison, the result of the comparison will be printed. $a and $b are the same value; thus, the first string is displayed.

```
    <?php
        $a = 36; $b = 24;
        echo $a <=> $b ? "They are equal" : "$a is greater than $b" :
        "$b is greater than $a";
?>
```

Output: 36 is greater than 24.

Why: You can also evaluate for equal (0), greater than (-1), and less than (1) using the spaceship operator. This comparison becomes very short and efficient to determine whether the values are equal or who is greater. Since $a is greater than $b, the statement between the two colons (:) is displayed. If $a were less than $b, the statement between the last colon and the semicolon would be displayed. Otherwise, when the values are equal, the statement between the question mark (?) and first colon would be displayed.

Let us take a look at some invalid comparisons and the resulting error messages.

E-1:

```
"ten" > "eleven";
```

Result: Error: "Unsupported type string for comparison"
E-2:

```
"eleven" > 10;
```

Result: Error: "Operator type mismatch string and int for comparison"
E-3:

```
"ten" == 10;
```

Result: Error: "Operator type mismatch string and int for comparison"
E-4:

```
"120" > "99.9";
```

Result: Error: "Unsupported type string for comparison"
E-5:

```
"120" <=> "99.9";
```

Result: Error: "Unsupported type string for comparison"

The *switch statement* can be used to eliminate embedded if-then-else statements when determining a value within a variable.

```
switch (value to compare) {
    case value:
        // code to execute if true
    break;
    case value;
        // code to execute if true
    break;
    default:
        // code to execute if there are no matches
    break;
}
```

The structure of the switch statement requires break commands (break;) at the end of each possible case situation. The colon (:) is used in each header of the case(s) after the value to compare.

```php
<?php

    $a = 36;

    switch ($a) {

        case 10:
            echo "10";
        break;

        case 20:
            echo "20";
        break;
        case 30:
            echo "30";
        break;

        default:
            echo "Number was not found";
        break;
    }

?>
```

Result: Number was not found.

Why: The value 36 is not caught in any of the case statements. PHP will do conversion, when possible. In this example, it will compare the value in the strings to the number presented. The flow of the structure will drop into the default statement since there are no matches. The default statement acts in a similar fashion to the else statement; it catches all remaining possibilities. It is a good idea to include a default statement in all case structures to handle the unexpected values rather than the possibility of causing an exceptional situation.

**Exercise**: Create a program which uses a conditional statement that will determine what color is contained in a string. If the color is green, display "I love the earth." If the color is blue, display "The sky is beautiful." If the color is yellow or orange, display "I love sunsets." For any other color, display "selectedcolor is my favorite color." Replacing the selectedcolor with the color chosen.

---

**Hint**    You can put a variable inside of a string.

---

# Functions

In addition to the 1000s of built-in or easily importable PHP functions available for your use, you can also create your own functions.

```
function function_Name(attribute1, attribute2, …) {

    // code goes here

}

function_name(attribute, attribute, …);
// next statement after function has completed
```

The general format of a function is shown in the preceding. The function keyword is lowercase. The name you provide for the function uses almost the same format as variables, except you do not include the $. Variables or values can be passed as parameters into the function in the parentheses. All code goes between the brackets {}. The function is called using the function name and the passing of any required attributes. When a function is called, the execution of the program jumps to the function. After all code has been executed, the program flow jumps to the instruction after the call to the function.

Let us look at some examples.

F-1:

```php
<?php

        function display_hello() {

            echo "Hello";

        }

        display_hello();

?>
```

Output: Hello

Why: No values are passed into the function. However, the print statement is executed.

The function can also be placed at the bottom of the code. However, be consistent. Either place your functions at the top of the code of the bottom of the code. Functions can also be included in a separate file that can then be imported into the main PHP program. We will look at that example soon.

F-2:

```php
<?php

function display_hello($value) {

          echo $value;

}

display_hello("Hello");

?>
```

Output: Hello

Why: This example accomplishes the same task. However, it allows some flexibility by allowing the user to pass the value to be displayed. Notice that the string was passed within the parentheses when the function was called. The string will drop into the variable $value (it determines where values go by the position they are passed). The print statement in the function then uses the variable $value to display the information. This function would actually display almost anything passed (including numbers), even though it is called display_hello.

F-3:

```php
<?php

    function display_names( $first_name, $last_name = "none") {

        echo "Your first name is $first_name";

        if ($last_name != "none") {

        echo  "Your last name is $last_name";

    }
```

```php
}

display_names("James");

display_names("Jackie", "Jones");

?>
```

Output: Your first name is James
Your first name is Jackie
Your last name is Jones

Why: The preceding display_names function accepts two values ($first_name, $last_name). However, it also provides a default value for the second parameter. In the first call to the function, "James" will pass into $first_name. Since there is not a second parameter passed, $last_name will contain "none." "Your first name is James" will be displayed. The if statement will determine that a second value has not been passed and will not attempt to display $last_name. In the second call, both values are passed. "Jackie" will be passed into $first_name. "Jones" will be passed into $last_name. The function will display "Your first name is Jackie" and "Your last name is Jones."

F-4:

```php
<?php

        function addtwo( $first_value, $second_value) {

                $result = $first_value + $second_value;

                return $result;

        }

        echo addtwo( 12, 14);

?>
```

Output: 26

Why: In the addtwo example, two numerical values are passed into the function. The call to the function causes 12 to be passed into $first_value and 14 to be placed into $second_value. The two numbers are added together, and the result is placed into $result. A return statement returns the value back to the program that called it (instead of displaying it). This allows the calling code the flexibility to determine what to do with the returned value. In this example, the function was called within a print execution. This will cause the value returned by the addtwo function (26) to be displayed.

F-5:

```php
<?php

function addtwo( int $first_value, int $second_value) : int {

        $result = $first_value + $second_value;

        return $result;

        }

        echo addtwo( 12, 14);

?>
```

Output: 26

Why: We can add scalar type hints to restrict the type of information passed into and out of a function. In the preceding example, the parameters passed in are restricted to integers only as indicated by the int keyword before the variable's names. The return value is also restricted to integers as indicated by the : int as part of the function header.

F-6:

```php
<?php

function addtwo( int | float $first_value, int | float $second_value) : int
| float {

        $result = $first_value + $second_value;

        return $result;

        }

        echo addtwo( 12.1, 14);

?>
```

Output: 26.1

Why: This example demonstrates the *union* of different data types. The function now provides the ability to accept either integers or floating-point numbers for $first_value and $second_value. It also provides the ability to return either an integer or a float. This provides added validation of data while still allowing flexibility of the actual use of the function itself.

As of PHP 8, the current valid data types are

- array
- bool
- callable
- int
- float
- null
- object
- resource
- string

As you use functions, you will discover that some could be used in other applications. You can move these functions in a separate file and imported into an application.

```php
<?php

    function addtwo( int $first_value, int $second_value) : int {

        $result = $first_value + $second_value;

        return $result;

}

?>
```

Functions that reside within their own files should still include the opening and closing php tags as shown in the preceding.

```php
<?php
```

```
    include "addtwo.php";

    echo addtwo( 12, 14);

?>
```

The preceding program will import the addtwo.php file (which contains the addtwo function). Once it is imported, it can call the function as shown.

---

**Caution**   *When importing more than one file, you can cause a conflict if more than one function imported has the same signature (name and parameters).*

---

The include keyword will search for the file and attempt to include it in the program. If the file does not exist, the program will continue. The include_once keyword is similar to the include. However, it makes an additional check to discover if the file has already been imported. If it has, it ignores the request (does not produce an error). include would produce errors if the file has already been imported.

The require keyword is similar to the include keyword. However, if the file does not exist, an error will be produced. The require_once keyword is similar to the require keyword with the additional check to not load the file if it has already been loaded.

The examples shown do not attempt to handle any errors. There are multiple possible problems with these examples, if the user does not enter what it expected. We can adjust the calling program to handle possible problems by adding a *try/catch* structure.

```php
    <?php

        try {
            include "addtwo.php";
            echo dividetwo( 12, 14);
        }

        catch(zeroException $e) {
            echo "Don't try to divide by zero!";
        }

        catch(Throwable $t) {
            echo $t->getMessage();
```

```
    }

    finally {
        echo "This message is over.";
    }
?>
```

In the preceding example, both the include statement and the print statement are placed in a *try block*. The program will execute statements in a try block until it runs into a problem. When a problem occurs, it will look for a *catch block* to handle the problem. Since the include statement depends on a file existing external to the program, it is important that the program be able to handle the possibility that the file might not exist. This example also places the dividetwo function within the try block. If this dividetwo function attempts to divide by zero, PHP will raise an exception.

The code specially captures the zeroException exception which would be raised by PHP if an attempt were made to divide by zero. If that occurs, the message shown in the block would be displayed and the program would shut down properly (not crash).

Additional catch blocks are shown. The Throwable catch captures all other exceptions caused by the program. If the execution of the code jumps the flow into one of these blocks, the standard error message would be displayed, and the program will execute the finally block. The *finally block* is executed even when no exceptions are discovered. It is important to assure that live programs do not crash. It is better to capture any problems and then display a message to the user requesting that they try using the system again later.

**Exercise**: Create a function which accepts two numbers and a symbol to indicate if the user wants to add, subtract, multiply, or divide. Use a switch statement to determine which operation will take place. Include the call to the function in a try/catch structure to capture any attempt to divide by zero.

# Arrays

Arrays hold multiple related information in memory. The ability to save information in arrays greatly reduces the amount of coding that would be necessary to create multiple variables to store information. Arrays also provide the ability to easily increase the amount of storage locations when needed. In PHP, arrays can be created on the fly, when needed, or formatted before actual use. The data type for each individual item in a PHP array is determined at the time when a value is stored.

Let us look at an example; an array might contain class information such as class number, class name, description, room, instructor, and size (number of students).

```
$class_array[0] = "CS122"; // class number

$class_array[1] = "Programming Concepts 1"; // class name

$class_array[2] = "Basic concepts of the PHP language."; // description

$class_array[3] = "B123"; // room

$class_array[4] = "Dr. Abraham Excel"; // instructor

$class_array[5] = 50; // number of students
```

This array has been created dynamically (on the fly). All numerical arrays in PHP begin with a *subscript* (index) of zero. However, when dynamically creating an array, you can start at any subscript and even skip positions. Array names require the same syntax as variables with the addition of the array subscript which is contained in square brackets ([]).

We can also allow PHP to create the subscript numbering for us, using the following format.

```
$class_array[ ] = "CS122"; // class number

$class_array[ ] = "Programming Concepts 1"; // class name

$class_array[ ] = "Basic concepts of the PHP language."; // description

$class_array[ ] = "B123"; // room

$class_array[ ] = "Dr. Abraham Excel"; // instructor

$class_array[ ] = 50; // number of students
```

We can also accomplish the same task with a more common format used in other programming languages.

```
$class_array = array (  "CS122",

                        "Programming Concepts 1",

                        "Basic concepts of the PHP language.",
```

```
                       "B123", "Dr. Abraham Excel", 50);
```

This format will also create the array, using fewer lines of code. The array keyword must be located to the right of the assignment operator followed by the items to be stored with parentheses. Each item is separated by a comma. PHP will place the first item in subscript position zero (0) and each additional item will be placed in the next positions, which will result in the same array structure as in the previous example.

The array itself actually behaves in exactly the same way as the previous array. Both of these arrays require us to remember what content is placed in which position. We as humans tend to remember words better than numbers. Thus, PHP provides us with associative arrays, which allow us to name our position (key) instead of using numbers (although technically we could name them with a number) and to associate the *key* with a *value*.

```
$class_array["class number"] = "CS122";

$class_array["class name"] = "Programming Concepts 1";

$class_array["description"] = "Basic concepts of the PHP language.";

$class_array["room"] = "B123";

$class_array["instructor"] = "Dr. Abraham Excel";

$class_array["number of students"] = 50;
```

This provides an easier-to-understand relationship between the values and the array itself. We can also create the same relationship with the other more common format.

```
$class_array = array (  "class number" =>"CS122",

                        "class name" => "Programming Concepts 1",

                        "description"  => "Basic concepts of the PHP
                        language.",

                         "room"  => "B123",  "instructor" => "Dr.
                        Abraham Excel",
                         "number of students" => 50);
```

The *arrow (=>) symbol* provides a visual association between the key and the value in each position in the array.

Let us take a moment to look at *multidimensional arrays.*

```
$class_array = array (

    array (  "CS122", "Programming Concepts 1",

        "Basic concepts of the PHP language.",

        "B123", "Dr. Abraham Excel", 50),

            array (  "CS123", "Programming Concepts 2",

            "Advanced concepts of the PHP language.",

            "B124", "Dr. Abraham Excel", 50)

);
```

Arrays can also be multidimensional. The preceding array contains two rows representing two different classes. Arrays are not limited to two dimensions. However, once we go beyond three or four dimensions, it is harder for us humans to associate the relationships between the dimensions. Also, the more dimensions you define, the more memory the program consumes to store the data and the associations between the dimensions. Keep your structures as simple as possible.

## Loops

Let's review what we have learned about loops. Loops provide the ability to execute the same code multiple times. As we will see in a moment, loops work hand in hand with retrieving and storing information into arrays.

```
for ($I = 1; $I <= 10; $I++) {

            echo "$I times ";

}
// next statement after loop has completed
```

```
Output: 1 times 2 times 3 times 4 times 5 times 6 times 7 times 8 times 9
times 10 times
```

The for loop works well when you know exactly how many times you want to loop. In the preceding example, $I is initially set to 1. Then the loop iterates as long as $I is less than or equal to 10. Each time the loop reaches the top, the value of I is increased by 1. When the value of $I reaches 11, the loop stops. The program will then execute any statements following the end of the loop.

```
$I = 1;

while ($I <= 10) {

            echo "$I times";
            $I++;

}
```

Output: 1 times 2 times 3 times 4 times 5 times 6 times 7 times 8 times 9 times 10 times

The same task can be accomplished with a while loop. However, as you can see, it does take slightly more code. You have to remember to include the incrementing of the counting variable ($I++). If that statement is forgotten, it will become an infinite loop. With the for loop, you are easily reminded to increment the variable in the top statement in the loop. While loops are good for conditions that might change – such as looping until you reach the end of a file or end of an array.

```
foreach( $class_array as $value)
{
    echo $value;
}
```

foreach loops work well with arrays. The preceding example loops through the one-dimensional numerical array ($class_array) shown in previous examples and displays each value. $value represents the current value that the loop is looking at in the array. foreach loops do not require the programmer to create code that checks for the end of the array. This eliminates any possibility that an "out of bounds" error message could occur. Also, foreach loops automatically skip over any positions in the array that have not yet been declared. This eliminates any possible "null value" messages being displayed when it loops through the array.

There are lots of php functions available to work with arrays. Let us take a moment to look at a couple of examples. *array_merge* can be used to add the contents of one or more arrays to the end of any existing array or to an array that has been defined but does not currently contain any values.

```php
<?php
    $colors1 = array("red", "green");
    $colors2 = array("blue", "yellow");
    $result = array_merge($colors1, $colors2);
    print_r($result);
?>
```

The $color2 array is merged to the end of the $color1 array, and the result is placed into the new $result array. The original arrays do not change. The print_r function is a handy tool that will display the contents of the array $result as follows.

```
Array
(
    [0] => red
    [1] => green
    [2] => blue
    [3] => yellow
)
```

You can also use the *spread operator* to merge two arrays together.

```php
<?php
$fords = ['falcon', 'mustang'];
$cars = ['civic', 'smart', ...$fords, 'tuson'];
var_dump($cars);
?>
```

The spread operator (…) allows you to place one array inside of another array at any location. The *var_dump* function is a great tool to discover what is inside of any array and the data type for the position in the array. It provides more details than the print_f function. The $cars array now contains

```
array(5) {
    [0]=>
```

```
    string(5) "civic"
    [1]=>
    string(5) "smart"
    [2]=>
    string(5) "falcon"
    [3]=>
    string(7) "mustang"
    [4]=>
    string(5) "tuson"
}
```

# Enums

Enumerations (enums) are a collection of a type with a fixed number of possible values. As an example, let us define a Food enum with certain allowed food types.

```
enum Food {
    case: Hotdog;
    case: Fish;
    case: Steak;
    case: Salad;
}
```

Once declared, you can use enums as type hints to restrict the values accepted or returned from a function.

```
function eating( Food $type)
{
    echo "I like $type";
}
```

To pass a value or return a value, you must include the enum and its value )with (::) or it will produce an error.

For more information on enums, visit www.zend.com/blog/php-8-1.

# Summary

As we stated in the beginning of the chapter, the goal was to introduce you to the basic structure of the language. We have reviewed the use and creation of functions, conditional statements, and variables. We do not expect you to be a php expert, yet. There are plenty more chapters ahead which will build your knowledge. Now that you have a general understanding, we are ready to explore the use of databases. We will soon use this knowledge to build a blogging system.

# Projects

1. Create a numerical array which contains the information about your house or apartment including number of bedrooms, number of bathrooms, and the street address. Use one of the looping structures to output the information in a well-formatted table. Hint: You can use HTML and CSS code within print or echo statements to create your table.

2. Complete #1 using an associative array.

3. Change #1 to include a two-dimensional array which will include all houses on your street or apartments in your complex. To output the information, you will need two embedded loops. You can either skim ahead in the book to discover examples or research "displaying a php two-dimensional array" in your favorite search engine on the Web.

# PART II

# CHAPTER 6

# Databases, MVC, and Data Objects

## Objectives

After completing this chapter, you will be able to

- Understand how to create MySQL/MariaDB databases

- Manipulate data in MySQL/MariaDB tables

- Design a database table structure

- Use PHP for secure interaction with MySQL/MariaDB databases

- Organize PHP scripts with a model-view-controller approach

- Create and use PHP Data Objects

Modern websites are incredibly powerful, and much of this power derives from their ability to store information. Storing information creates highly customizable interactions between software and the user. These interactions can range from entry-based blogs and commenting systems to high-powered banking applications that handle sensitive transactions securely.

This chapter covers the basics of MySQL/MariaDB, a powerful, open source database platform. We will also explore an object-oriented approach to accessing data within PHP projects.

© Jason Lengstorf, Thomas Blom Hansen, Steve Prettyman 2022
J. Lengstorf et al., *PHP 8 for Absolute Beginners*, https://doi.org/10.1007/978-1-4842-8205-2_6

**Note**    In 2009, Sun Microsystems purchased MySQL. Within a brief period of time, Oracle purchased Sun Microsystems. There was a concern that MySQL would not continue to be open source. Some of the developers of MySQL banded together to create a free and open source database system, MariaDB, which would be highly compatible with MySQL. While over the years, each product has added additional features not replicated in the other product, the basic commands and routines used to access and manipulate databases have remained the same. Many WAMP, MAMP, and LAMP stack software packages actually include MariaDB instead of MySQL (even though there is still a free version of MySQL available). Some of these products even use commands and references which indicate the database used is MySQL when it is actually MariaDB. However, since both products use virtually the same commands to access and manipulate databases, the code shown in this book and many others will work with either database system.

# The Basics of MySQL/MariaDB Data Storage

MySQL/MariaDB is a relational database management system that lets us store data in multiple tables. Each table contains a set of named columns, and each row consists of a data entry into the table. Tables will often contain information about other table entries. This allows tables to be linked together using a value stored in both tables.

When comparing Tables 6-1 and 6-2, the value in one table (`artist_id` in the artist table) can be associated with the same value (`artist_id` in album table) in another table. `artist_id` in the artist table is the *primary key* for that table as it uniquely identifies each row. `artist_id` in the album table is the *secondary key* because it is not used to uniquely identify the rows in the album table (`album_id` uniquely identifies the rows; it is the primary key). However, it is used to link to another table.

***Table 6-1.*** *The Artist Table*

| artist_id | artist_name |
|-----------|-------------|
| 1         | Bon Iver    |
| 2         | Feist       |

***Table 6-2.*** *The Album Table*

| album_id | artist_id | album_name |
|----------|-----------|------------|
| 1 | 1 | For Emma, Forever Ago |
| 2 | 1 | Blood Bank - EP3 |
| 3 | 2 | Let It Die |
| 4 | 2 | The Reminder |

The artist table includes two columns. The first column, `artist_id`, stores a unique numerical identifier for each artist. The second column, `artist_name`, stores the artist's name.

The album table stores a unique identifier for each album in the `album_id` column and the album name in – you guessed it – the `album_name` column. The album table includes a third column, `artist_id`, that relates the artist and album tables. This column stores the unique artist identifier that corresponds to the artist who recorded the album.

At first glance, it might seem like a silly way of storing data. Why keep an abstract, incomprehensible number, instead of simply writing the artist's name for every album? Table 6-3 gives an example of why this is not a good idea.

***Table 6-3.*** *The Badly Designed Album Table*

| album_id | artist | album_name |
|----------|--------|------------|
| 1 | Bon Iver | For Emma, Forever Ago |
| 2 | Bon Iver | Blood Bank - EP3 |
| 3 | Feist | Let It Die |
| 4 | fiest | The Reminder |

Did you notice the spelling error for `album_id`? Because the artist's name is spelled out separately for every album, it is possible to store different names for the same artist. In a tiny table with four entries, like the one preceding, it is easy to spot and correct errors. But tables are rarely that small in the real world. Imagine building a database for a music store. We would have to keep track of thousands of albums.

This problem also demonstrates the need to design databases in *third-normal form*. Without going into too much detail, a database is in third-normal form if data redundancy is reduced, and records can easily be uniquely identified. By creating an artist table, we eliminate the need to duplicate the artist's name in the album table. We also eliminate the possibility that two artists might have the same name. Using an artist id keeps each artist name unique, even if the spelling of the name is the same. If we did not use an id, to uniquely identify an album row, we would need to include both the album id and the artist's name (hopefully spelled correctly).

By designing tables that store one piece of data once, and only once, you design a robust database with data integrity. Joe Celko, a prominent figure in the SQL community, has aptly coined the slogan "One simple fact, in one place, one time." Memorize that slogan and let your database tables follow this one rule.

# Manipulating Data with SQL

We can manipulate the data in a MySQL/MariaDB table via the *Structured Query Language (SQL)*. SQL is a language which manages data in a *relational database system*. A relational database system (such as MySQL/MariaDB) formats data into tables and builds relationships between the tables, using primary and secondary keys. In this section, we will discover the basics of SQL, including the ability to create a database, create tables, insert data, update data, and display data.

*phpMyAdmin* is provided in many WAMP, LAMP, and MAMP stacks to easily create and maintain databases. In addition, other tools, such as *MySQL Workbench* (`www.mysql.com/products/workbench/`), provide additional ways to design, develop, and secure MySQL/MariaDB databases. We will start by looking at phpMyAdmin because it is included in the XAMPP stack. But first, we must activate both Apache and MySQL from the XAMPP control panel.

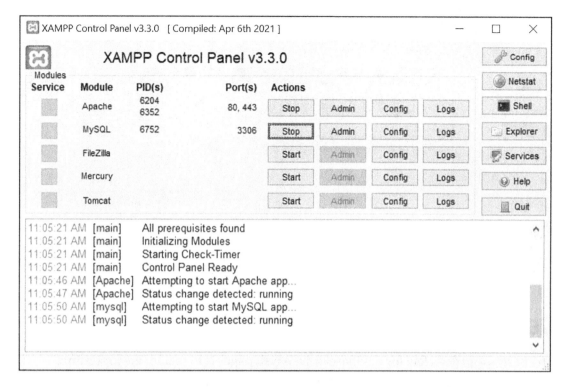

***Figure 6-1.*** *The XAMPP control panel*

To start both Apache and MySQL, simply click the start button to the right of each. Once they have properly started, each will be highlighted in green, and the start button will change to a stop button. If there are problems, the program will be highlighted in red, with error messages displayed in the view box. If this occurs, copy the error message into a browser to discover what others have done to fix the problem.

With MySQL and Apache running, open a browser and navigate to `http://localhost/`. The XAMPP Dashboard will display. On the menu of the dashboard, select phpMyAdmin to open the phpMyAdmin control panel.

**Figure 6-2.** *The phpMyAdmin control panel*

We are now ready to create our first MySQL/MariaDB database!

# Developing a Database for the Poll

The best way to get a feel for database-driven web pages is to create one for testing. Over the next pages, we will create a database-driven site poll. It is a simple example of database-driven development, but it is quite sufficient to demonstrate the essential principles. The simplest possible site poll will present one question to which site visitors can reply *yes* or *no*. All replies from users will be displayed, so every site user can see how others replied.

As simple as the example is, it will use many of the skills we have gained so far, and it will teach us how to integrate database-driven data in PHP projects.

The site poll relies on a database table to store the poll question and the poll replies. PHP will connect to MySQL/MariaDB and retrieve the relevant data, so it can be displayed in a browser. Using PHP, we will output an HTML form allowing site visitors to interact with the site poll. Whenever a visitor submits the form, PHP will then submit the answer and update the MySQL/MariaDB database table accordingly. Let's begin by creating a database with a table and some poll data.

# Building a Database Using CREATE

SQL uses the keyword CREATE to build a database or a database table. The CREATE statement must include the CREATE keyword and a keyword to indicate if we want to build a database or table. Logically, we must first create the database before we place any tables within it. Thus, we will use the keyword DATABASE along with the CREATE keyword to build a database. Of course, we also need to provide a name for our database.

```
CREATE DATABASE playground
```

To execute an SQL statement, we can select the SQL tab in the phpMyAdmin control panel (Figure 6-3). Once selected, a text field will be displayed to enter in any valid SQL commands. To execute the SQL, click the Go button beneath the text field.

***Figure 6-3.***  *The SQL tab in phpMyAdmin*

We can also create a database by selecting the Databases tab.

**Figure 6-4.** *The Databases tab in phpMyAdmin*

Just enter the database name and click CREATE. We could also select the type of collation to use with the database. However, the default is acceptable.

---

**Note**   A collation is a set of rules that specify which characters in the character set come first. We know that *a* comes before *b*, but how about the character *7*? Should that come before or after alphabetical characters? What about special characters such as *#"#€%&*? A collation explicitly states how characters should be ordered.

---

# The CREATE TABLE Statement

As mentioned earlier, since MySQL/MariaDB is a relational database, it stores data in tables. Naturally, after creating the database, we need to create a table. We need a little more SQL knowledge to accomplish this. The general syntax for creating a table is as follows:

```
CREATE TABLE table_name (
    column_name datatype [any constraints or default values],
    column_name datatype [any constraints or default values]
)
```

Again, we use the CREATE statement to build a table, in a similar format to building the database. We will declare names for our attributes (columns) and the data type for each column or attribute. We can always add or delete columns or attributes at any time. The CREATE statement can also declare constraints or default values.

## Secure Programming

When creating columns within databases, special care and consideration should be given to the data types, constraints, and default values. A secure database will restrict values entered that do not meet these parameters. If the program using the database is dependent on a value existing within a field, default values should be provided. Remember, the program might reject an invalid value before attempting to update the table. It might be acceptable to use the default value when this occurs. However, there may be cases in which the value is required in order for enough information to exist within the record created. In this case, the database column should be set to require the information. If it is not provided, the database management system will reject the attempt to enter the data.

Let's access the playground database by clicking its name in the left column of the phpMyAdmin control panel. Click the SQL tab at the top of the screen, and we're ready to create our first table.

```
CREATE TABLE poll (
    poll_id INT NOT NULL AUTO_INCREMENT,
    poll_question TEXT,
    yes INT DEFAULT 0,
    no INT DEFAULT 0,
    PRIMARY KEY (poll_id)
)
```

Notice the format of the CREATE statement. It is very vital that the proper parentheses and commas are included between each statement. The last line does not require a comma. Once we have entered the SQL into the text field, we can click Go to execute it. This will create the new table.

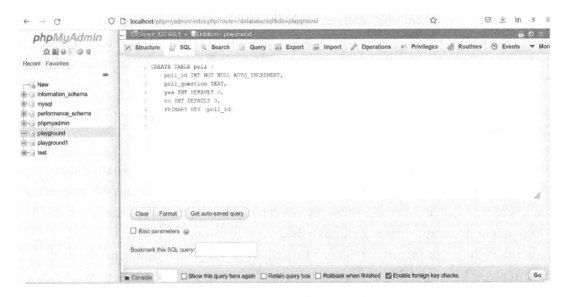

**Figure 6-5.** *Create a new table in the playground database*

We can also create a table using the default window after selecting the database from the left-hand column. Once the table name is entered, we must also select the number of columns to create. After clicking the button, the next screen will display boxes to enter in the attributes for each column. The information entered is the same as what was shown in the preceding program code.

Let's explore the new table we created by selecting the poll table from the panel at the left side of phpMyAdmin. Next, we will select the Structure tab from the menu.

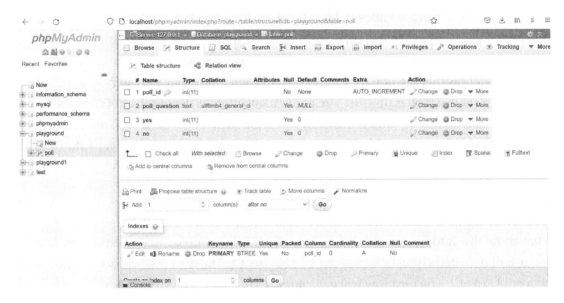

**Figure 6-6.** *Poll table structure*

The poll table has four attributes or columns: `poll_id`, `poll_question`, yes, and no. Each attribute has a *type* (data type). The fields of a table can only hold data of the correct type. For example, we can only store integers in `poll_id`, yes, and no as indicated by the int type. The number 11 is the default size of the integer. This can be adjusted with SQL code or by making changes when clicking the Change keyword to the right of the column. We will use the default settings. The type setting for `poll_question` restricts entries to text only. Finally, the yes and no attributes are created with a default value of 0. None of the other attributes has default values.

## Understanding PRIMARY KEY

The `poll_id` attribute includes a visual key to the right of the name. Also, it is listed at the bottom of the screen with a PRIMARY keyname. This indicates `poll_id` is now the *primary key* of poll entities. When an attribute is declared as the primary key, it must hold a unique value. So, however many rows of data the poll table will eventually contain, there can be no two identical `poll_id` values.

If we have a row of data with a `poll_id` of 1. Then if we attempt to insert another row of data also with a `poll_id` of 1, the new row will display an error message. A primary key is used to unambiguously identify one row of data. As an example, think about how many John Smiths there are. We could not use name as a unique identifier. However, we could give each a unique id to determine which John Smith we want to explore.

We can actually create tables in MySQL/MariaDB without a primary key, but such tables are special cases. Most of the time, you will want to create tables with a primary key, because data isn't really useful if you can't identify entries uniquely.

We now know that the poll table is created in such a way that a primary key `poll_id` must have a value which is unique. The `poll_id` attribute is declared as NOT NULL, meaning that a null value (null is basically the same as no entry at all) will not be accepted for `poll_id`. The `poll_id` attribute must invariably hold an integer value. The `poll_id` attribute cannot be left empty.

## Understanding AUTO_INCREMENT

What about the auto-increment setting for poll id? It is a simple but powerful tool: The first row of data in the poll table will get a `poll_id` of 1. The next row will automatically get a `poll_id` of 2. The next row will get a `poll_id` of 3, and so forth. The value of `poll_id` will automatically increment! A great way to make sure each row is identified by a unique value.

# The INSERT Statement

With our table created, we're ready to start storing data. Every new entry into the poll table will be stored as a separate row. For the sake of simplicity, we can start with inserting a single row of data.

```
INSERT INTO poll (
    poll_question
) VALUES (
    "Is PHP hard fun?"
)
```

This SQL statement will insert a new row of data into the table called `poll`. It will declare a value for the `poll_question` column or attribute. More specifically, the `poll_question` column will get a value of *Is PHP hard fun?* Remember how the poll table has a total of four attributes or columns? The remaining columns `poll_id`, yes, and no will simply be created with default values. `poll_id` will get a value of 1, while yes and no will both get a value of 0.

We can execute the SQL statement in the same manner as we did when creating the table. First, we select the playground database in the phpMyAdmin control panel. Then, we click the SQL tab and enter the preceding SQL statement. Finally, we click Go to execute the entered SQL statement. The system will then indicate that one row has been inserted.

Alternatively, we can select the database from the control panel. Then click insert in the menu provided. Text fields will be presented to allow us to enter data. We can then enter the "Is PHP hard fun?" statement in the pool_question text box. Then click the "Go" button at the bottom of the screen. This will generate an SQL statement similar to the one presented earlier. The system will also include the default values not previously shown. To execute the generated statement, click the "Go" button at the bottom of the screen.

To insert values for more than one column (attribute), the syntax of the INSERT statement will slightly vary.

```
INSERT INTO `poll` (`poll_id`, `poll_question`, `yes`, `no`) VALUES
(NULL, '"Is PHP hard fun?" ', '0', '0');)
```

As shown, we can specify the attribute (such as 'yes') in the first set of parentheses and then its related setting ('0') in the second set of parentheses. The positions must be the same. 'yes' is in the third position, and its value is also in the third position. For any attribute listed, there must be an associated value. Remember that any attributes not listed will be given a default value if one was defined in the table. Notice that in this example, poll_id is set to NULL. This setting is required for any auto numerated attributes. The NULL setting (remember, we set the restrictions to not allow NULL) will be rejected which prompts the system to generate a new number by incrementing the previous number. There are other formats that can be used to insert data. However, we will use this format because we can see clearly which value is associated with which attribute.

## The SELECT Statement

Once we have inserted a row of data into the poll table, it would be nice to see the new row displayed. To retrieve data from database tables, we will use the SQL SELECT statement.

```
SELECT column_name, column_name FROM table_name
```

The SELECT keyword is used to retrieve data. The FROM keyword specifies the table in the database to retrieve the information. The SELECT statement returns a temporary table populated with any retrieved data. The temporary table will have exactly the properties indicated immediately after the SELECT keyword.

```
SELECT poll_id, poll_question, yes, no FROM poll
```

We can then paste this statement into the SQL text box, as previously mentioned, to produce the required results.

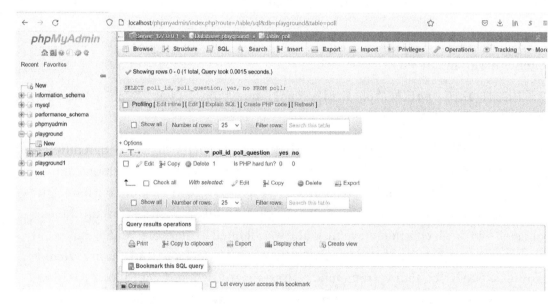

***Figure 6-7.*** *Poll table with one row inserted*

There is one row of data in the table. It has a poll_id of 1 and a poll_question. The yes and no columns are 1 and 0, respectively.

## Secure Programming

Alternatively, we could have used the * symbol to request all fields be displayed.

```
SELECT * FROM poll
```

While this format is certainly quick and easy to create, it can cause possible vulnerabilities. Remember that a temporary table will be created with all attributes returned by the SELECT statement. This table might be accessible to hackers. Only expose those columns that are necessary for the completion of the task at hand. We can use the * symbol for quickly testing that the data was stored. But we don't want to use it in the final product.

It is not much to look at in its present state, but this is all the data required to have a site poll displayed on a website. The website will display the poll question. Site visitors can then post their responses through an HTML form. Possible options would be *yes* or *no*. All responses from site visitors will then be stored in the yes or no fields. So, with a tiny bit of math, we could calculate the relative responses and display a message such as the following: *79% of all site visitors think PHP is hard and fun to learn.*

**Exercise**: Using phpMyAdmin, execute code to accomplish the following. You can accomplish this task without coding, but this exercise is designed to help you practice your SQL coding skills. Start by creating a database named Students. Within that database, create a student table. Within the table, create the following attributes (fields): StudentID, Name, Address, City, State, Zip code, and Major. Populate at least three rows of information. Now display the information using the SELECT statement.

## The UPDATE Statement

As you can probably determine, the yes or no values in the poll table will change every time a site visitor submits a response. We need one more SQL statement to make these changes. Let's assume a site user just agrees that PHP is hard to learn. We would need to generate an SQL statement to increase the stored value for the yes property by a value of 1.

```
UPDATE poll SET yes = yes + 1
WHERE poll_id = 1
```

We can execute this statement in the same matter as previously discussed.

**Figure 6-8.** *Result after update to poll table*

We can see that the *yes* property of the first row of data in the poll is incremented to 1. If we run the same SQL statement again, yes will be incremented to a value of 2.

Note how the WHERE clause limits which rows will be affected by the update. Only the row with a poll_id of 1 will be affected. Any other rows in the table will not be updated, because of the WHERE clause.

## Secure Programming

An UPDATE statement without a WHERE clause would update the yes attribute of all rows in the poll table. In this case, there is just one row, so the WHERE clause isn't absolutely necessary. However, most tables you will work with will have much more than just one row, so it's vital that the row(s) be explicitly declared. Otherwise, attributes might be updated that should not have, which will corrupt the data in the database.

Now that we have gained some basic SQL knowledge, it is time to code for our database-driven site poll.

## Coding a Database-Driven Site Poll

Obviously, our program will connect to a database from PHP, and additional PHP scripts will display the content for the site. PHP is a very forgiving language, and we can approach this task in many ways. But some ways are more scalable than others. Some that seem easy at first can transform code into a completely disorganized, tangled, spaghetti mess. Let's use a tried-and-tested approach to code architecture that can be scaled to accommodate complex projects. While this is overkill for our simple site poll, it gives us an opportunity to introduce the *model-view-controller* (*MVC*) design technique.

## Separating Concerns with MVC

The model-view-controller (MVC) design pattern is a common approach to organizing scripts consistently. Using a consistent approach to organizing your scripts can help you develop and debug faster and more efficiently.

The *MVC framework* is built upon the basic principles as defined by model-view-controller. Once you are familiar with the basic concepts, there are many MVC frameworks available to logically organize your PHP projects. Some of these include CodeIgniter, CakePHP, and Yii. These frameworks will aid in designing and developing more complex web applications.

At its most basic, MVC separates coding concerns into, you guessed it, three categories: models, views, and controllers. A *model* is a piece of code that represents data. Your models should also hold most logic involved in the system you're building. A *view* is a piece of code that shows information visually. The information to be displayed by the view is received from a model. A *controller* is a piece of code that retrieves input from users and sends commands to relevant model(s). In short, *MVC separates user interactions from visual representation from system logic and data.* This provides the ability to divide large projects in which an HTML expert can create the views, a database expert can create the models, and a PHP programmer can create the controllers. We can also include multiple views which allow the code to be used both on the Web and in applications, without any major changes.

---

**Note**    You can read much more about MVC at `http://en.wikipedia.org/wiki/Model-view-controller`.

---

We have already seen examples of separating code into model, view, and controller. Remember how we made a template for HTML pages? We worked with a view that held a bare-bones HTML page skeleton. You can find it in the gallery we started building in Chapter 4. The view is located in `ch4/templates/page.php`.

In the same project, we created a model related to that view: the ch4/classes/ Page_Data.class.php, which declares a number of methods and properties related to the content of the HTML pages.

The model and view were hooked up through a controller. In ch4/index.php, we assigned values to the model and made the model available to the view. It displayed a well-formed HTML5 page. Thus, index.php was our controller.

In this book, the aim is to use a simple implementation of MVC. Most other MVC implementations you will come across are likely to be much more elaborate. You can easily find many MVC examples that are not meant for beginning programmers. Once you understand the basic MVC principles and have gained some experience working with those principles in a simple context, you will find it much easier to understand the more elaborate implementations.

**Exercise**: Now that we have discovered that we have used MVC for our previous projects, return to the last project in Chapter 4. Change the folder names to indicate the model, view, and controller for the project. Make the necessary coding changes (it should not be very much) to reference the proper files within the new folders.

## Planning the Logic

Let's keep the poll simple. We will create an index.php to output a valid HTML5 page that will show the poll. The index will be a *front controller*.

A front controller is a design pattern very often seen in MVC web applications. A front controller is a single "entrance door" to a web application. We have already used a front controller in previous projects. Remember how index.php has been the only script loaded directly in your browser? It's a front controller.

---

**Note**   The front controller design pattern is well documented online. You could start your own research at http://en.wikipedia.org/wiki/Front_ Controller_pattern.

---

As in the previous projects, index.php will output a valid HTML5 page, and it will load the poll controller. The poll controller should return the poll as HTML, so it can be displayed on index.php. Note how every one view has its own model and its own controller (Figure 6-7).

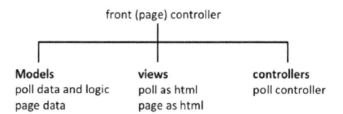

*Figure 6-9.* *Distribution of responsibilities*

Notice the poll model, the poll controller, and the poll view. These three work together to display a functional poll. We can also see that the page has its own model, view, and controller. The front controller is the page controller.

# Creating the Poll Project

Let's organize our project logically using the basic MVC structure. We will create a new folder, ch6, in our executable folder (in XAMPP it's the htdocs folder) and another folder, poll, inside this folder. We will also create three folders inside of the poll folder: models, views, and controllers. We can now copy the Privatepage.php program from the template folder in ch4 to the views folder under poll (rename it page.php). We can also copy the Private_Page_Data.class.php program from the ch4 classes folder into the models folder (rename it Page_Data.class.php). Of course, we could also download the files for this chapter from the publisher's website.

Now let's create our first version of the index.php program to test everything. It will be placed directly under the poll folder.

*Listing 6-1.* index.php

```php
<?php
//complete code for index.php
$nav = "";
$info = "";
include_once "models/Page_Data.class.php";
$pageData = new Page_Data();
$pageData->setTitle("PHP/MySQL site poll example");
$pageData->setContent("<h1>Everything works so far!</h1>");
$pageData->appendContent("<div>...and content goes here.</div>");
```

```php
require "views/page.php";
echo $page;
?>
```

This index program is just a slight modification from the original `privateindex` program seen previously. Some content has been removed, and the folder names and the values for title and content have changed! Let's test it.

# Everything works so far!

...and content goes here.

***Figure 6-10.*** *Output of new index.php program*

Our view has now changed. We are now looking at this code with a model-view-controller perspective. We can see how the created HTML page is a combination of a *view* merged with a *model*. We can see how the *front controller* hooks up the model and the view and outputs a well-formed HTML5 page to the browser for the user to see.

## Making a Poll Controller

With a nearly blank page created with its own model and view and a front controller setup, we can prepare a file for displaying our poll example in the browser. Sticking to the MVC approach, we will eventually need a poll model, a poll view, and a poll controller. Let's create a bare-bones poll controller and load that from the front controller (index. php). Let's create a new file, `poll.php`, in the `controllers` folder.

***Listing 6-2.*** poll.php

```php
<?php
//complete code listing for controllers/poll.php
$info = "<h1>Poll will show here soon</h1>";
?>
```

Next, we will load the poll controller from the front controller (which we will now name pollindex.php).

***Listing 6-3.*** pollindex.php

```php
<?php
//complete code for index.php
$nav = "";
$info = "";
include_once "models/Page_Data.class.php";
$pageData = new Page_Data();
$pageData->setTitle("PHP/MySQL site poll example");
include_once "controllers/poll.php";
$pageData->setContent($info);
$pageData->appendContent("<div>...and content goes here.</div>");
require "views/page.php";
echo $page;
?>
```

This format should look familiar, as it is very similar to the previous index examples in this textbook.

**Poll will show here soon**

...and content goes here.

***Figure 6-11.***  *Output from pollindex.php*

Now our front controller and poll controller are working together to create a dynamic web page for our poll! Let's work on our poll model next.

# Making a Poll Model

With a preliminary poll controller in place, we can develop a preliminary poll model.

***Listing 6-4.*** Poll.class.php

```php
<?php
//complete code for models/Poll.class.php
class Poll {
    private string $poll_question = "Default Question";
    private int $yes = 0;
    private int $no = 0;
    public function getPollData() {
        return $this;
    }

    public function getPollQuestion() : string {
        return $this->poll_question;
    }

    public function getYes() : int {
        return $this->yes;
    }

    public function getNo() : int {
        return $this->no;
    }
}
?>
```

The Poll class defines a blueprint for all Poll objects. The Poll class includes a method, getPollData(), which returns $this. What does the return accomplish? The simple answer is that it returns a *pointer* (address in memory) to the object for whatever code calls this method. What object, there is not one in this program? Before this method is called, an instance of this class (which we will see soon) must be created. Once it is created, then the getPollData() method can be called. At that point, an object with the contents of this class will exist in its own space in memory. The return statement passes a reference (pointer) to the object to the code that has called the function. This will allow the calling code to directly access and use the object and its contents.

The $pollData object has properties and get methods for poll_question, yes, and no. The $pollData object *represents* all the content required to show a poll. In other words, the $pollData *models* poll data.

# Making a Poll View

We can now create a poll view to look at our data (contained in the model we just created).

***Listing 6-5.*** poll-html.php

```php
<?php
//complete code for views/poll-html.php
$info = "
<aside id='poll'>
<h1>Poll results</h1>
<ul>
<li>" . $pollData->getYes() . " said yes</li>
<li>" . $pollData->getNo() . " said no</li>
</ul>
</aside>";
?>
```

This view uses the get methods to retrieve the results of the poll (currently defaulting to zero values) and places them into an unordered list.

# Hooking Up Poll View with Poll Model

With a preliminary poll model and poll view created, we can update the poll controller to hook up model and view and, finally, show something in the browser.

***Listing 6-6.*** newpoll.php

```php
<?php
//complete code listing for controllers/poll.php
include_once "models/Poll.class.php";
$poll = new Poll();
$pollData = $poll->getPollData();
include_once "views/poll-html.php";
?>
```

The Poll class model is included into the controller, and an instance ($poll) is created. The getPollData method is called which creates the reference to the $poll object named $pollData. We say that $pollData is now a pointer which points to the object. We can now access anything in the object using $pollData. Finally, the poll-html.php view is attached which displays the poll results. That's it! We have an MVC poll.

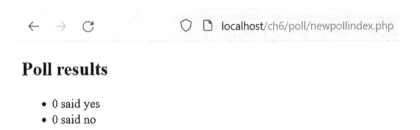

**Figure 6-12.**    *Output from newpollindex.php*

Perhaps you're dying to ask a question such as, *Why should I create three different files to show a simple* <ul> *element?* It would be a completely justified question to ask. If all you wanted was to show a <ul> element with a few hard-coded values, the MVC approach would be complete overkill. The best approach would probably be to write a short HTML program.

The point here is to introduce the MVC design pattern with a very simple example, so there is no overly complex code hiding the basic principles of MVC from your eyes. With the MVC approach, you are perfectly set up for creating a database-driven web application. The MVC architecture is hardly necessary for something this simple, but it can really solve some challenges you will come across with projects of greater complexity, such as the blogging system we will start making in the next chapter.

MVC encapsulates views from models and from controllers. That means we can change a view without changing anything else. Imagine we didn't want a <ul> element for the poll. We could simply change the HTML tags used in views/poll-html.php and trust the rest of the code to run correctly. We can easily change a view without changing anything else.

Similarly, we could change the content and still trust our code to run as expected. It would be a simple task to set the no property to 9. We would only need to change a tiny bit of code. This poll application is built with self-contained elements.

# Connecting to MySQL/MariaDB from PHP

The MVC architecture will make it a fairly straightforward task to connect the database and use database-driven data for the poll. Once we have established such a connection, we can retrieve data from our database and view it with HTML. That is the essence of an MVC database-driven website.

## PHP Data Objects (PDO)

PHP provides several ways to access MySQL/MariaDB databases. In this book, we will exclusively use PHP Data Objects (PDO). It is a very safe and efficient way of connecting to a database from PHP. PDO supports multiple databases and provides a uniform set of methods for handling most database interactions. This is a great advantage for applications that have to support multiple database types, such as PostgreSQL, Firebird, or Oracle.

## Opening a Connection

It is time to connect to our database. Remember that models contain all code that retrieves data. Thus, we will create a model program to connect to our database, and soon, a program to retrieve our database information. The following code assumes that the database does not require a userid and password for access. However, in production, it is essential that the database be secured with login credentials. This requires only a simple change to update the code with the proper userid and password.

***Listing 6-7.*** database.php

```php
<?php
$dbInfo = "mysql:host=localhost;dbname=playground";
$dbUser = "root";
$dbPassword = "";
try {
    //create a database connection with a PDO object
    $db = new PDO( $dbInfo, $dbUser, $dbPassword );
    }
    catch (PDOException $e) {
        $error_message = $e->getMessage();
```

```php
        $pageData->setContent ("<h1>Connection failed!</h1><p>$e</p>");
        exit();
    }
?>
```

The preceding code uses the try/catch blocks introduced previously to handle any code which might throw exceptions. When attempting to open the database, we might not be successful. Thus, this line of code is placed in the try block. If an exception is raised, the catch block will execute, displaying the exception message, our own message and exiting the program. If all works correctly, we can proceed with attempting to retrieve the data. If successful, the code creates a PDO object and stores it in the $db variable.

---

**Note**   There are other possible settings you might use for creating a PDO connection to a database. You can consult www.php.net/manual/en/book.pdo.php for complete and detailed coverage.

---

We will import this program into our controller soon.

# Sharing the Database Connection with the Poll Model

We can use a constructor with arguments to share a database connection with the poll model.

***Listing 6-8.*** NewPoll.class.php

```php
<?php
//complete code for models/Poll.class.php
class Poll {
    private string $poll_question = "Default Question";
    private int $yes = 0;
    private int $no = 0;
    private $db;
    //new code: declare a constructor
    //method requires a database connection as argument
    public function __construct( $dbConnection ){
```

```php
        //store the received connection in the $this->db property
        $this->db = $dbConnection;
    }
    public function getPollData() {
        return $this;
    }
    public function getPollQuestion() : string {
        return $this->poll_question;
    }
    public function getYes() : int {
        return $this->yes;
    }
    public function getNo() : int {
        return $this->no;
    }
}
?>
```

The constructor now accepts the pointer to the database connection object and places it in $db. Next, we will call the Poll class's constructor and pass the PDO object pointer as an argument. Take a pause to reflect. Where in our code would we load the poll model?

From the poll controller!

***Listing 6-9.*** newestpoll.php

```php
<?php
//complete code listing for controllers/poll.php
include_once "models/Poll.class.php";
$poll = new Poll( $db );
$pollData = $poll->getPollData();
include_once "views/poll-html.php";
?>
```

Now, we have passed the database connection to the poll model. The code shares a database connection, but it doesn't use it for anything yet. Let's update the index.php file to now include our database connection.

***Listing 6-10.*** newestpollindex.php

```php
<?php
//complete code for index.php
$nav = "";
$info = "";
include_once "models/Page_Data.class.php";
$pageData = new Page_Data();
$pageData->setTitle("PHP/MySQL site poll example");
include_once "models/database.php";
include_once "controllers/newestpoll.php";
$pageData->setContent($info);
require "views/page.php";
echo $page;
?>
```

There are only a couple of minor changes. The database.php program has been included and the controller has been updated to the newest version. If we execute this index file, we will see no changes in the output. However, we have connected to the database and passed the pointer to the data object. We are getting close to a complete program!

The variable $db is declared in newestpollindex.php. It is available in newestpoll.php because it is included in newestpollindex.php. Including a file is a lot like copying all the code from one file and pasting it into another file. As a consequence, all variables declared in any including file can be available in other included files, if those files are included afterward.

# Retrieving Data with a PDOStatement

Inside the database, we have a poll table with a poll_question and values for its yes and no attributes. We are ready to retrieve data from the database.

Remember, code dealing with the data for the poll belongs in the poll model. Thus, we need to modify the getPollData method in the Poll class. At this point, the method returns hard-coded poll data; we want to return database-driven poll data.

***Listing 6-11.*** NewestPoll.class.php

```php
?php
//complete code for models/Poll.class.php
class Poll {
    private $db;
    //method requires a database connection as argument
    public function __construct( $dbConnection ){
        //store the received connection in the $this->db property
        $this->db = $dbConnection;
    }
    public function getPollData() {
    $sql = "SELECT poll_question, yes, no FROM poll WHERE poll_id = 1";
    $statement = $this->db->prepare($sql);
    $statement->execute();
    $pollData = $statement->fetchObject();
    return $pollData;
    }
}
?>
```

The Poll class actually becomes a much smaller program. We no longer need to store the values for the question and the responses because we are passing the object which contains the information from the database back to the calling program. Thus, the properties and get methods are no longer required. It only takes a few lines of code to retrieve our information.

```php
$sql = "SELECT poll_question, yes, no FROM poll WHERE poll_id = 1";
```

The property $sql contains the SQL statement to retrieve the information needed.

```php
$statement = $this->db->prepare($sql);
```

The SQL string is converted to a PDOStatement object before it can be executed. prepare() converts a simple SQL string to a PDOStatement object.

```php
$statement->execute();
```

The PDOStatement method called execute() executes the SQL against the MySQL/MariaDB database.

```
$pollData = $statement->fetchObject();
```

fetchObject() retrieves the one row of data from the queried database table creating a StdClass object ($pollData). This object will publicly expose all the data we have retrieved. However, this is not much of a security concern, since we only intend to display the data to everyone, anyways. If we intended to use this data to update our database, we would need to use a more secure approach. The returned StdClass object is automatically created with properties for poll_question, yes, and no.

```
return $pollData;
```

The object is returned to the calling program (finalpoll.php).

---

**Note**    You can consult the official documentation for PDOStatement objects at www.php.net/manual/en/class.pdostatement.php.

---

***Listing 6-12.*** finalpoll.php

```php
<?php
//complete code listing for controllers/poll.php
include_once "models/NewestPoll.class.php";
$poll = new Poll( $db );
$pollData = $poll->getPollData();
include_once "views/finalpoll-html.php";
?>
```

finalpoll.php has only been modified to call the updated Poll class and a slightly modified HTML view.

***Listing 6-13.*** finalpoll-html.php

```php
<?php
//complete code for views/poll-html.php
$info = "
<aside id='poll'>
```

```
    <h1>Poll results</h1>
    <ul>
        <li> $pollData->yes said yes</li>
        <li> $pollData->no said no</li>
    </ul>
</aside>
";
?>
```

Since a StdObject is returned from the database, we can directly access the properties without using get methods. Therefore, a slight change has occurred in the view program (finalpoll-html.php).

***Listing 6-14.*** finalpollindex.php

```php
<?php
//complete code for index.php
$nav = "";
$info = "";
include_once "models/Page_Data.class.php";
$pageData = new Page_Data();
$pageData->setTitle("PHP/MySQL site poll example");
include_once "models/database.php";
include_once "controllers/finalpoll.php";
$pageData->setContent($info);
require "views/page.php";
echo $page;
?>
```

The index file (controller) was also only slightly modified to call the new version of the poll controller. If we execute the finalpollindex.php program in our browser, we will discover the same output format as Figure 6-12. However, the one big difference is now the data is being pulled from the database. A true database-driven website!

# Showing a Poll Form

We don't have much of a site poll yet. Site visitors should be allowed to submit their opinions and, thus, contribute to the poll results. We must provide a form for the site visitors. Remember, all displays are views. So, let's update our view not only to display poll results but also to accept the site visitor's opinion.

***Listing 6-15.*** completepoll-html.php

```php
<?php
//complete code listing for views/poll-html.php
$dataFound = isset( $pollData );
if( $dataFound === false ){
    trigger_error( 'views/completepoll-html.php needs an $pollData
    object' );
}

$info = "
<aside id='poll'>
    <form method='post' action='completepollindex.php'>
            <p>$pollData->poll_question</p>
            <select name='user-input'>
                <option value='yes'>Yes, it is!</option>
                <option value='no'>No, not really!</option>
            </select>
            <input type='submit' value='post' />
    </form>
    <h1>Poll results</h1>
    <ul>
        <li>$pollData->yes said yes</li>
        <li>$pollData->no said no</li>
    </ul>
</aside>
";
?>
```

```
$dataFound = isset( $pollData );
if( $dataFound === false ){
    trigger_error( 'views/completepoll-html.php needs an $pollData
    object' );
}
```

To increase reliability of the program, we have added an if statement which determines if the $pollData information was properly created. We assumed it was previously. But we should never assume. Always expect the unexpected and check for the possibility that something went wrong. trigger_error will create a custom error message. You can create a try/catch to capture this possible error whenever the form is used in another program (such as the controller).

```
form method='post' action='completepollindex.php'>
            <p>$pollData->poll_question</p>
            <select name='user-input'>
                <option value='yes'>Yes, it is!</option>
                <option value='no'>No, not really!</option>
            </select>
            <input type='submit' value='post' />
    </form>
```

A form was created to obtain the customer's opinion. Once the customer responds by clicking the submit button, the response is passed, via post, to the index (controller).

## Updating a Database Table According to Form Input

There is one final step required to complete the site poll example. We need to retrieve any user input submitted through the form and update the poll table with the received input. If a site visitor submits a *no*, we will increment the value of the no attribute in the poll database table.

All data interactions are a task for a *model*. Let's update the poll model class with a method for updating the database table.

***Listing 6-16.*** FinalPoll.class.php

```
<?php
//complete code for models/Poll.class.php
```

```php
class Poll {
    private $db;
    //method requires a database connection as argument
    public function __construct( $dbConnection ){
        //store the received conection in the $this->db property
        $this->db = $dbConnection;
    }
    public function getPollData() {
    $sql = "SELECT poll_question, yes, no FROM poll WHERE poll_id = 1";
    $statement = $this->db->prepare($sql);
    $statement->execute();
    $pollData = $statement->fetchObject();
    return $pollData;
    }

    public function updatePoll ( $input ) {
    if ( $input === "yes" ) {
        $updateSQL = "UPDATE poll SET yes = yes+1 WHERE poll_id = 1";
    } else if ( $input === "no" ) {
        $updateSQL = "UPDATE poll SET no = no+1 WHERE poll_id = 1";
    }
    $updateStatement = $this->db->prepare($updateSQL);
    $updateStatement->execute();
}
}
?>
```

The new method updatePoll() is similar to the getPollData method. However, if the user submitted a *yes,* we format an SQL string that can update the yes attribute in the poll table. If the user submitted a *no,* we format a different SQL string to update the no attribute. Notice that the yes or no values are incremented by one to add the user's choice into the proper location in the database table. Whichever SQL string is created, it is stored in a variable called $updateSQL. Once the $updateSQL string is created, we again use the PDO method prepare() to convert the SQL string to a PDOStatement object, which is stored in the variable $updateStatement. We then call execute() to update the poll table.

# Secure Programming

We should always be aware that a hacker can attempt to use *SQL Injection* to corrupt our tables and databases. SQL Injection is an attempt to insert SQL statements into a program's use of SQL to insert or update data in the database. In future chapters, we will use prepared statements to create our SQL commands, which will reduce the possibility of successful injection. We will also validate the data before making any updates to the database. In the previous example, we did not use any information gathered from the user to format the SQL statement. Thus, the SQL statement created was secure and resistant to SQL Injection.

# Responding to User Input

Controllers are responsible for dealing with user interactions. So, the poll controller is the right place to intercept user input from the poll form. There are a couple of things to add to the script.

***Listing 6-17.*** completepoll.php

```php
<?php
//complete code listing for controllers/poll.php
include_once "models/FinalPoll.class.php";
$poll = new Poll( $db );

//check if form was submitted
$isPollSubmitted = isset( $_POST['user-input'] );
//if it was just submitted...
if ( $isPollSubmitted ) {
    //get input received from form
    $input = $_POST['user-input'];

    //...update model
    $poll->updatePoll( $input );
}

$pollData = $poll->getPollData();
include_once "views/completepoll-html.php";
?>
```

```
//check if form was submitted
$isPollSubmitted = isset( $_POST['user-input'] );
//if it was just submitted...
if ( $isPollSubmitted ) {
```

We will use the isset method to determine if the user has chosen to give their opinion in the survey. If they have, we will update the results.

```
    //get input received from form
    $input = $_POST['user-input'];

    //...update model
    $poll->updatePoll( $input );
}
```

If they did, we will retrieve the value selected and place it into $input. Then we will pass that value to the updatePoll method, which will make the changes to the database table.

```
$pollData = $poll->getPollData();
include_once "views/completepoll-html.php";
```

Whether or not the user provides their opinion, the program will get the current poll results and display them by calling the HTML page.

---

**Note**    A minor change has occurred to the index (controller) program to call completepoll.php. You can view this change in the files downloaded from the publisher's website.

---

To see the results, run completepollindex.php in the browser.

Is PHP hard fun?

**Poll results**

- 2 said yes
- 0 said no

***Figure 6-13.*** *Output from completepollindex.php*

We now have a completely functional poll site!

There is one weakness to this final version. Can you see it? Once the user has entered their opinion, the program allows them to enter it again. How can this be corrected? We can change the output to only display the question the first time the page is shown. Once the opinion has been given, then we can display the page that does not ask the question again, but does display the results. We can change the results to use `finalpoll-html.php` which was created earlier. This will require just a change to the include statement discussed earlier.

**Exercise**: Adjust the final poll project to accept more than one input from the user. Adjust the controller, model, and view to request, store, and display this information.

# Summary

In this chapter, we've learned the basics of SQL statements, as well as how to interact with a database using PHP. We learned how MVC provides a logical structure to creating programs which require data and interfaces. In the next chapters, we'll learn how to build a blog with a basic entry manager that will allow us to create, modify, and delete entries, as well as display them on a public page.

# Projects

1. The power of MVC design is the ability to change the model or view with little or no changes to the other components of the project. Review the PHP documentation (www.php.net/manual/en/function.file.php) on reading and writing to files. Change the model code from the examples to read and store the poll information into a file, instead of a database. You should be able to make these changes within very minimal changes to the controller or the viewer. Most of your changes should occur within the model.

2. Visit www.w3schools.in/laravel-tutorial/ and discover how Laravel can help create robust data-driven web applications using PHP and other tools.

# CHAPTER 7

# Building the Basic Blog System

## Objectives

After completing this chapter, you will be able to

- Create a view, containing an HTML form to accept a new blog entry

- Create a controller, to handle input from the form

- Create a model, to save and retrieve any entry using a database table

- Design and create a MySQL/MariaDB database with a table

- Use a design pattern for the front controller

- Use the table data gateway design pattern for database access

- Use a while loop to iterate through a data set

In this chapter, we will begin to build our blog system. We will start by creating an entry manager (front controller). We will create two front pages for the blog system, one for the administrator and one for the user. By the end of the chapter, the basic blog system will be able to save new blogs and display all entries stored within a database. Along the way, we will use the concepts and topics we have previously covered: database design, SQL, and MVC. We will also learn new techniques including design practices and prepared SQL statements.

© Jason Lengstorf, Thomas Blom Hansen, Steve Prettyman 2022
J. Lengstorf et al., *PHP 8 for Absolute Beginners*, https://doi.org/10.1007/978-1-4842-8205-2_7

# Creating the blog_entry Database Table

One of the most important steps with any new application is the planning of the tables that will hold data. This has an enormous impact on the ease of scaling the application later. *Scaling* is the expansion of an application to manage more information and/or users, and it can be a tremendous pain, if we do not look ahead when starting a new project. At first, the blog needs to store several types of entry information to function, including the following:

- Unique ID

- Entry title

- Entry text

- Date created

The first step is to determine the types of fields for the entries table.

- `entry_id`: A unique number identifying the entry. This will be a positive integer, and it makes sense for this number to increment automatically, ensuring the number is unique. The `entry_id` will be the primary key for the table.

- `title`: An alphanumeric string that will be relatively short. We'll limit the string to 150 characters.

- `entry_text`: An alphanumeric string of indeterminate length. We won't limit the length of this field (within reason).

- `date_created`: The timestamp generated automatically at the original creation date of the entry. We'll use this to sort the entries chronologically, as well as for letting the users know when an entry was posted originally.

Now that we have determined the fields needed, it's time to create the database. Using the techniques we learned in the previous chapter, let us begin. Remember that both Apache and MySQL/MariaDB need to be running for our application to work properly.

```
CREATE DATABASE simple_blog
```

We can enter the preceding code into the SQL window of phpMyAdmin or create the database using the phpMyAdmin Databases menu item.

The next step is to create the entries table. Remember to select the simple_blog database from the menu at the left side of the phpMyAdmin control panel.

```
CREATE TABLE blog_entry (
    entry_id INT NOT NULL AUTO_INCREMENT,
    title VARCHAR( 150 ),
    entry_text TEXT,
    date_created TIMESTAMP DEFAULT CURRENT_TIMESTAMP,
    PRIMARY KEY ( entry_id )
)
```

We can enter the preceding code in the SQL window. Alternatively, we can use the create table text boxes provided by phpMyAdmin after selecting the database. If you choose to enter the values using the text boxes, make sure all information entered is the same as what is provided in the preceding code.

The title attribute has a new data type: VARCHAR(150). As a consequence, any title must contain CHARacters of VARiable length. Blog entry titles can be a string of characters between 0 and 150 characters long. If we insert a title that is 151 characters long, only the first 150 characters would be saved in the blog_entry table. The database has ensured that our value entered is valid before it is saved.

The date_created attribute is also declared with a new data type: TIMESTAMP. A TIMESTAMP holds precise information about a moment in time. It stores *year, month, day, hour, minute,* and *second* as YYYY-MM-DD HH:MM:SS.

We have already discussed using default values in our MySQL tables. Here, it is used again for the date_created attribute. When a new entry is inserted for the first time, MySQL/MariaDB will automatically store the current TIMESTAMP based on the server's clock. The server clock will be based on the time zone in which the server is located.

# Planning the PHP Scripts

Our next logical step is to create a blog entry editor, so that we can create new blog entries. This blog entry editor is only meant for the blog author. Ordinary site visitors will not be able to create new entries. Normal site visitors should simply see the blog entries, without being able to edit existing entries or create new ones.

One approach to such a task is to create two main site entrances: index.php for regular visitors and admin.php. In MVC terminology, index.php and admin.php will both be *front controllers*. In a later chapter, we will learn how to restrict access to admin.php, with a login.

The admin page will list all blog entries, and provide access to the entry editor, to create new entries and edit or delete existing entries. This will require separate views: one for listing all entries and one for showing the editor.

The program admin.php will display an HTML5 page. It will allow the administrator to decide whether to show the editor or list all entries. Figure 7-1 uses the MVC architecture to develop a schematic overview of the blog administration module.

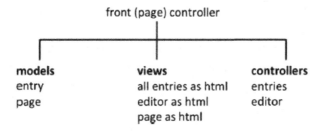

**Figure 7-1.** *Distribution of responsibilities*

Notice that every view has a corresponding controller. The entry model displays all entries and saves any new entry.

# Admin View: Creating the Admin Blog Site

Let us create a new folder called ch7 and a folder blog inside the ch7 folder. Inside the blog folder, we will also create four other folders: models, views, controllers, and CSS.

We can now copy the page.php program from the template folder in ch4 to the views folder under blog. We can also copy the Page_Data.class.php program from the ch4 classes folder into the models folder. We will create a blank style sheet, which we will code later, and place it in the CSS folder with the name of blog.css. Of course, we can download the files for this chapter from the publisher's website.

Now it is time to create a test version of admin.php, our front controller, to see if everything works together properly.

***Listing 7-1.*** admin.php

```php
<?php
//complete code for blog/admin.php
include_once "models/Page_Data.class.php";
$pageData = new Page_Data();
$pageData->setTitle("PHP/MySQL blog demo");
$pageData->setCss("<link rel='stylesheet' href='css/blog.css'>");
$pageData->setContent("<h1>YES!</h1>");
include_once "views/page.php";
echo $page;
?>
```

> **Note**    If you copied the Page_Data.class.php from the ch4 folder, the validation using the if statements will need to be adjusted to allow the values passed in this listing and future listings in this chapter. If you don't see the expected results, check the security restrictions within this file. The Page_Data.class.php file from the publisher's website already has the required adjustments.

This code should look familiar, as it is similar to the basic front controllers that we created in previous chapters. The only addition is the included style sheet.

When testing this program, everything should work as expected; we should get a well-formed HTML5 with a `<title>` of *PHP/MySQL blog demo* and an `<h1>` element happily exclaiming *YES!* Seeing YES in the browser is visual confirmation that the project is set up correctly. If we view the source code, we will also see the HTML link for accessing the CSS style sheet has been properly located in the title section.

# Creating the Admin Entry Manager Navigation

The entry manager (front controller) will have two views: one to list all entries and one to show an entry editor. Let us make a navigation to access these views.

But first, we can expect this project to contain many PHP files before we are done. Let us create some folders to keep scripts related to the administration module grouped together. We will create a folder called admin in the existing views folder. We will place our first version of the admin navigation in this folder.

***Listing 7-2.*** admin-navigation.php

```php
<?php
//complete code for views/admin/admin-navigation.php
$nav = "
<nav id='admin-navigation'>
    <a href='admin.php?page=entries'>All entries</a>
    <a href='admin.php?page=editor'>Editor</a>
</nav>";
?>
```

We can see that the entry manager navigation is very similar to the navigation we made previously.

The admin navigation is a *static view*, meaning there is no dynamic or database-driven information in the script. We do not need a model for the navigation because all content is hard-coded. We do need a controller to load the navigation whenever it should be loaded. The navigation will be loaded and displayed all the time. We will control this from a new version of the front controller.

***Listing 7-3.*** adminWithNavigation.php

```php
<?php
//complete code for blog/admin.php
    include_once "views/admin/new-admin-navigation.php";
    include_once "models/Page_Data.class.php";
    $pageData = new Page_Data();
    $pageData->setTitle("PHP/MySQL blog demo");
    $pageData->setCss("<link rel='stylesheet' href='css/blog.css'>");
    $pageData->setContent($nav . "<h1>YES!</h1>");
    include_once "views/page.php";
    echo $page;
?>
```

Only three minor adjustments have been made to the program. The navigation program has been included at the top of the code. The $nav variable has been added to the string passed into the setContent method. The navigation program has also been adjusted to call this new version of admin.

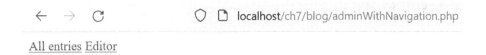

All entries Editor

# YES!

*Figure 7-2.* *Output from adminWithNavigation.php*

When running the program within our browser, we should see the navigation displayed in the top of the browser window. Clicking a navigation item will not have any immediately visible effect; the navigation is just a view. Clicking any navigation item will encode a URL variable named page. We can see it if we look in the browser's address bar. Next, we will create the controller code to respond to these user interactions.

## Loading Admin Module Controllers

As already mentioned, the admin.php program is our front controller. As such, it will load any other controller(s) associated with the navigation item the user clicked. There are two links in the navigation, so we will need two controllers.

Let us create two preliminary controllers so we can see visible changes in the browser when we click a navigation item. Let us add an admin folder to the controllers folder. We will create a program for the editor view within this folder.

*Listing 7-4.* editor.php

```php
<?php
//complete source code for controllers/admin/editor.php
$info = "<h1>editor controller loaded!</h1>";
?>
```

The editor controller will not be doing a whole lot to start. Initially, we just want to check that it hooks up the right files. With that in place, we can develop code of greater complexity. Let us create another file for controlling the view that will eventually list all entries.

***Listing 7-5.***  entries.php

```php
<?php
//complete source code for controllers/admin/entries.php
$info = "<h1>entries controller loaded!</h1>";
?>
```

Now we can adjust the admin program to process these controllers.

***Listing 7-6.***  newadminWithNavigation.php

```php
<?php
//complete code for blog/admin.php
$nav = "";
$info = "";
include_once 'views/admin/newest-admin-navigation.php';
include_once "models/Page_Data.class.php";
$pageData = new Page_Data();
$pageData->setTitle("PHP/MySQL blog demo");
$pageData->setCss("<link rel='stylesheet' href='css/blog.css'>");
$pageData->setContent($nav);
//new code begins here
$navigationIsClicked = isset( $_GET['page'] );
if ( $navigationIsClicked ) {
    //prepare to load corresponding controller
    $contrl = $_GET['page'];
} else {
    //prepare to load default controller
    $contrl = "entries";
}
//load the controller
include_once "controllers/admin/$contrl.php";
$pageData->appendContent($info);
include_once "views/page.php";
echo $page;
?>
```

Again, the style of this front controller should look very familiar. It is similar to previous chapters. Remember the file names `entries.php` and `editor.php`. These names are essential. They must be matched with corresponding values of the URL variable `page` declared when a user clicks a navigation item. Let us take a closer look at the `href` values used in the navigation:

```
<a href='admin.php?page=entries'>All entries</a>
<a href='admin.php?page=editor'>Editor</a>
```

When a user clicks the `All entries` item, the URL variable `page` gets a value of `entries`. The URL variable `page` is fetched using `$_GET`. The string value `entries` are stored inside a variable called `$contrl` and subsequently used to include `controllers/admin/$contrl.php`, which will really translate to including `controllers/admin/entries.php`, because the variable `$contrl` holds the value `entries`. If the `user clicks the Editor item`, `controllers/admin/editor.php` will be included.

At this point, we can test the system again to make sure everything is still working properly. By default, we will see the message returned from the entries controller. If we click the navigation item for the editor, we will see the returned message from the editor controller.

## Creating the Admin Entry Input Form

Now that we have dynamic navigation, it's time to create a form to accept blog entries. While we are at it, let us create a button for deleting an entry. We will create code for deletion in a later chapter.

***Listing 7-7.*** editor-html.php

```php
<?php
//complete source code for views/admin/editor-html.php
return "
<form method='post' action='admin.php?page=editor' id='editor'>
    <fieldset>
        <legend>New Entry Submission</legend>
        <label>Title</label>
        <input type='text' name='title' maxlength='150' />
        <label>Entry</label>
        <textarea name='entry'></textarea>
```

```
        <fieldset id='editor-buttons'>
            <input type='submit' name='action' value='save' />
            <input type='submit' name='action' value='delete' />
        </fieldset>
    </fieldset>
</form>
";
?>
```

If you have used HTML before, most of the preceding code should be familiar. We included two <fieldset> elements. They are used to group related form fields together. The main <fieldset> has a <legend> element. A <legend> is like a heading for a <fieldset> element.

The <input> element for the entry title has a maxlength attribute set to 150. You can probably guess that the displayed text field will only accept 150 characters. That is perfect, because our entry table in the database accepts a maximum of 150 characters for new title attributes. We should always make sure that any limits placed in HTML forms match the limits placed in the database table that will store this information.

The maxlength attribute enhances form usability, in that it becomes harder for users to create an invalid title through the form. The maxlength attribute performs client-side validation and will only allow submission of valid titles. One thing to keep in mind is the fact that client-side validation is great for enhancing usability.

A first attempt is made to validate information before it is sent to the server. This increases efficiency because the information is not sent to the server until it is valid. However, it does not improve security, because a malicious user can override client-side validation. We will also need to validate the information submitted to the server, within PHP, to make sure we received the information we expected.

With a new editor view created, we must update the controller, so it shows the new view. You can now test our current progress by placing the following controller in your browser.

***Listing 7-8.*** neweditor.php

```php
<?php
//complete source code for controllers/admin/neweditor.php
include_once "views/admin/editor-html.php";
?>
```

At the moment, the editor simply includes the HTML page. We will also need to update the navigation to now call this new version.

***Listing 7-9.*** updatedadminWithNavigation.php

```php
<?php
//complete code for views/admin/admin-navigation.php
$nav = "
<nav id='admin-navigation'>
    <a href='newestadminWithNavigation.php?page=entries'>All entries</a>
    <a href='newestadminWithNavigation.php?page=neweditor'>Editor</a>
</nav>";
?>
```

A simple change has now set the page to `neweditor`. Finally, we need to update our front controller to use the new navigation. The line changed is included in the following. The new front controller is now `newestadminWithNavigation.php`.

```php
include_once 'views/admin/updatedadminWithNavigation.php';
```

After completing these changes, we can open the front controller, and click the Editor menu item to see the form. However, let us add a little CSS to make the form look better.

## Styling the Admin Editor

You will probably agree that the unstyled entry editor form is not professional. A little CSS can take us a long way toward improved aesthetics.

***Listing 7-10.*** newblog.css

```css
/* code listing for blog/css/blog.css */
form#editor{
    width: 300px;
    margin-top:10px;
    padding:0px;
    background-color: #dedede;
}

form#editor label, form#editor input[type='text']{
```

```
    display:block;
}

form#editor #editor-buttons{
    border:none;
    text-align:right;
}

form#editor textarea, form#editor input[type='text']{
    width:90%;
    margin-bottom:2em;
}

form#editor textarea{
    height:10em;
}
```

One line in the front controller must be updated to use the new CSS style sheet.

```
$pageData->setCss("<link rel='stylesheet' href='css/newblog.css'>");
```

Finally, we can see our results by loading updatedadminWithNavigation.php into our browser and by clicking the Editor menu item.

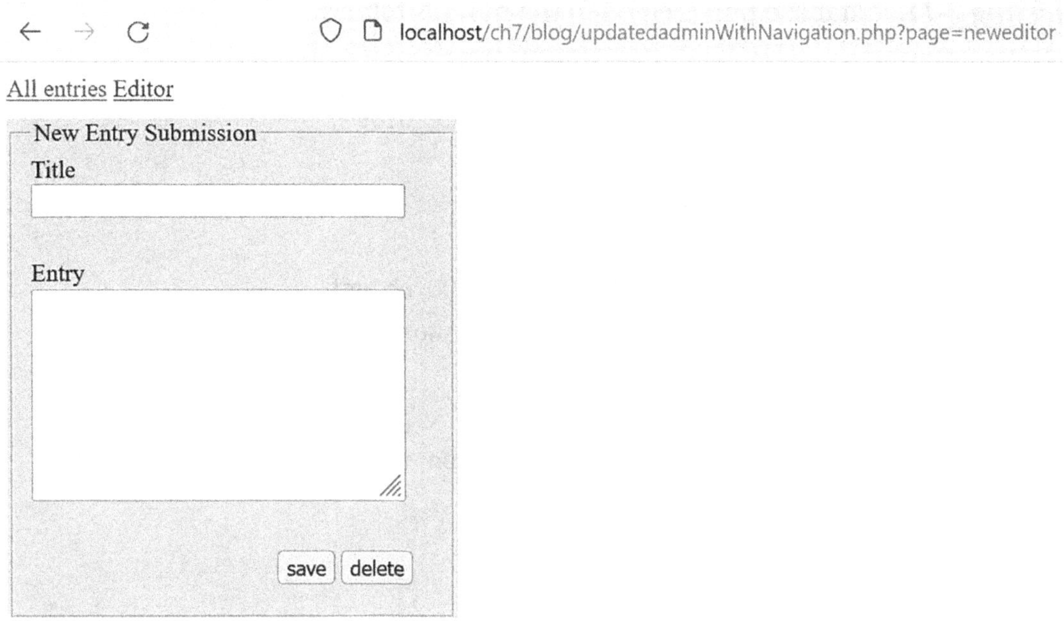

*Figure 7-3.* *Output after clicking the Editor menu item*

The best way to learn CSS is by using an existing style sheet and adjusting it to what you like. This sheet gives a simple display of the form – enough to make it look more professional.

**Exercise**: Adjust the CSS file to make the form more appealing. Make the buttons more rounded and curve off the edges of the form box. Adjust the menu items so they display a more professional look.

# Connecting to the Database

We have completed the basic editor view. Soon, we will be able to insert new blog entries into the blog_entry database table through the editor form. To do that, we will need a database connection from the application to the database.

We will take the same approach we used for the poll: use PDO for making a connection and include the connection in the front controller to share it with subsequently loaded controllers.

***Listing 7-11.*** database.php located in the models folder

```php
<?php
$dbInfo = "mysql:host=localhost;dbname=simple_blog";
$dbUser = "root";
$dbPassword = "";
try {
    //create a database connection with a PDO object
    $db = new PDO( $dbInfo, $dbUser, $dbPassword );
}catch (PDOException $e) {
        $error_message = $e->getMessage();
        $pageData->setContent("<h1>Connection failed!</h1><p>$e</p>");
        exit();
    }
?>
```

We can use the database.php file located in the models folder of the poll program from Chapter 6 to access our database. The only change we need to make is to change the database to simple_blog. We will soon include it into our front controller.

# Using Design Patterns

A design pattern is a general, best-practice solution to a common task. Some design patterns are defined comprehensively. As your experience grows, you will come across more design patterns. As an absolute beginner, you do not need a comprehensive treatment of design patterns – that would likely be more confusing than helpful.

This book uses simple implementations of a few design patterns. We have already seen a simple implementation of the *front controller design pattern* and an equally simple implementation of MVC. It is possible to combine several design patterns in the same project.

---

**Note**    For more information on design patterns, visit http://en.wikipedia. org/wiki/Software_design_pattern.

---

## The Table Data Gateway Design Pattern

The *table data gateway* design pattern is a relatively simple design pattern to understand. The table data gateway pattern specifies that one PHP class be created for every one table in a database. The idea is that all communication between the system and the one table happens through one specific object. The table data gateway encapsulates data communication between the system and a specific database table.

All SQL statements for this communication will be declared in a table data gateway class definition. This has a couple of advantages: One is that we know where to write your SQL statements. Consequently, we also know where to find our SQL statements related to the particular database table.

If you as a PHP developer keep all your SQL encapsulated in relatively few class definitions, then any database expert on your team will only have to work with these few classes. That is a huge advantage over having your SQL statements scattered all through your code base. Always remember, keep your coding as clean and simple as possible. This helps to reduce logical coding errors.

## Writing the Entry_Table Class

Initially, we will need to be able to insert new blog entries received from the editor form. We can create a new table gateway class definition for the blog_entry table.

Let us create the new class definition in the models folder; we will call it Blog_Entry_Table.class.php.

***Listing 7-12.*** Blog_Entry_Table.class.php

```php
<?php
//complete code listing for models/Blog_Entry_Table.class.php

class Blog_Entry_Table {

    private $db;
    //notice there are two underscore characters in __construct
    public function __construct ( $db ) {
        $this->db = $db;
    }
```

```php
public function saveEntry ( $title, $entry ) {
//notice placeholders in SQL string. ? is a placeholder
//notice the order of attributes: first title, next entry_text
$entrySQL = "INSERT INTO blog_entry ( title, entry_text )
            VALUES ( ?, ?)";
$entryStatement = $this->db->prepare( $entrySQL );
//create an array with dynamic data
//Order is important: $title must come first, $entry second
$formData = array( $title, $entry );
try{
    //pass $formData as argument to execute
    $entryStatement->execute( $formData );
} catch (Exception $e){
    $msg = "<p>You tried to run this sql: $entrySQL<p>
            <p>Exception: $e</p>";
    trigger_error($msg);
}
}
}
?>
```

The `Blog_Entry_Table` will not do anything until it is used from another script. The `Blog_Entry_Table` has one property db and two methods: the `constructor` and `saveEntry()`. The constructor takes a PDO object as argument. The received PDO object will be stored in the db property. This way, all methods of `Blog_Entry_Table` will have access to the PDO object and access to the `simple_blog` database.

In object-oriented terminology, `Blog_Entry_Table` and PDO are now associated through a `has-a` relationship. The `Blog_Entry_Table` `has-a` PDO object.

At this point, we will only be saving new entries. So, the `Blog_Entry_Table` class has just one method besides the constructor. The `saveEntry()` method takes two arguments: the `title` and the `blog_entry`.

The code provided uses *prepared statements* to insert data into the table. When we created the poll application, we did not directly insert any information the user provided into the database. However, in our blog, we want to save the title and blog entry information.

# Secure Programming

You might discover some PHP and SQL code on the Internet that directly save information into a database. However, this is a major security risk. A hacker can use *SQL Injection* to destroy our database information. Simply stated, the hacker can alter the SQL statement we intended to create, change, or delete information.

---

**Note**   For more information on SQL injections, visit `http://en.wikipedia.org/wiki/SQL_injection`.

---

Prepared statements also have a positive side effect of allowing the user to pass information containing quotes into the database. Prepared statements treat all input as nonexecutable strings which eliminates both of these concerns.

There are three equally important requirements for our use of prepared statements:

1. Characters are used as placeholders in the SQL string.

   ```
   $entrySQL = "INSERT INTO blog_entry ( title, entry_text )
   VALUES ( ?, ?)";  // ? ? are used as placeholders
   ```

2. An array is created with the dynamic data. The order of items must match the order used in the SQL string.

   ```
   //$formdata is an array with dynamic data
   //Order is important: $title must come first, $entry second
   $formData = array( $title, $entry );
   ```

3. The array with dynamic data is passed as an argument to the execute() method.

   ```
   // pass $formData as argument to execute
   $entryStatement->execute( $formData );
   ```

When the statement is executed, the values in the array will be inserted where the placeholders existed. The information inserted will not allow any SQL Injection.

```
} catch (Exception $e){
        $msg = "<p>You tried to run this sql: $entrySQL<p>
```

```
            <p>Exception: $e</p>";
        trigger_error($msg);
    }
```

In case an exception occurs, the code will trigger an error showing the SQL string that caused the exception and a more detailed look at the exception. In production, we do not want to display all this information to the user, but it's a good technique to help us debug any problems doing development.

## Processing the Admin Form Input and Saving the Entry

With the Blog_Entry_Table class created, we can continue development. A logical next step is to process input received from the editor form and use a Blog_Entry_Table object to save a new blog entry in the database. Let us update our editor controller.

*Listing 7-13.* newesteditor.php

```php
<?php
//complete source code for controllers/admin/editor.php
//include class definition and create an object
include_once "models/Blog_Entry_Table.class.php";
$entryTable = new Blog_Entry_Table( $db );
//was editor form submitted?
$editorSubmitted = isset( $_POST['action'] );
if ( $editorSubmitted ) {
    $buttonClicked = $_POST['action'];

    if ( $buttonClicked === 'save' ) {
        //get title and entry data from editor form
        $title = $_POST['title'];
        $entry = $_POST['entry'];
        //save the new entry
        $entryTable->saveEntry( $title, $entry );
    }
}
include_once "views/admin/insert-editor-html.php";
?>
```

```
include_once "models/Blog_Entry_Table.class.php";
$entryTable = new Blog_Entry_Table( $db );
```

The class is included, and the database connection is passed into the constructor.

```
if ( $buttonClicked === 'save' ) {
    //get title and entry data from editor form
    $title = $_POST['title'];
    $entry = $_POST['entry'];
    //save the new entry
    $entryTable->saveEntry( $title, $entry );
}
```

If the save button is clicked, the title and entry are retrieved and passed to the saveEntry method to insert them into the database.

---

**Note**    The following programs have been updated to link to the newest versions. All code changes are minor. The insertadminWithNavigation. php front controller also now includes an include_once statement to insert the database.php program.

```
insert-editor-html.php, insert-admin-navigation.php,
insertadminWithNavigation.php
```

---

We can now test the insert process by executing the insertadminWithNavigation. php program in our browser. Then we can click the Editor menu item, enter some test data, and click the save button. The information will now be properly placed into the blog_entry table in the database. The form will automatically clear all data, which is a common indication to the user that the data was inserted. You can browse the content of the blog_entry table using the phpMyAdmin control panel.

**Exercise**: Use either the code provided or the code you have developed and do a complete test on the current system. Try to break the system. Enter in SQL information and see if you can hack the program. Did you find any weaknesses?

# User View: Getting Data for All Blog Entries

Let's now provide the ability for our users to see the blog entries. We are switching from what the administrator will see (which eventually will be controlled with a userid and password) to what the user will see. Thus, we will create a different entrance (front controller) for the user, which does not require a userid and password, a different model, and a different view. We can use a stripped-down version of the administrator's front controller for the user controller.

***Listing 7-14.*** index.php

```php
<?php
//complete code for blog/index.php
$info = "";
include_once "models/Page_Data.class.php";
$pageData = new Page_Data();
$pageData->setTitle("PHP/MySQL blog demo");
include_once "models/database.php";
include_once "controllers/blog.php";
$pageData->setContent($info);
include_once "views/page.php";
echo $page;
?>
```

As we can see, currently, there is no need for navigation, as the user only has permission to view blog entries. The same Page_Data class, database.php, and page.php scripts are used. Since there is no menu, the determination of what menu item was selected is not currently needed. Of course, the controller and view are changed to the user versions.

Let us work on the changes required in the blog_entry class. We will show a list of all blog entries found in the database. Let us display the title, the first 150 characters of the entry_text, and a *Read more* link for each of the blog entries.

Let us start by creating a new method to retrieve the blog entries from the blog_entry table.

***Listing 7-15.*** Partial Listing of New_Blog_Entry_Table.class.php

```php
//declare a new method inside the Blog_Entry_Table class
public function getAllEntries () {
```

```
$sql = "SELECT entry_id, title,
        SUBSTRING(entry_text, 1, 150) AS intro
        FROM blog_entry";
$statement = $this->db->prepare( $sql );
try {
    $statement->execute();
} catch ( Exception $e ) {
    $exceptionMessage = "<p>You tried to run this sql: $sql <p>
            <p>Exception: $e</p>";
    trigger_error($exceptionMessage);
}
return $statement;
}
```

This method will be placed right before the saveEntries method within the class. This method has a similar format to the previous saveEntry method. There are a few minor changes, such as retrieving the information, instead of inserting it.

The getAllEntries() method will return a PDOStatement object, through which we can get access to all blog entries, one at a time. The statement involves some SQL we have not seen before, so it might be a bit tricky to understand initially. Let us go through it step by step.

## Using an SQL SUBSTRING Clause

```
$sql = "SELECT entry_id, title,
        SUBSTRING(entry_text, 1, 150) AS intro
        FROM blog_entry";
```

The first thing to notice is that the SELECT statement selects three columns – entry_id, title, and entry_text – from the blog_entry table. But we are not selecting everything from the entry_text column. We are only selecting the first 150 characters. We can accomplish this with the SQL SUBSTRING() function. The general syntax for the SUBSTRING() function is as follows:

```
SUBSTRING( string, start position, length )
```

The SUBSTRING() returns the part of a string requested: a substring. The string argument indicates which partial string to return. As you might guess, the start position argument indicates at which position to start the substring. The length argument specifies how long a substring to return. Thus, in the SELECT statement, we are selecting the first 150 characters from the string found in the entry_text field.

## Using an SQL Alias

In SQL statements, we can use an alias to rename a table or a column. In the SQL used to select all blog entries, we have named the substring result intro. It was not necessary to rename it, but it provides us with a straightforward way to access the information in the substring.

## Preparing a User View for All Blog Entries

It is time to create a user view. This view will list all blog entries. The number of blog entries is likely to change, so it would be a bad idea to create a view for a specific number of entries. The view should automatically change to accommodate however many – or few – blog entries are found in the database. We will iterate over blog entries by using a loop.

***Listing 7-16.*** list-entries-html.php

```php
<?php
//complete code for views/list-entries-html.php
$entriesFound = isset( $entries );
if ( $entriesFound === false ) {
    trigger_error( 'views/list-entries-html.php needs $entries' );
}

//create a <ul> element
$info = "<h1>Blog Entries</h1>";
$info .= "<ul id='blog-entries'>";

//loop through all $entries from the database
//remember each one row temporarily as $entry
//$entry will be a StdClass object with entry_id, title and intro
```

```php
while ( $entry = $entries->fetchObject() ) {
    $href   = "index.php?page=blog&id=$entry->entry_id";
    //create an <li> for each of the entries
    $info .= "<li>
        <h2>$entry->title</h2>
        <div>$entry->intro
            <p><a href='$href'>Read more</a></p>
        </div>
    </li>";
}
//end the <ul>
$info .= "</ul>";
?>

$entriesFound = isset( $entries );
if ( $entriesFound === false ) {
    trigger_error( 'views/list-entries-html.php needs $entries' );
}
```

$entries will contain the blog entries contained in the database. If they are missing, an error will be raised to indicate the problem. In production, this will need to be replaced with an informative statement to the user that there are not currently any blogs.

```php
while ( $entry = $entries->fetchObject() ) {
    $href   = "index.php?page=blog&id=$entry->entry_id";
    //create an <li> for each of the entries
    $info .= "<li>
        <h2>$entry->title</h2>
        <div>$entry->intro
            <p><a href='$href'>Read more</a></p>
        </div>
    </li>";
}
```

The while loop first attempts to fetch the next object (entry from the database table) and places it in $entry. The while loop considers a successful fetch as a true status. If the fetch is not successful (there are no more records), a false value is placed into

$entry and the loop will stop. As long as the status is true, the loop will dynamically create an <li> element for however many rows are in the blog_entry database table. If there is one blog entry in the database, there will be one <li>. If there are ten blog entries in your database, there will be ten <li> elements.

The $href variable contains a link which will recall the index page, passing the two attributes – page which is set to blog and id which is set to the entry_id contained in the record in the database table. This information will be used if the user wants to read more of the blog entry. In addition to the title and the intro (substring) being displayed, the actual href link is provided, allowing the user to click Read more for the complete blog entry.

## Hooking Up the User View and User Model

The last step is to hook up the user view with the data from the user model. It does not take much code, but it will produce a simple display of our entries.

***Listing 7-17.*** blog.php

```php
<?php
//complete code for controllers/blog.php
include_once "models/New_Blog_Entry_Table.class.php";
$entryTable = new New_Blog_Entry_Table( $db );
$entries = $entryTable->getAllEntries();
//load the view
include_once "views/list-entries-html.php";
?>
```

We simply include the model, make an instance of the class, pass the database connection object to the entry table object, call the getAllEntries method, and use the viewer to display the results. That is it!

← → C          ○ ▢ localhost/ch7/blog/

# Blog Entries

- **New Blog**

  My new blog!

  Read more

- **Another Blog**

  My new blog!

  Read more

***Figure 7-4.*** *Output from index.php*

Our view could use some CSS, but we can see that the test is successful. We can visit `http://localhost/blog/insertadminWithNavigation.php`, to create new entries, and then reload the index in the browser, to see the newly created blog entries listed. The blogging system is really starting to look like a proper blog.

It is very tempting to click *Read more*, isn't it? Don't you just want to click it and read a blog entry? Well, clicking *Read more* at this point will not have a significant impact. We have not written the code to display all content of individual blog entries, so nothing will change when you click.

**Exercise**: Update the navigation in the `admin` front controller to use this program to display all entries. Evaluate the results. What is missing? When displaying all entries from the admin controller, we currently lose the navigation. We will correct this later in the book.

# Responding to User Requests to Read More

We will show all the content for one blog entry when the user clicks *Read more*. We can find individual blog entries in the database table by the `entry_id`, the primary key. It is already available in the code, as mentioned before.

Which part of the code should respond when a user clicks *Read more*: model, view, or controller? The controller! A controller manages user interactions. Clicking a link is a user interaction. So, we need to make changes to the blog controller to deal with users who click *Read more*.

# Getting Entry Data

Let us tackle the problem of displaying the entry. To do that, we will retrieve data from the blog_entry table. We already have a class that provides access to the blog_entry table. We will continue to use this class to maintain a single point of access to the table.

```
$href   = "index.php?page=blog&id=$entry->entry_id";
```

Remember, the entry_id is passed through the URL call to the index page (blog controller) from the fetchObject() method we created previously. We can access this value to retrieve the record requested from the database table. Thus, we can declare a method that takes this entry_id as an argument (currently stored in the id attribute) and returns a StdClass object with all the content for the corresponding blog entry.

***Listing 7-18.*** Partial Listing of Newest_Blog_Entry_Table.class.php

```php
public function getEntry( $id ) {
    $sql = "SELECT entry_id, title, entry_text, date_created
            FROM blog_entry
            WHERE entry_id = ?";
    $statement = $this->db->prepare( $sql );
    $data = array( $id );
    try{
        $statement->execute( $data );
    } catch (Exception $e) {
        $exceptionMessage = "<p>You tried to run this sql: $sql <p>
                <p>Exception: $e</p>";
        trigger_error($exceptionMessage );
    }
    $model = $statement->fetchObject();
    return $model;
}
```

We can place this method within the class just above the getAllEntries() method. Now we have two methods to access entries: one which pulls all entries and one which pulls a specific entry. This new method is quite similar to the getAllEntries() method.

```
$sql = "SELECT entry_id, title, entry_text, date_created
          FROM blog_entry
          WHERE entry_id = ?";
```

The SQL string is almost the same as the one created in getAllEntries, except that the WHERE clause will restrict the selection to only one record with the correct entry_id.

```
$statement = $this->db->prepare( $sql );
```

The prepare() method converts the SQL string to a PDOStatement object.

```
$data = array( $id );
```

An array is declared to hold the value in $id, which will be populated with the entry_id.

```
$statement->execute( $data );
```

The execute method will replace the placeholder (?) with the value in $id and attempt to retrieve the requested record.

```
$model = $statement->fetchObject();
```

The fetchObject() method will attempt to retrieve the first row of data from the returned table. The return method will pass the StdClass object created to the blog controller. It was not necessary to include a loop since we are only retrieving one record from the database table.

# Secure Programming

Why did we use a prepared statement?

The $id came from a URL variable and as such can be manipulated; it should be treated as unsafe. A malicious hacker might try to change the value in the variable and attempt an SQL Injection attack. A prepared statement stops any such attempts.

Now we are ready to create our view for the specific entry selected by the user.

## Creating a Blog View

Again, the code we create for our single entry will be similar to the code we created to view all entries.

***Listing 7-19.*** entry-html.php

```php
<?php
//complete source code for views/entry-html.php
$entryFound = isset( $entryData );
if ( $entryFound === false ) {
    trigger_error( 'views/entry-html.php needs an $entryData object' );
}
$info = "<h1>Detailed Blog</h1>";
//properties available in $entry: entry_id, title, entry_text, date_created
$info .= "<article>
    <h1>$entryData->title</h1>
    <div class='date'>$entryData->date_created</div>
    $entryData->entry_text
</article>";
?>

$info .= "<article>
    <h1>$entryData->title</h1>
    <div class='date'>$entryData->date_created</div>
    $entryData->entry_text
</article>";
```

$info is populated from retrieving the title, date created, and entry text for the individual entry. This process is similar to the method which retrieves all the blog entries, except we did not need a loop. The essence is quite familiar: merge some data stored in a StdClass object with a predefined HTML structure. The view requires a StdClass object saved in a variable called $entryData. So, the first few lines of code check the availability of $entryData. If it is not found, the code will trigger a custom error. Remember, in production, we will display a different more user-friendly message if a problem occurs. However, during development, this provides us the information needed to correct the problem.

# Displaying an Entry

We have got the model; we have got the view. The last step is to update the blog controller. It is responsible for fetching entry data from the model, sharing it with the entry view, and returning the resulting HTML string to index controller, where it will be displayed.

***Listing 7-20.*** newblog.php

```php
<?php
//complete code for controllers/blog.php
include_once "models/Newest_Blog_Entry_Table.class.php";
$entryTable = new Newest_Blog_Entry_Table( $db );
$isEntryClicked = isset( $_GET['id'] );
if ($isEntryClicked ) {
    $entryId = $_GET['id'];
    //new code begins here
    $entryData = $entryTable->getEntry( $entryId );
    include_once "views/entry-html.php";
    //end of code changes
} else {
    $entries = $entryTable->getAllEntries();
    include_once "views/new-list-entries-html.php";
}
?>
```

```php
$isEntryClicked = isset( $_GET['id'] );
```

If the user clicks the *More details* link, the id will be populated in the URL used to call the index page. isset will return a true value into $isEntryClicked.

```php
if ($isEntryClicked ) {
    $entryId = $_GET['id'];
    //new code begins here
    $entryData = $entryTable->getEntry( $entryId );
    include_once "views/entry-html.php";
```

If it was clicked, the id is fetched from the URL using $_GET. This value is then passed into the getEntry() method. The entry view is then included to display the single entry retrieved. If the link is not clicked, the else part of the if statement is executed, which displays all entries.

---

**Note**   list-entries-html.php has been updated to now call newindex. php instead of index.php. It is now named new-list-entries-html.php. index.php has also now been updated to include newblog.php, instead of blog.php. It is now named newindex.php.

---

We can now test our program by loading newindex.php in our browser and by clicking the *Read more* link.

localhost/ch7/blog/newindex.php?page=blog&id=1

# Detailed Blog

## New Blog

2022-03-17 12:38:14
My new blog!

***Figure 7-5.*** *Results from clicking the Read more link in newindex.php*

Again, we could use some CSS, but we do now have a functional blog which allows users to select more information. It includes both administrative abilities (adding new blog entries) and normal user abilities. Now would be an enjoyable time to celebrate our progress! We have come a long way since the first chapter. But...

**Exercise**: Update the project, by adding code similar to previously seen in this chapter, to use the same CSS style sheet to professionally design the display of all the entries and the detailed display of an individual entry. Add CSS to the style sheet which will display all current views in a similar professional user-friendly design.

# Code Smell: Duplicate Code

Can you smell it? There is a bad smell coming from our code. It is one of those classic code smells every coder knows about. It is one of those things you should learn to avoid, as your proficiency with code grows.

---

**Note** Find a long list of typical code smells at `http://en.wikipedia.org/wiki/Code_smell`.

---

Duplicate code is *when identical or similar code exists in multiple places*. Do you already know where to find the smell? It is in models/Newest_Blog_Entry_Table.class. php. Here is an example:

```
//partial code for models/Blog_Entry_Table.class.php
public function getEntry( $id ) {
    $sql = "SELECT entry_id, title, entry_text, date_created
            FROM blog_entry
            WHERE entry_id = ?";
    $statement = $this->db->prepare( $sql );
    $data = array( $id );
    try{
        $statement->execute( $data );
    } catch (Exception $e) {
        $exceptionMessage = "<p>You tried to run this sql: $sql <p>
                <p>Exception: $e</p>";
        trigger_error($exceptionMessage );
    }
    $model = $statement->fetchObject();
    return $model;
}
```

There are a couple of other similar methods in the Newest_Blog_Entry_Table class. They all prepare() a PDOStatement and try() to execute() it. In all three methods, we can find many lines of code that are nearly identical. That is bad!

## Staying DRY with Curly

Duplicate code is bad for a number of reasons. One is that it is not efficient; we are simply using more lines than necessary. The code is unnecessarily long. Longer code can invariably cause more potential errors. Less code means fewer chances for errors. Another reason duplicate code is bad is that it complicates the maintenance of the program over time. It is highly likely, over time, that the code will need to be updated. If the code is identical or remarkably similar code in multiple different methods, changes might need to occur in all of those methods. We always should create code that is as easy as possible to maintain.

We can place the duplicate code in a separate method, so any change to the code can be made in one place. Each method can then call the new method. This decreases maintenance time and increases reliability.

It is really just another case of coding by Curly's law or at least a variant of Curly's law. Curly's original law was: *Do one thing*. This particular variant should be: *Do one thing once*. There is another geek expression for it: staying DRY. *DRY* is an acronym that means "don't repeat yourself."

## Refactoring with Curly

*Refactoring* is the process of changing code without changing what it does. It is a big deal for coders. We should refactor our code whenever we realize the project requirements have outgrown the code architecture, or, in other words, when the code architecture does not support the features, your project needs in a beautiful way. Simply, when we discover duplicate logic in multiple places, it needs to be fixed.

It is time to refactor the Newest_Blog_Entry_Table class, so it becomes DRIER. Let us begin by encapsulating the code that prepares an SQL statement into a separate method.

```
//$sql argument must be an SQL string
//$data must be an array of dynamic data to use in the SQL
private function executeSQL ( $sql, $data) {
    //create a PDOStatement object
    $statement = $this->db->prepare( $sql );
    try{
        //use the dynamic data and run the query
        $statement->execute( $data );
```

```
    } catch (Exception $e) {
        $exceptionMessage = "<p>You tried to run this sql: $sql <p>
                <p>Exception: $e</p>";
        trigger_error($exceptionMessage);
    }
    //return the PDOStatement object
    return $statement;
}

public function executeSQL ( $sql, $data) {
```

This new method accepts the prepared statement in $sql and the array of data to be placed into the prepared statement when called from another program or method. It then uses this information in the same manner that we discovered in the other methods contained within the Blog Entry class.

With the new method declared, we can refactor one of the existing methods to use the new method.

***Listing 7-21.*** getEntry Method of Updated_Blog_Entry_Table.class.php

```
public function getEntry( $id ){
    $sql = "SELECT entry_id, title, entry_text, date_created
            FROM blog_entry
            WHERE entry_id = ?";
    $data = array($id);
    //call the new DRY method
    $statement = $this->executeSQL($sql, $data);
    $model = $statement->fetchObject();
    return $model;
}
```

The new executeSQL() method makes the getEntry() method a little shorter. The code is also easier to follow as it only creates the prepared statement, and the array, then it calls the executeSQL method. It then fetches the results and returns them.

There is a little syntactical detail to notice. See how we used the $this keyword when one method calls another method declared in the same class? It is not really different from using $this to get to a property. In both cases, $this is an object's reference to itself. It is the object-oriented way of saying "my."

Let us refactor the saveEntry() method.

***Listing 7-22.*** saveEntry of Updated_Blog_Entry_Table.class.php

```
public function saveEntry ( $title, $entry ) {
    $entrySQL = "INSERT INTO blog_entry ( title, entry_text )
                VALUES ( ?, ?)";
    $formData = array($title, $entry);
    //changes start here
    //$this is the object's way of saying 'my'
    //so $this->makeStatement calls makeStatement of Blog_Entry_Table
    $entryStatement = $this->executeSQL( $entrySQL, $formData );
    //end of changes
}
```

Finally, let us refactor the getAllEntries() method.

***Listing 7-23.*** getAllEntries of Updated_Blog_Entry_Table.class.php

```
public function getAllEntries () {
    $sql = "SELECT entry_id, title, SUBSTRING(entry_text, 1, 150) AS
intro  FROM blog_entry";
    $statement = $this->executeSQL($sql);
    return $statement;
}
```

We have a slight problem here. We only need the SQL string and not the array to retrieve all the records because we are not using a prepared statement. However, when we call the executeSQL(), it requires two arguments. We only want to pass one.

Sometimes, we want to call executeSQL() with one argument, and sometimes we want to call it with two arguments. The second argument needs to be optional. Luckily, PHP has a very easy way to make an argument optional. We simply declare the argument with a default value, which will be used if nothing is passed. Let us update the executeSQL method to allow this.

***Listing 7-24.*** executeSQL of Updated_Blog_Entry_Table.class.php

```
private function executeSQL ( $sql, $data = NULL ){
    //end of code changes
```

```
    $statement = $this->db->prepare( $sql );
    try{
        $statement->execute( $data );
    } catch (Exception $e){
        $exceptionMessage = "<p>You tried to run this sql: $sql <p>
                <p>Exception: $e</p>";
        trigger_error($exceptionMessage );
    }
    return $statement;
}
```

In the preceding code, the argument $data gets a default value of NULL. So, if executeSQL() is called without a second argument, the created PDOStatement object will execute with NULL. No dynamic values will replace placeholders in the prepared statement. And that is exactly what we want, because there are no placeholders in the SQL for this statement.

---

**Note**    You can consult www.w3schools.com/php/php_functions.asp to learn a little more about function arguments with default values.

---

In the other cases where executeSQL() is called with two arguments, the second argument will be used to replace SQL placeholders with actual values. Using optional arguments is a very powerful concept in code. It can often lead to a clean solution when encapsulating nearly duplicate code into a single separate method.

---

**Note**    Minor changes have been made to the following files to properly use the new Blog Entry Table class.

updated-entries-html.php, updatedblog.php, updatedindex.php

---

We can test our changes by executing updatedindex.php in our browser. The same output will occur when displaying all entries and retrieving more information for an individual entry.

Remember: Refactoring is to change code without changing what it does. So, a successful test confirms when the code behaves exactly as it did before refactoring. Refactoring is done with the sole purpose of making the code easier to maintain and more efficient.

## Secure Programming

You may have noticed that the executeSQL() method is private instead of public. It is a fragile member of the Blog Entry Table class. It is only meant to be called internally and only by other methods in the class. It is certainly not meant to be called from outside the class.

The executeSQL() method is a *submethod* used by the other methods. This method makes the actual changes to the data in the database table. It is very vulnerable to attacks by hackers. Thus, it needs to be protected from any attempt to use it outside of the class. Simply setting it to private provides this extra protection. It can only be used by a method within the class itself.

Remember: The single responsibility principle, also known as Curly's law, applied to classes. A class should have a single purpose, and all its properties and behaviors should be strictly aligned with that purpose. A class with one responsibility is simpler than a class with many, and a simple class is easier to use than a complex class. By hiding some properties and methods using a private access modifier, we present a public interface that's even simpler and easier to use. So, as a rule of thumb, use private by default, public when you need it.

---

**Note**   There is a third access modifier: protected. In PHP, it is similar to private, except it can be shared with subclasses through *inheritance*. You can find a nice tutorial covering inheritance, access modifiers, and other central OOP topics at www.killerphp.com/tutorials/object-oriented-php/.

---

# Summary

In this chapter, we have created a basic blog. The blog provides administrative ability to create new entries and user ability to display blog entries. In the process, we learned about prepared statements, and we were introduced to design patterns. We also discovered how to refactor duplicate code. We created a Blog Entry Table class which is the data gateway that provides a single point of access from the PHP code to the blog_ entry database table. We have eliminated smelly code and have produced DRY code in the process.

While our code provides us a good functioning blog, it is missing some key components. For example, we do not have the ability to update or delete a blog entry. We will enhance the features of this blog next.

# Projects

1.  Using the design practices from this and previous chapters, create a student registration system. The basic system will accept student information (name, address, date of birth, and major) and save the information in a database. The system will also display the name of all students registered. Next to each student name will be a link to provide additional student information. When the link is clicked, the name, address, date of birth, and major will be displayed.

2.  Using MVC, create a web page that the user can use to request more information. The page should accept the user's name, email, subject, and detailed description. This information will be stored in a database. Create administrator pages to display the subjects entered by all users. Next to each subject provides a link to display the user's name, email, and detailed description. For an extra challenge, search www.php.net to discover how to send emails using PHP. After the user submits the information, send an email to your email address (in addition to saving the information in the database).

# CHAPTER 8

# Basic Blog: Entries and Comments

## Objectives

After completing this chapter, you will be able to

- Create a view containing an interactive HTML form

- Create a controller to handle input from the form

- Create a model to save and retrieve any entry using a database table

- Use a foreign key to associate rows and tables comments in a database

- Use inheritance to avoid redundant code

- Create a search algorithm to find data in a database table

In this chapter, we will make improvements to both the administrator module and the user (blog) module. We will begin with the administrator module.

The second iteration of the administration module will update and delete existing entries through the entry editor (front controller). In the process of improving the entry manager, we will start by writing small, informal code tests. These tests check the logical flow of the information between the controller, model, and view before adding additional code which can complicate the debugging process. Integrating testing into the development process will improve the overall code quality and decrease debugging time.

© Jason Lengstorf, Thomas Blom Hansen, Steve Prettyman 2022
J. Lengstorf et al., *PHP 8 for Absolute Beginners*, https://doi.org/10.1007/978-1-4842-8205-2_8

# Creating a Model for the Administrative Module

When looking at the version of our administrative module from the previous chapter, we can clearly see that there are already buttons that can be used for saving or deleting existing entries. We can also see that something is missing. Where would we click to load an existing entry into the entry editor, so that we could edit or delete it?

Let us start our development process to solve this problem by copying the files from the publisher's website. You can choose to copy files from the ch7 folder and modify them, as discussed in the next paragraph. However, due to the number of changes, this is not recommended. If you do want to venture into that swamp, follow the directions in the following.

Start by creating a ch8 folder. Under this folder, create a blog folder. Under the blog folder, create the controllers, css, models, and views folders. Under the controllers folder, create an admin folder. Under the views folder, create an admin folder. Then copy the programs from the ch7 folder as shown in the following table.

| Original Name | New Name | Location |
|---|---|---|
| newesteditor.php | editor.php | controllers/admin |
| database.php | database.php | Models |
| Page_Data.class.php | Page_Data.class.php | Models |
| Updated_Blog_Entry_Table.class.php | Blog_Entry_Table.class.php | Models |
| updated-admin-navigation.php | admin-navigation.php | views/admin |
| insert-editor-html.php | editor-html.php | views/admin |
| insertadminWithNavigation.php | admin.php | Blog |
| newblog.css | blog.css | css |
| page.php | page.php | views |

**Note**   Each file copied will need to be updated to use any of the renamed programs.

Next, to accomplish the task for update and delete, let us display a list of all entries to our administrators. Clicking one entry will load it into the entry editor. We can use the `getAllEntries()` method from the Blog Class to accomplish our task.

## Displaying Administrative Links

With the previous model (`Blog_Entry_Table.class.php`) tried, tested, and understood, we can start working on the view. Let us create a list of clickable blog entry titles. This allows us to take an approach similar to logic used with the `blog.php` program. We can use a `while` loop to iterate through database records using the `PDO Statement` object. Every row of data from the database table will be represented by a separate `<li>` element. We can wrap the individual blog titles in `<a>` elements to create a clickable list of entries. Let us make these adjustments to the Chapter 7 `updated-entries-html.php` program.

***Listing 8-1.***  entries-html.php

```php
<?php
//complete code for views/admin/entries-html.php
$entriesFound = isset( $entries );
if ( $entriesFound === false ) {
    trigger_error( 'views/admin/entries-html.php needs $entries' );
}
//create a <ul> element
$info = "<h1>Blog Entries</h1>";
$info .= "<ul id='blog-entries'>";
$info .= "<ul>";
//loop through all $entries from the database
//remember each one row temporarily as $entry
//$entry will be a StdClass object with entry_id, title and intro
while ( $entry = $entries->fetchObject() ) {
    $href  = "admin.php?page=editor&id=$entry->entry_id";
    //create an <li> for each of the entries
    $info .= "<li><a href='$href'>$entry->title</a></li>";
}
//end the <ul>
$info .= "</ul>";
?>
```

Clicking an entry will request a URL like `admin.php?page=editor&id=2`. This way, the editor controller will have access to the `entry_id` of the clicked entry. This code is similar to the code we created previously.

Now we can create an entries controller for administration access.

***Listing 8-2.*** entries.php

```php
<?php
//complete code for controller/admin/entries.php
include_once "models/Blog_Entry_Table.class.php";
$entryTable = new Blog_Entry_Table( $db );
$entries = $entryTable->getAllEntries();
include_once "views/admin/entries-html.php";
?>
```

This code is similar to `updatedblog.php` in Chapter 7. It is actually a simplified version because we are not checking to see if the user has clicked a button. We are displaying all entries by default.

We can test the logical flow of our program by loading `http://localhost/ch8/blog/admin.php?page=entries` into a browser. Once we are satisfied that everything works, we can add additional details to our code.

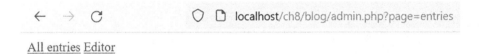

All entries Editor

# **Blog Entries**

- New Blog
- Another Blog

***Figure 8-1.*** *Output from admin.php?page=entries*

We now see a list of clickable blog entry titles. If we click a title, the empty entry editor will be displayed. We can change this, so that the entry editor will be loaded with the contents of the clicked blog entry displayed inside the editor.

# Populating the Form with the Entry to Be Edited

Sometimes, the entry editor form should be displayed with blank fields, so that we can create new entries. At other times, the editor should display an existing entry, so that it can be edited. A user can click a blog title to load the values into the editor. Clicking the blog title will encode the entry's entry_id into the HTTP request as a URL variable. It follows that if an entry's entry_id is available as a URL variable, we can load the corresponding entry into the editor. If no such URL variable is found, we can display a blank editor.

Let us adjust the editor view to display the contents when an id is found; otherwise, it will still display an empty form.

***Listing 8-3.*** new-editor-html.php

```php
<?php
//complete source code for views/admin/editor-html.php
//new code added here
//check if required data is available
$entryDataFound = isset( $entryData );
if( $entryDataFound === false ){
    //default values for an empty editor
    $entryData = new StdClass();
    $entryData->entry_id = 0;
    $entryData->title = "";
    $entryData->entry_text = "";
}
$info = "
<form method='post' action='admin.php?page=neweditor' id='editor'>
    <input type='hidden' name='id' value='$entryData->entry_id' />
    <fieldset>
        <legend>New Entry Submission</legend>
        <label>Title</label>
        <input type='text' name='title' maxlength='150'
            value='$entryData->title' />

        <label>Entry</label>
        <textarea name='entry'>$entryData->entry_text</textarea>
```

267

```
        <fieldset id='editor-buttons'>
            <input type='submit' name='action' value='save' />
            <input type='submit' name='action' value='delete' />
        </fieldset>
    </fieldset>
</form>";
?>

$entryDataFound = isset( $entryData );
if( $entryDataFound === false ){
    //default values for an empty editor
    $entryData = new StdClass();
    $entryData->entry_id = 0;
    $entryData->title = "";
    $entryData->entry_text = "";
}
```

If there is information contained in $entryData (which will be populated from pulling a record from the database, if the user clicked the title), then that information will be placed into $entryDataFound. The information is contained in a StdClass. If there was no information pulled (the user wants to enter a new blog), then default values are used.

```
<input type='hidden' name='id' value='$entryData->entry_id' />
```

The entry_id is saved into a hidden variable id since the value has no meaning to the user. It will be hidden from view when displaying the page. However, if the user looks at the HTML code formed in the browser (view source), the value will be visible. Thus, it is hidden, but not considered secure.

```
<input type='text' name='title' maxlength='150'
        value='$entryData->title' />
```

```
<label>Entry</label>
<textarea name='entry'>$entryData->entry_text</textarea>
```

Both the title and entry fields are populated with values from the StdClass. This will display the blog data to be updated or the default values if the user wants to enter a new blog.

The last step is to update the editor.php program to use the getEntry() method from the Blog_Entry_Table to retrieve the data for any blog entry the user requested.

***Listing 8-4.*** neweditor.php

```php
<?php
//complete source code for controllers/admin/editor.php
//include class definition and create an object
include_once "models/Blog_Entry_Table.class.php";
$entryTable = new Blog_Entry_Table( $db );
//was the editor form submitted?
$editorSubmitted = isset( $_POST['action'] );
if ( $editorSubmitted ) {
    $buttonClicked = $_POST['action'];

    if ( $buttonClicked === 'save' ) {
        //get title and entry data from editor form
        $title = $_POST['title'];
        $entry = $_POST['entry'];
        //save the new entry
        $entryTable->saveEntry( $title, $entry );
    }
}
$entryRequested = isset( $_GET['id'] );
//create a new if-statement
if ( $entryRequested ) {
    $id = $_GET['id'];
    //load model of existing entry
    $entryData = $entryTable->getEntry( $id );
    $entryData->entry_id = $id;
}
include_once "views/admin/new-editor-html.php";
?>

$entryRequested = isset( $_GET['id'] );
//create a new if-statement
if ( $entryRequested ) {
```

```
$id = $_GET['id'];
//load model of existing entry
$entryData = $entryTable->getEntry( $id );
$entryData->entry_id = $id;
}
```

isset is used to determine if the hidden id value has been set. If it has, then it is retrieved and placed into $id. The $id value is then passed into the getEntry() method to retrieve the data from that particular record in the database table. The $id value then is added to the entry_id property in the StdObject named $entryData which was created when the data was retrieved.

---

**Note**    The following new versions, with minor changes, have been created to access neweditor.php and new-editor-html.php: new-entries-html. php, newentries.php.

---

Let us take time to test the logic of our code before we continue. We can test our code by entering http://localhost/ch8/blog/admin.php?page=newentries into a browser – then by selecting one of the blogs that are displayed.

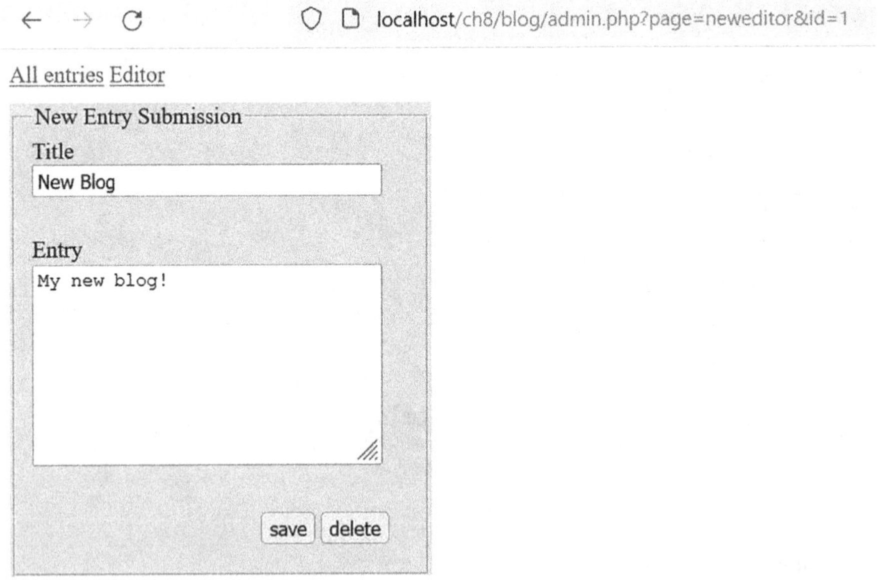

*Figure 8-2.* *Output from calling neweditor.php via admin.php and selecting a blog*

The editor is not perfect yet. We can see any existing entry in the editor, but we cannot save any changes. If we click the Save button, a new entry will be inserted, but an existing blog cannot be updated. The editor cannot properly handle existing entries yet, nor can it delete existing entries. Deleting is easy, so we will implement that first.

## Handling Entry Deletion

The model will logically contain code to delete entry data from the database. The view already has a Delete button, so no changes are necessary. The controller must also be updated to execute code when a user clicks the Delete button.

## Deleting Entries from the Database

To delete a row of data from the blog_entry table in the database, we will need to create more SQL. Let us take a minute to reflect. Where would we write the code to delete an entry? The PHP code to delete an entry in the blog_entry table belongs in the Blog_Entry_Table class, our single gateway to the database table. We will create a new method to accomplish this task.

***Listing 8-5.*** Partial Listing from New_Blog_Entry_Table.class.php

```
//partial code for models/New_Blog_Entry_Table.class.php

//declare a new method inside the Blog_Entry_Table class
public function deleteEntry ( $id ) {
    $sql = "DELETE FROM blog_entry WHERE entry_id = ?";
    $data = array( $id );
    $statement = $this->executeSQL( $sql, $data );
}
```

The code within this method should look familiar. It uses the same logic as other methods in the Blog Entry Table. The only difference is the SQL statement.

Deleting data from a database is a final action; there is no undo! It is important that we never accidentally delete something. The database table is properly designed: every record has a primary key. That means every single record can be uniquely identified if we have the primary key of an entry. It follows that we also know which record to delete by the entry_id.

# Responding to Delete Requests

With the editor model ready to delete entries, it is time to update the controller with code, to determine if the Delete button was clicked. If the Delete button was clicked, the controller should call the model, to have the relevant entry deleted.

```
//partial code for views/admin/editor-html.php
//two buttons, one name, different values
<fieldset id='editor-buttons'>
    <input type='submit' name='action' value='save' />
    <input type='submit' name='action' value='delete' />
</fieldset>
```

Clicking any of the submit buttons in the editor form will encode a URL variable named action. The action will have a value of save, if the Save button is clicked, and a value of delete, if the Delete button is clicked. Knowing this, let us update the editor program.

***Listing 8-6.*** newesteditor.php

```php
<?php
//complete source code for controllers/admin/newesteditor.php
include_once "models/New_Blog_Entry_Table.class.php";
$entryTable = new New_Blog_Entry_Table( $db );
//was the editor form submitted?
$editorSubmitted = isset( $_POST['action'] );
if ( $editorSubmitted ) {
    $buttonClicked = $_POST['action'];
    $id = $_POST['id'];
    if ( $buttonClicked === 'save' ) {
        //get title and entry data from editor form
        $title = $_POST['title'];
        $entry = $_POST['entry'];
        //save the new entry
        $entryTable->saveEntry( $title, $entry );
    } else if ($buttonClicked === 'delete' ) {
```

```
        $entryTable->deleteEntry( $id );
    }
}
$entryRequested = isset( $_GET['id'] );
//create a new if-statement
if ( $entryRequested ) {
    $id = $_GET['id'];
    //load model of existing entry
    $entryData = $entryTable->getEntry( $id );
    $entryData->entry_id = $id;
}
include_once "views/admin/new-editor-html.php";
?>
```

There are actually only a few changes necessary.

```
$id = $_POST['id'];
```

The hidden value in id is saved into $id.

```
    } else if ($buttonClicked === 'delete' ) {
        $entryTable->deleteEntry( $id );
    }
```

An else if statement is added to check if the Delete button was clicked. If it was, then the $id value is passed to the new deleteEntry() method.

---

**Note**    The following programs have been updated to call the new versions of newesteditor.php and New_Blog_Entry_Table.php: new-entries-html. php, newestentries.php, newadmin.php, newest-editor-html.php, newest-admin-navigation.php.

---

We can pause again to test our updates to the model, controller, and view. We can check our progress by entering http://localhost/ch8/blog/newadmin. php?page=newestentries into a browser.

After selecting a blog to delete and clicking the Delete button, the form will clear. This gives the user an indication that the record has been deleted. We can click the All entries menu item to discover that the entry is no longer listed. We can also verify this by looking in the database table.

---

**Note**    The entry_id can be found in two different places. In one part of the program, the code looks for the entry_id using $_POST['id']; in another part of the program, the code looks for it using $_GET['id']. It is a little peculiar that they hold identical values but serve different purposes.

---

The $_GET['id'] gets encoded every time a user clicks a blog title listed. So, $_GET['id'] represents the entry_id of a blog entry a user would like to see in the entry editor.

The $_POST['id'] gets encoded every time an entry has been loaded into the entry editor. It represents the entry_id of the entry the user has just seen in the editor. So, $_GET['id'] represents the entry to be loaded, whereas $_POST['id'] represents the already loaded entry.

We now have an editor that can create new entries and delete existing ones. Let us complete the process by allowing the administrator to update entries.

# Preparing a Model to Update Entries in the Database

Updating an existing entry in the database is definitely a job for the model. Let us add an update method to our Blog Entry Table.

*Listing 8-7.* Partial Listing of Newest_Blog_Entry_Table.class.php

```
//Partial code for models/Newest_Blog_Entry_Table.class.php

//declare new method
        public function updateEntry ( $id, $title, $entry) {
    $sql = "UPDATE blog_entry
            SET title = ?,
            entry_text = ?
            WHERE entry_id = ?";
```

```
    $data = array( $title, $entry, $id );
    $statement = $this->executeSQL( $sql, $data) ;
    return $statement;
}
```

The logic of this function and the basic structure of the SQL should look familiar.
We used the update SQL statement when we updated our poll. However, we are using a
prepared statement to place the changes into the record in the database table to ensure
that any attempt at SQL Injection will fail. Now we can update the code to call this
method when the user clicks the Save button. The Save button will accept both a new
entry and an updated entry.

## Controller: Should I Insert or Update?

When the user clicks Save, the displayed entry should either be inserted or updated in
the database. Which action to take depends on which entry was displayed in the entry
editor form.

Remember the hidden input from the editor view? It stores the currently displayed
entry's entry_id, or 0, if the editor fields are blank (set to the defaults). We can use this
information to check whether the administrator is trying to insert a new row in the blog_
entry table or update an existing row.

When the Save button is clicked, we will retrieve the value from the hidden
input. If the editor was empty, the hidden input holds a value of 0. This indicates the
administrator has just created a new entry. The code will then insert a new row into
blog_entry. If it holds any other integer, the code will update the blog_entry with the
corresponding entry_id. Let us update the controller to accomplish these tasks.

***Listing 8-8.*** updatededitor.php

```php
<?php
//complete source code for controllers/admin/updatededitor.php
include_once "models/Newest_Blog_Entry_Table.class.php";
$entryTable = new Newest_Blog_Entry_Table( $db );
//was the editor form submitted?
$editorSubmitted = isset( $_POST['action'] );
if ( $editorSubmitted ) {
```

```php
    $buttonClicked = $_POST['action'];
    $id = clean_input($_POST['id']);
    $title = clean_input($_POST['title']);
    $entry = clean_input($_POST['entry']);
    if ( ($buttonClicked === 'save') and ($id === '0' ) ) {
        $entryTable->saveEntry( $title, $entry );
    } else if  (($buttonClicked === 'save') and ($id != '0')) {
     $entryTable->updateEntry( $id, $title, $entry );
     } else if ($buttonClicked === 'delete' ) {
         $entryTable->deleteEntry( $id );
     }
}
$entryRequested = isset( $_GET['id'] );
//create a new if-statement
if ( $entryRequested ) {
    $id = $_GET['id'];
    //load model of existing entry
    $entryData = $entryTable->getEntry( $id );
    $entryData->entry_id = $id;
}
include_once "views/admin/updated-editor-html.php";
//New function to remove invalid code
function clean_input($value) {
  $value = trim($value);
  $value = stripslashes($value);
  $value = strip_tags($value);
  return $value;
}
?>
```

## Secure Programming

```php
    $id = clean_input($_POST['id']);
    $title = clean_input($_POST['title']);
    $entry = clean_input($_POST['entry']);
```

...

```php
function clean_input($value) {
  $value = trim($value);
  $value = stripslashes($value);
  $value = strip_tags($value);
  return $value;
}
```

In addition to the changes mentioned, we have taken the opportunity to improve the validity of the data being entered by using three PHP functions: `trim()`, `stripslashes()`, and `strip_tags()`. `trim()` will remove extra spaces, tabs, and/or newline characters. Backslashes will be removed using `stripslashes()`. `strip_tags()` will remove any PHP or HTML tags entered, which will keep it from being executed.

---

**Note**    The following programs have been updated to access the most current versions of the updated files: `updated-editor-html.php`, `updated-entries-html.php`, `updatedentries.php`, `updatedadmin.php`, `updated-admin-navigation.php`.

---

The code must be able to differentiate between two user actions (save, update). When the user clicks the Save button, and `entry_id` is 0, the user is really trying to insert a new entry.

```php
$id = clean_input($_POST['id']);
$title = clean_input($_POST['title']);
$entry = clean_input($_POST['entry']);
```

All three values are saved if the user clicked a button. The values will be default values, and `$id` will contain a zero, if the user wants to save a new entry. `$id` will contain the entry id number if the user wants to update an existing entry.

```php
if ( ($buttonClicked === 'save') and ($id === '0' ) ) {
    $entryTable->saveEntry( $title, $entry );
} else if ( ($buttonClicked === 'save') and ($id != '0')) {
  $entryTable->updateEntry( $id, $title, $entry );
} else if ($buttonClicked === 'delete' ) {
  $entryTable->deleteEntry( $id );
}
```

If it is a new entry, then the saveEntry() method is called, with $title and $entry passed. If it is an updated entry, the updateEntry() method is called, with $id, $title, and $entry. If the Delete button was clicked, deleteEntry() is called, with $id.

We can now take another pause and test our changes by entering http:// localhost/ch8/blog/updatedadmin.php?page=updatedentries into our browser.

After clicking on a blog listed, we can make updates to the blog and click the submit button. The form will be clear which is an indication that the changes took place. Then we can use the navigation menu to display all blogs (again) and click on the updated blog to see that the update did occur.

## Insisting on a Title

We have a usability flaw in our logic; it is possible to create a new blog entry without specifying a title for it!

*Figure 8-3.*  *Entering a blog without a title*

The problem is that a blog entry without a title cannot be clicked, and consequently, such an entry is not loaded into the entry editor form. If we really wanted to edit the blog entry, we could change the entry in the database table. We might say that this is a usability problem rather than a functional problem. Functionally speaking, it *is* possible to edit the entry, but it would be much more convenient, and much easier for users, if all blog entries could be edited through the entry editor.

## Secure Programming

This might be considered a security flaw in our program or, at least, a validation flaw. Remember, we must make sure all data is valid before it is entered into the database. We certainly have not done so here. For secure validation, it must occur in two locations:

the client side and the server side. We must remember that hackers can bypass our forms and attempt to send information directly to our program on the server. If we only validate on the client machine, we leave a hole for this to occur.

So why not validate everything on the server, and just skip validation on the client?

The answer is efficiency. Every time we use PHP code, we are interacting with the server. Thus, if we only validate using PHP, we must pass the information to the server, validate, pass back the information and error messages to the form on the client machine, and do it again if the user still does not enter correct information. If we validate on the client machine first, we can make sure that valid information (when sent from the form) is only sent to the server – thus reducing the server calls and making the program more user-friendly and more efficient. Of course, we still will validate using PHP to make sure that the data was not corrupted on the way to the server or that a hacker is not attempting to send invalid data to the server.

Let us start by making a small change to our editor HTML code for client-side validation. Although we already cleaned our data on the server side, let us update the user side to not allow special characters, which may indicate an attempt to enter HTML code. We also will require that a title be entered. This will eliminate the problem shown in Figure 8-3.

```
//partial code for views/admin/another-editor-html.php

<input type='text' name='title' maxlength='150' ";
if ( $entryData->title !="") {
        $info .= "value='$entryData->title' ";
}

        $info .= "pattern='[A-Za-z]{,150}'"
      title='Title can contain only alphabetic letters, no special
      characters. Title is required.'
       required />
```

The pattern

```
pattern='[a-z][A-Z]{,150}'
```

will allow only alphabetic characters, and requires at least one character, with a maximum of 150 characters. The HTML **required** attribute also checks that the user has entered information. The **title** attribute defines the error message to be displayed if the user does not enter the correct required information. The title text box will only be set with a value if it is not the default value. Otherwise, the pattern test will fail.

***Figure 8-4.*** *Output from another-editor-html.php with invalid input*

---

**Note**   The following files have been updated with minor changes to use the modified form: `another-admin-navigation.php, anothereditor.php, anotheradmin.php, another-entries-html.php, anotherentries.php`.

For more information on input patterns, visit `www.w3schools.com/tags/att_input_pattern.asp`.

---

This solution will work beautifully in most modern browsers. However, any older browsers will ignore HTML that it cannot execute and simply pass the values entered to the PHP program on the server.

To verify that the title has a value, we only need to change one code line in the `anothereditor.php` program.

```
if (( $editorSubmitted ) && (isset( $_POST['title']))) {
```

**Exercise**: Adjust the HTML code for the text field in the `another-editor-html.php` form and the PHP code in `anothereditor.php` to allow a few types of HTML (and/or CSS) formatting. To accomplish this, you will need to create a JavaScript function for validation on the user side and update the clean function on the server side.

# User View: Building and Displaying the Comment Entry Form

Let us switch over to the user side of our application and correct another missing required function of our blog. Any blogging system should allow the user to compose comments for existing blog entries. We will start by creating a comment form (*view*) to accept these user comments. This form will also need a corresponding model and a controller.

---

**Note**   The following files have been copied from the `ch7/blog` folder and renamed as shown in the following. The files have also been modified to use the current versions of other related files. It is recommended that you copy the files from the Chapter 8 folder on the publisher's website to avoid issues.

---

| Original Name | New Name | Location |
|---|---|---|
| updatedindex.php | index.php | Blog |
| updatedblog.php | blog.php | blog/controllers |
| updated-entries-html.php | entries-html.php | blog/views |
| entry-html.php | entry-html.php | blog/views |

Let us look at the code for the comments form.

***Listing 8-9.*** comments-html.php

```php
<?php
//complete code for views/comment-form-html.php
$idIsFound = isset($entryId);
if( $idIsFound === false ) {
    trigger_error('views/comments-html.php needs an $entryId');
}
```

```php
$info .= "
<form action='newindex.php?page=blog&id=$entryId' method='post'
id='comment-form'>
    <input type='hidden' name='entry-id' value='$entryId' />
     <label>Your name</label>
     <input type='text' name='user-name' maxlength='30'
         pattern='[a-zA-Z]{1,30}'
        title='Name can contain only alphabetic letters, no special
        characters. Name is required.'
           required />
    <label>Your Comment</label>
        <textarea name='new-comment'></textarea>
    <input type='submit' value='post!' />
</form>";
?>

$idIsFound = isset($entryId);
if( $idIsFound === false ) {
    trigger_error('views/comments-html.php needs an $entryId');
}
```

If an entry id is not passed, then no attempt will be made to accept comments. The user should only be on this form if they have selected a blog entry (which has an entry id) and are attempting to add a comment related to the blog. If the entry id is missing, an error is raised.

```php
<form action='newindex.php?page=blog&id=$entryId' method='post'
id='comment-form'>
     <input type='hidden' name='entry-id' value='$entryId' />
```

When the form is submitted, page is set to blog, and the id is set to the value in $entryid. $entryid is also stored in a hidden property, entry-id. This logic is similar to the logic shown in the previous chapter.

```php
<input type='text' name='user-name' maxlength='30'
        pattern='[a-zA-Z]{1,30}'
       title='Name can contain only alphabetic letters, no special
       characters. Name is required.'
          required />
```

282

The name text box also restricts entries to alphabetic characters, required, with a maximum of 30 characters. We will also filter out any invalid data in our PHP code which will reside on the server.

To display the comment form, we need a comment controller. Its job at this early stage is to simply load the view and return the HTML to have the comment form displayed.

***Listing 8-10.***  comments.php

```php
<?php
//complete code for controllers/comments.php
include_once "views/comment-form-html.php";
?>
```

So far, the code is short, to the point, and very much like previous code examples. The comment controller loads the comment view. But who should load the comment controller and actually show the comment form?

# A Combined View

A comment form should only be displayed when a complete entry is displayed (more details have been selected). So, the page that shows an entry should also show a comment form: it is a complex view composed of other views. Figure 8-5 shows a simple solution to combine views.

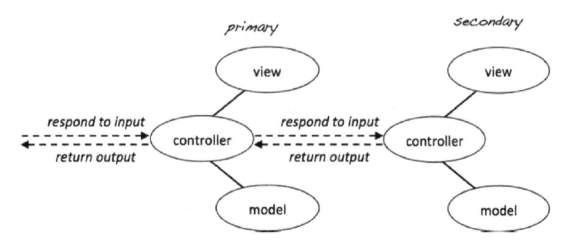

***Figure 8-5.***  *Constructing complex views*

Some of our previous front controllers also provided multiple views. The code in anotheradmin.php loads a model and a view for making HTML5 pages. Depending on conditions, anotheradmin.php loads either the editor controller or the list-entries controller, each of which will return some content to be embedded on the generated page. Thus, anotheradmin.php is the *primary controller*, and the subsequently loaded controller is a *secondary controller*.

In this example, the primary controller is the blog controller. The comment form is only meaningful in the context of a blog entry. The blog controller loads blog entries. Then the blog controller will load the comment controller (secondary controller).

***Listing 8-11.*** newblog.php

```php
<?php
//complete code for controllers/newblog.php
include_once "models/Newest_Blog_Entry_Table.class.php";
$entryTable = new Newest_Blog_Entry_Table( $db );
$isEntryClicked = isset( $_GET['id'] );
if ($isEntryClicked ) {
    $entryId = $_GET['id'];
    //new code begins here
    $entryData = $entryTable->getEntry( $entryId );
    include_once "views/entry-html.php";
    include_once "controllers/comments.php";
} else {
    $entries = $entryTable->getAllEntries();
    include_once "views/new-entries-html.php";
}
?>
```

```
include_once "controllers/comments.php";
```

The only change from our previous blog controller is the preceding one code line to include the comments.php secondary controller.

**Exercise**: The form is completely unstyled. It is not a pretty sight. Go ahead and style the comment form however you prefer. A little CSS has been included in the newblog. css file under the css folder. However, use your own creativity. Make sure to add the required code to use as CSS style sheet as shown in previous chapters.

Of course, we cannot yet display or store our comments. Let us create the database table which will hold this information provided by the user.

# Creating a Comment Table in the Database

Let us create a table named *comment* in the `simple_blog` database. We will use this to store all information about comments. We will include several different kinds of information in this table as follows:

- *comment_id*: A unique identifier for the comment. This is the table's primary key. We will use the `AUTO_INCREMENT` property, so that new comments are automatically assigned a unique id number.

- *entry_id*: The identifier of the blog entry to which the comment corresponds. This column is an `INT` (integer) value. The `entry_id` refers to a primary key in another table. The `entry_id` is a foreign key in the comments table.

- *author*: The name of the comment author. This column accepts a maximum of 30 characters and is of the `VARCHAR` (string) type.

- *txt*: The actual comment text. The column's data type is `TEXT`.

- *date*: The date the comment was posted is stored as a `TIME_STAMP`. We can set a default value for this column: the `CURRENT_TIMESTAMP`, which will provide a `TIME_STAMP` for the exact date and time when a user adds a new comment to the table.

To create this table, we will navigate to `http://localhost/phpmyadmin` in a browser, select the `simple_blog` database, and open the SQL tab. Then we will execute the following command to create the comment table:

```
CREATE TABLE comment (
    comment_id INT NOT NULL AUTO_INCREMENT,
    entry_id INT NOT NULL,
    author VARCHAR( 75 ),
    txt TEXT,
    date TIMESTAMP DEFAULT CURRENT_TIMESTAMP,
    PRIMARY KEY (comment_id),
    FOREIGN KEY (entry_id) REFERENCES blog_entry (entry_id)
)
```

---

**Note**    You can alternatively use the GUI screens within *phpmyadmin* to create the comment table and its contents as previously discussed in other chapters.

---

A comment is a user's response to one particular blog entry. So, every new comment must be uniquely associated with one blog entry. When a particular blog entry is displayed, only comments related to that blog entry will be displayed.

It follows that the database must be designed in such a way as to represent a relationship between blog entries and comments. The database design must support that any one comment can be related to only one blog entry. A logical solution is to create the comment table with a column for entry_id, as shown in Table 8-1. That way, one comment will know the related entry_id of the specific entry.

***Table 8-1.***  *Comment Rows Related to Specific Entries*

| comment_id | entry_id | Author | txt | date |
|---|---|---|---|---|
| 1 | 1 | Thomas | [...] | 2022-09-02 12:54:15 |
| 2 | 8 | Thomas | [...] | 2022-09-02 13:25:41 |
| 3 | 1 | Brennan | [...] | 2022-09-07 01:43:19 |

Let us take a look at the populated comment table shown in Table 8-1. See how anyone's comment will be explicitly related to a particular entry's entry_id? This way, every comment knows the associated blog entry. Notice also that one blog entry may have many associated comments. The entry with entry_id = 1 has two comments in the preceding example. This kind of relationship is known as a *one-to-many relationship* in relational database terminology.

# Using a Foreign Key

It is very common to use a *foreign key* when establishing relationships between two tables. You can see how a foreign key is declared in the previous SQL statement. But what is it really for?

A foreign key is also a *reference* to a primary *key* column in a *foreign* table. In the preceding example, the comment table's entry_id is a reference to the blog_entry table's entry_id column.

The foreign key helps maintain data integrity, because the comment table will only accept comments with an entry_id that can be found in the blog_entry table. In other words, the comment table will only accept comments related to blog entries that exist.

## Building a Comment_Table Class

Let us now create the model for our comments which will be used to access the new comment table in the database. We are continuing to use the table data gateway design which provides a single point of access from PHP code to one database table.

The Blog_Entry_Table class contains several items which we will also use in our comment table. This includes the constructor, which accepts the PDO object, and the executeSQL() method, which will execute our new SQL statements. We could simply copy the code we are reusing into the new class. However, this is not code efficiency. This situation provides us another opportunity to learn something new, using *inheritance* to share common code among different classes.

## Inheritance

When using *inheritance*, we can create a single class definition to keep the code to be shared among several classes. We will create separate *subclasses* which will contain the unique code for individual classes.

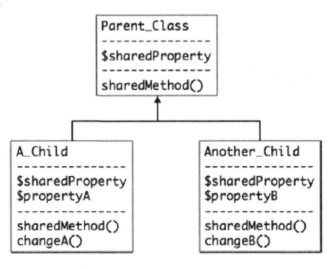

***Figure 8-6.*** *Subclasses inherit properties and methods from a parent class*

Figure 8-6 illustrates how some code to be shared among a number of classes can be declared in a *parent* class. All *children* of the parent will be *born* with these properties. In Figure 8-6, we can see that both A_Child and Another_Child have a $sharedProperty and a sharedMethod(). These were inherited from the parent class. In Figure 8-6, we can also see that A_Child and Another_Child each have special properties and methods. These are declared in the child class definition. For example, only A_Child has a changeA() method.

We will use this idea to share the contents of $db and the function executeSQL() between the Blog_Entry_Table and the Comment_Table classes. The Comment_Table and Blog_Entry_Table classes will both be born with a $db property and an executeSQL() method *inherited* from the Table class (parent class).

## Is-a Relationships

In object-oriented terminology, the relationship between a parent class and child class is referred to as an *is-a* relationship. A Comment_Table *is a* Table. The Table is a general abstraction that represents a database table. The Comment_Table is a representation of a specific database table.

The concept of is-a relationships between objects is something you use in your everyday thinking. Coffee is a beverage. Orange juice also is a beverage. Orange juice and coffee share some characteristics, though they are clearly different. A beverage is the abstract idea of a consumable liquid. Coffee and orange juice are specific kinds of consumable liquids. Object-oriented programming has borrowed a widely used human mode of reasoning and used it to bring hierarchical order to computer programs.

## Using Inheritance in Our Code

The code we will share among subclasses must have *public* or *protected* access modifiers. Any property or method with a private access modifier is not shared through inheritance. Let us create a general Table class which will contain those items shared by the subclasses.

*Listing 8-12.* Table.class.php

```php
<?php
//complete code listing for models/Table.class.php
class Table {
```

```
    protected $db;
    //notice there are two underscore characters in __construct
    public function __construct ( $db ) {
        $this->db = $db;
    }
    protected function executeSQL ( $sql, $data = NULL) {
    //create a PDOStatement object
    $statement = $this->db->prepare( $sql );
    try{
        //use the dynamic data and run the query
        $statement->execute( $data );
    } catch (Exception $e) {
        $exceptionMessage = "<p>You tried to run this sql: $sql <p>
                <p>Exception: $e</p>";
        .trigger_error($exceptionMessage);
    }
    //return the PDOStatement object
    return $statement;
}
}
?>
```

This code should look very familiar as it is copied from the Blog Entry class with just a few minor modifications.

```
protected $db;
...
protected function executeSQL ( $sql, $data = NULL) {
```

The *protected* access modifier is quite similar to the private access modifier we have already used. Protected methods and properties cannot be accessed from outside of a class. However, they can be accessed from inside the class itself. If we used private for these statements, they would not be accessible to the subclasses that need to use them.

To make this code available to a subclass such as Comment_Table, we will have to include the Table class script in our code and indicate it is used with the keyword extends.

***Listing 8-13.*** Table.class.php

```php
<?php
//complete code for models/Comment_Table.class.php
include_once "models/Table.class.php";

class Comment_Table extends Table{

  public function saveComment ( $entryId, $author, $txt ) {
        $sql = "INSERT INTO comment ( entry_id, author, txt)
                VALUES (?, ?, ?)";
        $data = array( $entryId, $author, $txt );
        $statement = $this->executeSQL($sql, $data);
        return $statement;

  }
  public function getAllById ( $id ) {
  $sql = "SELECT author, txt, date FROM comment
          WHERE entry_id = ?
          ORDER BY comment_id DESC";
  $data = array($id);
  $statement = $this->executeSQL($sql, $data);
  return $statement;
}
}
?>
```

Now the Comment_Table class contains only code that is specific to accessing and updating the comment table in the database. The saveComment() function uses familiar code to insert comments into the table. The getAllById() function uses familiar code to retrieve all comments related to a particular entry_id. Notice that both functions use the executeSQL() function contained in the Table class to execute each SQL command. This function was inherited from the Table class and, thus, is available for use by both functions. The getAllById() function also sorts the results in descending order (DESC), to display the most recent comments displayed at the top of the results.

**Note**    It is possible to code long inheritance chains. You could make a Dog class, which *is a* child of Wolf, which *is a* child of Canine, which *is a* child of Quadruped, which *is a* child of Mammal. But experience shows that shallow inheritance relationships are preferable. Long inheritance chains lead to dependency issues, because the Dog would depend on the presence of the Wolf, which, in turn, depends on Canine, which depends on the Quadruped. Keep inheritance chains short.

Take a moment to read the select SQL statement used in the preceding code. It will `SELECT` author, txt, and date columns for all comments associated with a particular `entry_id`. Remember that the `entry_id` was declared as a *foreign key*. It is a reference to the primary key of the `blog_entry` table. Through the `entry_id`, we can unambiguously identify one particular `blog_entry`: we know which comment is related to which blog entry.

In the insert SQL statement, the `comment_id` column is declared as `auto_incrementing`, which means the very first comment inserted will automatically get a `comment_id` value of 1. The next comment will get a `comment_id` value of 2, and so forth. So, the newest comments will have the highest `comment_id` value. Thus, descending order will list new comments first, older comments later.

Now that the model is created, it is time to create a view, to see if everything is working correctly.

## Creating a View for Listing Comments

The view we are creating will use similar logic to other views we have created previously.

*Listing 8-14.* comments-html.php

```php
<?php
$commentsFound = isset( $allComments );
if($commentsFound === false){
    trigger_error('views/comments-html.php needs $allComments' );
}
$allCommentsHTML = "<ul id='comments'>";
//iterate through all rows returned from database
```

```php
while ($commentData = $allComments->fetchObject() ) {
 //notice incremental concatenation operator
 //it adds <li> elements to the <ul>
     $allCommentsHTML .= "<li>
     $commentData->author wrote:
     <p>$commentData->txt</p>
     </li>";
   }
$allCommentsHTML .= "</ul>";
$info .= $allCommentsHTML;
?>

while ($commentData = $allComments->fetchObject() ) {
    //notice incremental concatenation operator .=
    //it adds <li> elements to the <ul>
    $allCommentsHTML .= "<li>
        $commentData->author wrote:
        <p>$commentData->txt</p>
    </li>";
}
```

The while loop will loop through the standard object containing the comments retrieved from the database table. As long as there is a comment, the contents of the txt property (the actual comment) are displayed from $commentData which contains the current record pulled from the standard object. The loop will continue until there are no more comments related to the particular blog entry.

## Hooking Up View and Model to Display Comments

The final step to displaying comments is to load the view that will display all comments retrieved from the database.

*Listing 8-15.*  newcomments.php

```php
<?php
//complete code for controllers/comments.php
include_once "models/Comment_Table.class.php";
```

```php
$commentTable = new Comment_Table($db);
include_once "views/comment-form-html.php";

$allComments = $commentTable->getAllById( $entryId );
include_once "views/comments-html.php";
?>
```

The preceding code will display a blog entry, then the comment form, and, finally, a list of all comments associated with that blog entry. We could manually enter a comment into the database table. However, let us go ahead and create the ability to do so with a form – especially since we already created our insert function.

# Inserting a Comment Through the Comment Form

Using PHP to retrieve form input is a very common task for web developers. It is something you should be starting to understand at this point of the book.

***Listing 8-16.*** comment-form-html.php

```php
<?php
//complete code for views/comment-form-html.php

$idIsFound = isset($entryId);

if( $idIsFound === false ) {
    trigger_error('views/comments-html.php needs an $entryId');
}
$info .= "
<form action='newindex.php?page=blog&id=$entryId' method='post'
id='comment-form'>
    <input type='hidden' name='entry-id' value='$entryId' />
     <label>Your name</label>
     <input type='text' name='user-name' maxlength='30'
        pattern='[a-zA-Z]{1,30}'
       title='Name can contain only alphabetic letters, no special
       characters. Name is required.'
          required />
```

```
    <label>Your Comment</label>
        <textarea name='new-comment'></textarea>
    <input type='submit' value='post!' />
</form>";
?>
```

```
<form action='newindex.php?page=blog&id=$entryId' method='post'
id='comment-form'>
```

The form method is post. The page attribute is set to blog, and the id attribute holds the value in $entryId.

There is also an <input> field named user-name, a hidden <input> named entry-id, and a <textarea> named new-comment. Knowing this, we can write a little PHP in the comment controller to insert new comments from users.

***Listing 8-17.*** updatedcomments.php

```php
<?php
//complete code for controllers/updatedcomments.php
include_once "models/Comment_Table.class.php";
$commentTable = new Comment_Table($db);
//new code here
$newCommentSubmitted = isset( $_POST['new-comment'] );
if ( $newCommentSubmitted ) {
    $whichEntry = $_POST['entry-id'];
    $user = clean_input($_POST['user-name']);
    $comment = clean_input($_POST['new-comment']);
    $commentTable->saveComment( $whichEntry, $user, $comment );
}
//end of new code
include_once "views/updated-comment-form-html.php";

$allComments = $commentTable->getAllById( $entryId );
include_once "views/comments-html.php";
function clean_input($value) {
  $value = trim($value);
  $value = stripslashes($value);
```

```php
    $value = strip_tags($value);
    return $value;
}
?>

$newCommentSubmitted = isset( $_POST['new-comment'] );
if ( $newCommentSubmitted ) {
    $whichEntry = $_POST['entry-id'];
    $user = clean_input($_POST['user-name']);
    $comment = clean_input($_POST['new-comment']);
    $commentTable->saveComment( $whichEntry, $user, $comment );
}
```

The new loop added to the code will now pull the comment left by the user, remove any invalid code, and pass the information to the saveComment() function. The function will then place the comment into the comment database table.

---

**Note**    The following files have been updated to use the most current versions of the comment's logic: updatedblog.php, updatedindex.php, updated-comment-form-html.php, updated-entries-html.php.

---

Let us take a moment to test our logic. Let us open our browser and execute updatedindex.php, then point our browser to any blog entry and submit a new comment through the form. We should expect to see the submitted comment listed alongside any other comments that exist for that blog entry. The commenting system works!

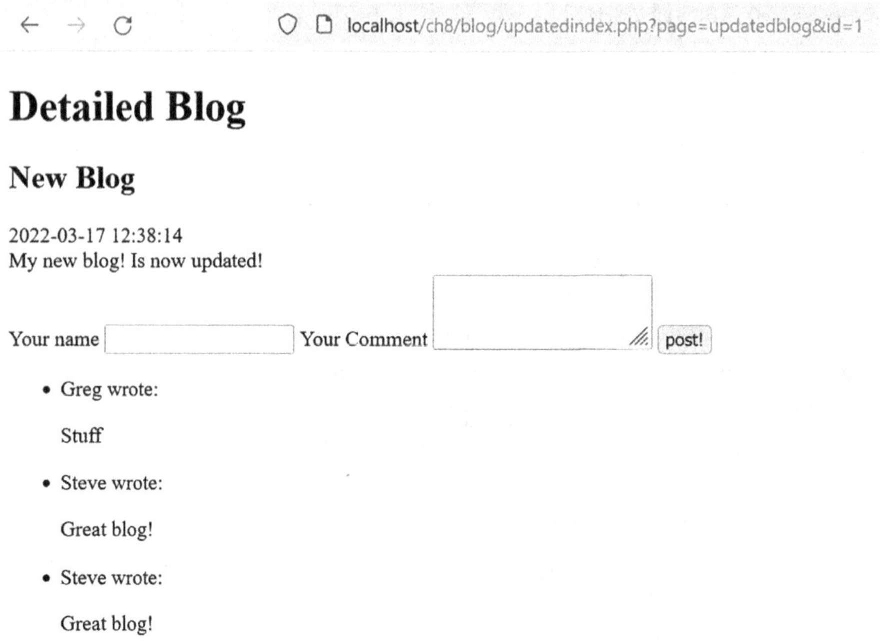
localhost/ch8/blog/updatedindex.php?page=updatedblog&id=1
Detailed Blog
New Blog
2022-03-17 12:38:14
My new blog! Is now updated!
Your name
Your Comment
post!
Greg wrote:
Stuff
Steve wrote:
Great blog!
Steve wrote:
Great blog!

***Figure 8-7.*** *Output from selecting more details in updatedindex.php*

**Exercise**: Change the `Blog_Entry_Table` class, so that it inherits from `Table`, to practice inheritance. It will be very similar to what we did with the `Comment_Table` class.

# Searching for Entries

We have come a long way with our blogging system. Somebody visiting the blog might want to look for something specific written at one time, and they might not remember which entry contained the information. We can provide them an option to search through entries.

We will show a search form, so that visitors can enter a search text. We will accept any entered search text to perform a search in our database and return any entries that match the entered search information.

We will need a *view* to show the search form and another *view* to show the search results. We will need a *model* to perform the database search and return a result. We will need a *controller* to respond to user interactions. If the form was submitted, the controller should show search results; if not, it will show the search form.

# The Search View

It is always a good idea to begin with a small step. We will start by creating an HTML form for the search view. We will keep it simple. It will be nothing fancy. Create a new file in views/search-form-html.php.

***Listing 8-18.*** search-form-html.php

```php
<?php
//complete code for views/search-form-html.php
$info .= "<aside id='search-bar'>
    <form method='post' action='index.php?page=search'>
        <input type='search' name='search-term' />
        <input type='submit' value='search'>
    </form>
</aside>";
?>
```

The view will display an HTML search form. A *search* input type is simply a special single-line text field. Search fields will remember a user's previous search terms and present the user with a drop-down list suggesting previous search terms. Older browsers may not support the search type. But any browser that does not support it will default to a basic <input type='text'>, so the search form will still work, even if a browser does not support the search type.

To display the search form, we should consider where we want it to be displayed. It would be nice to display the search form on every page view. To show the search form regardless of what else is displayed, we could load it from the front controller, from index.php. We will add one line of code near the end of index.php.

***Listing 8-19.*** searchindex.php

```php
<?php
//complete code for blog/index.php
$info = "";
include_once "models/Page_Data.class.php";
$pageData = new Page_Data();
$pageData->setTitle("PHP/MySQL blog demo");
include_once "models/database.php";
```

```
include_once "controllers/searchblog.php";
//new code: include the search view before the blog controller
include_once "views/search-form-html.php";
//end of new code
$pageData->setContent($info);
include_once "views/page.php";
echo $page;
?>
```

Let us take another break and test our logic. We can view our progress by loading `http://localhost/blog/searchindex.php` in a browser.

***Figure 8-8.*** *Output from searchindex.php*

We can see the search area displayed at the bottom of the listing. If we select one of the "Read more" links, we will also see the search area at the bottom of the information provided.

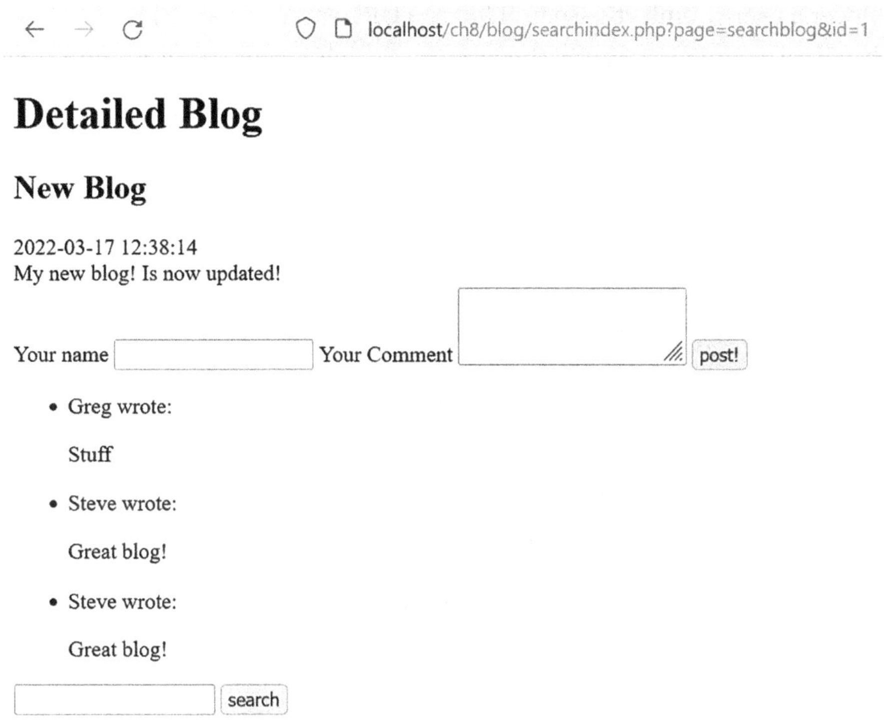

**Figure 8-9.** *Output from selecting "Read more" in searchindex.php*

We could alternatively place the search area at the top of the display and/or just display it in the initial display of searchindex.php. Of course, at the moment, the actual search does not work. But soon it will!

**Exercise**: Adjust the location of the search area to the top of the display. How can you only display it on the original display of searchindex.php?

# Responding to a User Search

We will load the search controller from the index, when a search has been performed. If no search has been performed, the index should load the blog controller. Notice the action attribute of the search form:

```
//partial code from views/search-form-html.php, don't change anything
<form method='post' action='index.php?page=search'>
```

Whenever a user submits the search form, a URL variable named page with a value of search will be encoded as part of the request. So, when a page has a value of search, the web application should show search results. This will be quite easy to achieve in the index program.

*Listing 8-20.*  searchingindex.php

```php
<?php
//complete code for blog/index.php
$info = "";
include_once "models/Page_Data.class.php";
$pageData = new Page_Data();
$pageData->setTitle("PHP/MySQL blog demo");
include_once "models/database.php";

$pageRequested =  isset( $_GET['page'] );
//default controller is searchingblog
$controller = "searchingblog";
if ( $pageRequested ) {
    //if user submitted the search form
    if ( $_GET['page'] === "search" ) {
        //load the search by overwriting default controller
        $controller = "search";
    }
}
include_once "controllers/$controller.php";
include_once "views/searching-form-html.php";
$pageData->setContent($info);
include_once "views/page.php";
echo $page;
?>

//default controller is searchingblog
$controller = "searchingblog";
if ( $pageRequested ) {
    //if user submitted the search form
```

```
if ( $_GET['page'] === "search" ) {
    //load the search by overwriting default controller
    $controller = "search";
}
}
```

By default, the searchingblog.php controller will be displayed. However, if the user has entered a value in the search box and clicked the search button, the search.php controller will be displayed.

## The Search Model

We have a search form view, and we have a preliminary search controller. It is time to work on a search model, so that we can perform an actual search. To perform a search, we will have to query our blog_entry database table. We already have a Blog_Entry_Table class to provide a single point of access to that table. The sensible thing to do would be to add another method to the Blog_Entry_Table.

*Listing 8-21.* Partial Listing Searched_Blog_Entry_Table.class.php

```
//Declare new method in Blog_Entry_Table class
public function searchEntry ( $searchTerm ) {
    $sql = "SELECT entry_id, title FROM blog_entry
            WHERE title LIKE ?
            OR entry_text LIKE ?";
    $data = array( "%$searchTerm%", "%$searchTerm%" );
    $statement = $this->executeSQL($sql, $data);
    return $statement;
}
```

Perhaps the $data array warrants a few words of explanation. Isn't it strange to create an array with two separate items *when the items are identical*? Well, the number of unnamed placeholders in your SQL must exactly match the number of items in the array executed. Because there are two placeholders in the SQL, we need an array with two values to use in the search. In the preceding example, the code will search for the same search term in two different table columns (title and entry_text).

## Searching with a LIKE Condition

The preceding SQL statement demonstrates an SQL keyword we have not used in the previous examples in this book: LIKE.

```
$sql = "SELECT entry_id, title FROM blog_entry
        WHERE title LIKE ?
        OR entry_text LIKE ?";
  $data = array( "%$searchTerm%", "%$searchTerm%" );
```

The % character represents a wildcard character. A wildcard character represents anything. The query would return a result set of all rows where the title or the entry_text contains the search value, wherever it exists within these columns. For example, if the search value is "test," a row with a title of "test if it works" could be returned. A row with an entry_text value of "This is a test" could also be returned. Since the wildcard character is both in the front and back of the term to be searched, both are possible results.

# A Search Result View

To show a search result in a way a user might appreciate, we will need a search view. We will wrap some HTML around the returned data.

***Listing 8-22.*** searched-results-html.php

```php
<?php
//complete code for views/searched-results-html.php
$searchDataFound = isset( $searchData );
if( $searchDataFound === false ){
    trigger_error('views/searched-results-html.php needs $searchData');
}

$searchedHTML = "<section id='search'> <h1>
    You searched for <em>$searchTerm</em></h1><ul>";

while ( $searchRow = $searchData->fetchObject() ){
    $href = "seaarchedindex.php?page=searchedblog&id=$searchRow->entry_id";
    $searchedHTML .= "<li><a href='$href'>$searchRow->title</li>";
}
```

```
$searchedHTML .= "</ul></section>";
$info .= $searchedHTML;
?>
```

The preceding code assumes the existence of a $searchData variable. If it is not found, an error will be triggered. If the $searchData variable is found, the code will iterate through the result set with a while statement. The while loop will create an <li> element for each blog_entry that matches the search.

# Loading a Search Result View from the Controller

To display the search results in a browser, we must load the search result view. Hooking up a view with a model is a task for a controller.

***Listing 8-23.*** searched.php

```php
<?php
//complete code for controllers/searched.php
include_once "models/Searched_Blog_Entry_Table.class.php";
$blogTable = new Searched_Blog_Entry_Table( $db );

$searchOutput = "";
if ( isset($_POST['search-term']) ){
    $searchTerm = $_POST['search-term'];
    $searchData = $blogTable->searchEntry( $searchTerm ) ;
    include_once "views/searched-results-html.php";
}
?>
```

That is it. The front controller will only show either the blog or the search page. The search page will show search results – even if there were no matches.

> **Note**    The following files have been updated to reference the most current
> versions of the search method: Searchedindex.php, searchedblog.php,
> searched.php, searchedcomments.php, Searched_Blog_Entry_
> Table.class.php, searched-comments-form-html.php, searched-
> comments-html.php, searched-entries-html.php, searched-form-
> html.php, searched-results-html.php.

***Figure 8-10.*** *Results from searching for "Blog" within searchedindex.php*

The search successfully finds all occurrences of the search string as shown when
searching for "Blog" in Figure 8-10.

## Exercise: Improving Search

Did you notice a minor problem with the search? Try to search for a term you absolutely
know has no match in the database. If we look at the generated HTML source code, we
find the following:

```
<section id='search'>
    <h1>You searched for <em></em></h1>
    <ul></ul>
</section>
```

Make changes to the code to detect when no results are returned. Hint: The
PDOStatement will contain FALSE. Display a message such as "No entries match your
search."

# Summary

We have covered a lot of ground in this chapter, both in terms of learning and in improving the blog. The commenting system is a game changer, as far as interactive communication is concerned. All of a sudden, the site is not just publishing blogs for the world to see. With a commenting system, we are inviting two-way communication between the author and the readers.

We still want to refine our blog system with additional security and the ability to post an image. We will complete our discussion of this system in the next chapter.

# Projects

1. Using the design practices from this and previous chapters, update the student registration system from Chapter 7. Provide a search program which will allow the user to search for a student record by name or major. The program should display all students with similar names or all students with the same major.

2. Update the information request site from Chapter 7 to allow the administrator to search for information contained in the detailed description field. The results should display all information (user's name, email, and complete description) for all records found which contain the data in the search string.

# CHAPTER 9

# Basic Blog: Images and Authentication

## Objectives

After completing this chapter, you will be able to

- Delete entries from related tables in a database

- Create a dynamic select drop-down box

- Hash passwords using `password_hash()`

- Determine the size of a string using `strlen()`

- Validate a string using `preg_match()`, regular expressions, and `filter_var()`

- Authenticate user access using `password_hash` and `password_verify()`

- Secure a web application using sessions

- Log errors and exceptions

The basic blog is almost complete! Sure, there's room for improvement, but it is fully functional. The administration module can be used to create blog entries, but there are some serious shortcomings:

- It cannot delete blog entries if there are comments in the database related to the entry.

- It cannot add images to blog entries.

© Jason Lengstorf, Thomas Blom Hansen, Steve Prettyman 2022
J. Lengstorf et al., *PHP 8 for Absolute Beginners*, https://doi.org/10.1007/978-1-4842-8205-2_9

Let's work on fixing these now.

Let us start our development process to fix these flaws by copying the files from the publisher's website. You can choose to copy files from the ch8 folder and modify them, as discussed in the next paragraph. However, due to the number of changes, this is not recommended. If you like living dangerously, follow the directions in the following.

Start by creating a ch9 folder. Under this folder, create a blog folder. Under the blog folder, create the controllers, CSS, models, and views folders. Under the controllers folder, create an admin folder. Under the views folder, create an admin folder. Then copy the programs from the ch8 folder as shown in the following table.

| Original Name | New Name | Location |
|---|---|---|
| anotheradmin.php | admin.php | Blog |
| anothereditor.php | editor.php | controllers/admin |
| updatedentries.php | entries.php | controllers/admin |
| blog.css | blog.css | Css |
| Comment_Table.class.php | Comment_Table.class.php | Models |
| Searched_Blog_Entry_Table.class.php | Blog_Entry_Table.class.ph | p models |
| database.php | database.php | Models |
| Page_Data.class.php | Page_Data.class.php | models |
| Table.class.php | Table.class.php | models |
| another-admin-navigation.php | admin-navigation.php | views/admin |
| another-editor-html.php | editor-html.php | views/admin |
| updated-entries-html.php | entries-html.php | views/admin |
| page.php | page.php | views |

**Note**    Each file copied will need to be updated to use any of the renamed programs.

# Deleting Entries in Related Tables

The commenting system is a great improvement. Unfortunately, the comments have also introduced unwanted system behavior in the administration module. It has become impossible to delete an entry with comments. We can test this by attempting to delete a blog that has comments. The system will ignore the request. This is an *integrity violation*.

You may even see the following error displayed, indicating the problem.

```
Exception: exception 'PDOException' with message 'SQLSTATE[23000]:
Integrity constraint violation: 1451 Cannot delete or update a parent row:
a foreign key constraint fails
```

# Understanding Foreign Key Constraints

It is always a bit annoying to come across errors, but this one is a friendly error. It is really preventing us from undermining the integrity of the database. Table 9-1 takes a look inside the blog_entry table.

***Table 9-1.*** *One Row from the blog_entry Table*

| entry_id | Title | entry_text | Created |
|----------|-------|------------|---------|
| 17 | delete me | Testing | 2022-07-23 10:26:18 |

A comment might be related to that particular blog entry. Table 9-2 shows the corresponding row from the comment table.

***Table 9-2.*** *One Row from the Comment Table*

| comment_id | entry_id | author | Txt | Date |
|------------|----------|--------|-----|------|
| 4 | 17 | Thomas | test comment | 2022-07-23 10:26:40 |

Imagine that the blog_entry with entry_id = 17 is deleted. There would be a comment related to a blog entry that no longer exists. Comments are only meaningful in the right context. The comment with comment_id = 4 would have lost its context;

it would have lost its integrity. Imagine what would happen if we inserted a new blog entry with entry_id = 17. That blog entry would be born with a completely irrelevant comment!

The purpose of a foreign key is to maintain data integrity. So, when we try to delete a blog_entry that has a comment, MySQL/MariaDB will stop us, because the delete action would leave a renegade comment floating around in the database, without a meaningful context. Remember, only blog entries without comments can be deleted without losing data integrity.

## Deleting Comments Before Blog Entry

When deleting a blog entry, we will first delete any comments related to the entry. We already have a class that provides a single point of access to the comment table. We can add a new method to delete all comments related to a particular entry_id.

***Listing 9-1.*** Partial Listing from Comments_Table.class.php

```
//partial code for models/Comment_Table.class.php

public function deleteByEntryId( $id ) {
    $sql = "DELETE FROM comment WHERE entry_id = ?";
    $data = array( $id );
    $statement = $this->executeSQL( $sql, $data );
}
```

This method will be called before a blog entry is deleted. Blog entries are deleted from the Blog_Entry_Table class.

***Listing 9-2.*** Partial Listing from Blog_Entry_Table.class.php

```
//partial code for models/Blog_Entry_Table.class.php

//edit existing method
public function deleteEntry ( $id ) {
    //new code: delete any comments before deleting entry
    $this->deleteCommentsByID( $id );
    $sql = "DELETE FROM blog_entry WHERE entry_id = ?";
```

```php
    $data = array( $id );
    $statement = $this->executeSQL( $sql, $data );
}

//new code: declare a new private method inside Blog_Entry_Table.class.php
private function deleteCommentsByID( $id ) {
    include_once "models/Comment_Table.class.php";
    //create a Comment_Table object
    $comments = new Comment_Table( $this->db );
    //delete any comments before deleting entry
    $comments->deleteByEntryId( $id );
}
```

Now, if there are any comments related to the blog_entry, those comments will be deleted first, to avoid violating foreign key constraints!

# Creating an Image Manager

The admin module has two different page views at this point: the list of entries and the entry editor. We will now add a third page for uploading and deleting the images that we will be using in our blog entries. We can start by creating the menu item for the image manager.

***Listing 9-3.*** admin-navigation.php

```php
<?php
//complete code for views/admin/admin-navigation.php
$nav = "
<nav id='admin-navigation'>
    <a href='admin.php?page=entries'>All entries</a>
    <a href='admin.php?page=editor'>Editor</a>
    <a href='admin.php?page=images'>Image manager</a>
</nav>";
?>
```

Clicking the Image manager link will encode a URL variable named page and set its value to images. The front controller admin.php will require a new controller script called images.php. As always, we will start with a tiny step to catch errors while they are still easy to correct.

***Listing 9-4.*** images.php

```php
<?php
//complete code for controllers/admin/images.php
$info = "<h1>Image manager coming soon!</h1>";
?>
```

If we load http://localhost/ch9/blog/admin.php?page=images in our browser, we should see a new menu and the message display.

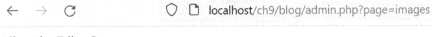

All entries Editor Image manager

# Image manager coming soon!

***Figure 9-1.*** *Output from http://localhost/ch9/blog/admin.php?page=images*

## Showing a Form for Uploading Images

Now that we have the image manager controller script, we can create an image manager view. Let us start with a basic HTML form, which we can eventually use to upload images.

***Listing 9-5.*** images-html.php

```php
<?php
//complete code for views/admin/images-html.php
if ( isset( $uploadMessage ) === false ){
    $uploadMessage = "Upload a new image";
}
```

```
$info = "<h1>Image Upload</h1>
<form method='post' action='admin.php?page=images'
      enctype='multipart/form-data'>
    <p>$uploadMessage</p>
    <input type='file' name='image-data' accept='image/jpeg' />
    <input type='submit' name='new-image' value='upload' />
</form>
";
?>
```

We can see that the views code is prepared with a placeholder for displaying upload messages to users. The default upload message is *Upload a new image*. Soon, the system will let our users know if an upload was successful or not.

Remember, to allow users to upload files such as images, we need an HTML form. We must use the HTTP method POST, and the form's encoding type must explicitly be declared, to allow for file upload. We must set the enctype of the form to multipart/ form-data, which will accept files *and* ordinary URL encoded form data.

As mentioned before, an <input> element with type=file will retrieve the file window from the operating system; this allows users to browse their local computers for a file to upload. The accept attribute has been set to allow only JPEG images.

Keep in mind that client-side validation can improve usability but not security. The file type can be changed to "All Files" within the file window. We should also expect that a malicious user will work around any client-side validation. To protect our system from attacks, we will also implement server-side validation. We will add this soon. But first, let us update the image manager controller, so the upload form is displayed.

***Listing 9-6.*** newimages.com

```
<?php
//complete code for controllers/admin/newimages.php
 include_once "views/admin/images-html.php";
?>
```

We can now point our browser to http://localhost/ch9/blog/newadmin. php?page=newimages, to confirm that the form is, in fact, displayed in the browser.

---

**Note**    The following files have been updated to access the new images controller: `newadmin.php`, `new-admin-navigation.php`.

---

# A Quick Refresher on the $_FILES Superglobal Array

We learned about the $_FILES superglobal in Chapter 4, but it might be helpful to review what it does, before moving on. Whenever a file is uploaded via an HTML form, that file is stored in temporary memory, and information about the file is passed in the $_FILES superglobal array. The array contains several important aspects about the file uploaded.

```
Array (
        [image-data] => Array (
        [name] => alberte-lea.jpg
        [type] => image/jpeg
        [tmp_name] => /Applications/XAMPP/xamppfiles/temp/phpYPcBjK
        [error] => 0
        [size] => 119090
    )
  )
```

The name and type are self-explanatory. The `tmp_name` is the temporary name of the file after it has been uploaded. If the file size is too big (according to the settings in php.ini), then this will be set to `"none."` An error code of 0 or `UPLOAD_ERR_OK` indicates that the file was uploaded successfully. The file size is the number of bytes.

Where did the name `image-data` come from?

```
//one line of code from views/admin/images-html.php
<input type='file' name='image-data' accept='image/jpeg' />
```

The answer is that we provided it! The `image-data` is there because of the name attribute for the file chooser window. If we look at the code in `views/admin/images-html.php`, we see that it was set in the file input.

We are just one or two lines of code away from uploading the image. All we have to do is to save the file data on the server. The file data is already uploaded and saved temporarily under `tmp_name`, inside `image-data` array, inside $_FILES. To grab the file data, we would simply have to write something similar to the following lines:

```
//don't write this anywhere...yet
$fileData = $_FILES['image-data']['tmp_name'];
```

Instead of reinventing a solution every time we need one, we can write a reusable class for uploading. That way, we can reuse the upload code in many projects without changing it.

Come to think of it, we already wrote an Uploader class back in Chapter 4. Let us copy the Uploader class from ch4/classes/ImagesUploader.class.php and save it into ch9/blog/models/Uploader.class.php. Alternatively, we can also download the class from the publisher's website. Let us also copy the checkImageFile.php program (used in the uploader) from ch4/views/CheckImageFile.php to ch9/blog/views/ CheckImageFile.php. We can also copy this file from the publisher's website.

# Uploading an Image

To upload an image using the Uploader class, we begin by creating a new folder for images (imgs) directly under the ch9/blog folder location.

When the image manager upload form is submitted, the code will attempt to upload the indicated file. Submitting a form is a user interaction, so the code belongs in a controller. We will copy the code from ch4/views/imagesUpload.php with only a very small modification. It is always logical to reuse code that has been well tested and used successfully.

*Listing 9-7.* newestimages.php

```php
<?php
//complete source code for controllers/admin/newestimages.php
function upload(){
    include_once "models/Uploader.class.php";
    //image-data is the name attribute used in <input type='file' />
    $uploader = new ImagesUploader( "image-data" );
    $uploader->saveIn("imgs");
    $fileUploaded = $uploader->save();
    if ( $fileUploaded ) {
        $out = "<h1>New image uploaded</h1>";
    } else {
```

```php
        throw new Exception("Error: File not uploaded to Imgs folder");
    }
    return $out;
}
$imageSubmitted = isset( $_POST['new-image'] );
//if the upload form was submitted
if ( $imageSubmitted ) {
$info = upload();
}
else {
include_once "views/admin/newest-images-html.php";
}
?>

<?php
//complete source code for controllers/admin/newestimages.php
function upload(){
    include_once "models/Uploader.class.php";
    //image-data is the name attribute used in <input type='file' />
    $uploader = new ImagesUploader( "image-data" );
    $uploader->saveIn("imgs");
    $fileUploaded = $uploader->save();
    if ( $fileUploaded ) {
        $out = "<h1>New image uploaded</h1>";
    } else {
        $out = "File not uploaded to Imgs folder. Check file size and
        type.");
    }
    return $out;
}
```

The upload function from Chapter 4 remains unchanged, except for changing the
display messages. The method uses the Uploader class to set location for the image to
be stored. Then the save() method of the Uploader class is called to attempt to save the
image. The corresponding message is then displayed, if the upload was successful or not.

```php
if ( $imageSubmitted ) {
$info = upload();
}
else {
include_once "views/admin/newest-images-html.php";
}
```

The function is called, only if an image has been selected from the newest-images-html.php page. If an image has not been selected, then the page is displayed to allow the user to select a file.

***Listing 9-8.***  Uploader.class.php

```php
<?php
//complete code for models/Uploader.class.php
require_once "views/checkImageFile.php";
class ImagesUploader {
    private $filename;
    private $fileData;
    private $destination;
     private $keyValue;

    //declare a constructor method
    public function __construct( string $key ) {
        $this->keyValue = $key;
      $this->filename = $_FILES[$key]['name'];
      $this->fileData = $_FILES[$key]['tmp_name'];
    }

    public function saveIn( $folder ) {
        $this->destination = $folder;
    }

    public function save(){
        $variableName = $this->keyValue;
        $tmp = $_FILES[$this->keyValue]['tmp_name'];
        $folderIsWriteAble = is_writable( $this->destination );
        $notValid = checkImageFile($tmp, $variableName);
```

```
        if ( !$notValid and $folderIsWriteAble) {
            $name = "$this->destination/$this->filename";
            $success = move_uploaded_file( $this->fileData, $name );
        } else {
            $success = false;
        }
    }
    return $success;
    }
}
?>
```

The Uploader class is unchanged from Chapter 4. However, it is worth reviewing the code that is included to validate the file which the user is attempting to upload.

```
        $folderIsWriteAble = is_writable( $this->destination );
          $notValid = checkImageFile($tmp, $variableName);
          if ( !$notValid and $folderIsWriteAble) {
              $name = "$this->destination/$this->filename";
              $success = move_uploaded_file( $this->fileData, $name );
          } else {
              $success = false;
          }
      }
```

The folder is checked to assure it is writable. The checkImageFile() function from checkimagefile.php is called to verify the file. If it is valid, the file is stored in the imgs folder. $success is set to true if the move is successful. It is set to false if the move was not successful or the file was not valid.

***Listing 9-9.*** checkImageFile.php

```
<?php
function checkImageFile($tmpName, $variableName) {

$valid_File_Types =  array('image/jpeg' => 'jpg');

$max_Size  = 40 * 1024 * 1024;
//  40MB must be the same size or less than the setting in php.ini

$errorStatus = false;
```

```php
if(!isset($_FILES[$variableName]) ) {
    // error $_FILE does not exist
    $errorStatus = true;
} else {
    $info = finfo_open(FILEINFO_MIME_TYPE);
    if (!$info) {
        // error Can't open finfo using mime type
        $errorStatus = true;
    } else {
        $mime_type = finfo_file($info, $tmpName);
            if (!in_array($mime_type, array_keys($valid_File_Types))) {
                // error invalid file type
                $errorStatus = true;
        } else {
    if (filesize($_FILES[$variableName]['tmp_name']) > $max_Size) {
                    // error file size too big
                    $errorStatus = true;
        }
            finfo_close($info);
        }
}
}
return $errorStatus;
}
?>
```

The function will check to see if the file exists (`if(!isset($_FILES[$variableName])` ) and if the mime information can be accessed ( `$info = finfo_open(FILEINFO_MIME_TYPE);`). If it does exist, it will check for the valid file type (`if (!in_array($mime_type, array_keys($valid_File_Types)))` and if the file does not exceed the maximum file size (`if (filesize($_FILES[$variableName]['tmp_name']) > $max_Size)` {). If any test fails, `$errorStatus` will be set to `true`. Otherwise, it will be sent to `false`. This status is then returned to the `Uploader` class.

We can test the upload procedure by entering `http://localhost/ch9/blog/newestadmin.php` in the browser and by selecting the `Image manager` menu item – then by selecting a file to upload.

The single most common error to encounter at this point relates to folder permissions. If the destination folder is write-protected, PHP cannot save the upload file. So, if we cannot upload a file, the permissions of the img folder must be changed to read & write.

## Exercises

1. We can improve the error messages further. We can check for the error codes (see the listing provided in Chapter 4) and provide custom error messages for them. To accomplish this task, you will need to learn how to trigger these errors and display meaningful error messages to the users.

2. It would be a significant improvement if we could check for name conflicts before upload. The system should throw an exception and prompt the user to rename the image before upload? Or we could even change the upload form to allow users to rename the image through the form?

# Displaying Images

We now have an image manager that allows image upload. It should be possible for a blog administrator to see all available images and use any one of those in a blog entry. We can reuse the code from Chapter 4, with some changes, to meet most of these requirements.

The following additional files have been copied and renamed from Chapter 4 and Chapter 8 to begin our journey into displaying the uploaded images. Each file has been adjusted to use additional files with their new names. It is recommended that you use the files from the editor's website to avoid any logical errors.

| Original Name | New Name | Location From->To |
|---|---|---|
| ImagesUploader.class.php | Uploader.class.php | ch4 classes -> models |
| gallery.php | gallery.php | ch4 views -> views/ admin |
| searchedblog.php | blog.php | ch8 controller-> controllers |
| searchedcomments.php | comments.php | ch8 controller->controller |
| searched.php | searched.php | ch8 controller->controller |
| searched-comment-form-html.php | comment-form-html.php | ch8 views-> views |
| searched-comments-html.php | comments-html.php | ch8 views-> views |
| searched-entry-html.php | entry-html.php | ch8 views-> views |
| searched-form-html.php | form-html.php | ch8 views-> views |
| searched-results-html.php | results-html.php | ch8 views-> views |

Let us review the contents of the gallery.php file now located in views/admin.

***Listing 9-10.*** gallery.php

```php
<?php
//complete source code for views/gallery.php
//edit existing function
function showImages() : string{
    $out = "<h1>Images Gallery</h1>";
    $out .= "<ul id='images'
      style='
      list-style-type:none;
      width: 550px;
      border: 5px solid black;
      padding: 5px;
```

```
margin: 20px;'
><li><p>";

$totalSize = 0;
$numberOfImages = 0;
$dir_name = "imgs";
chdir($dir_name);
$images = glob("*.jpg");

foreach($images as $image) {
    if((filesize($image) < 500000) and ($totalSize < 2500000)) {
$out .= '<img src="'.$dir_name. '/' .$image.'" alt="'.$image.'"
title="'.$image.'"
 style="
height: 200px;
width: 250px;
border: 2px solid black;
padding: 5px;
margin: 5px;
"/>';
$totalSize += filesize($image);
$numberOfImages++;
    }
    if (($numberOfImages % 2) == 0) {
        $out .= "</li><li>";
    }
}
$out .= "</li></ul>";
return $out;
}
$info = showImages();
```

Only a minor change was required from the original Chapter 4 gallery program. We will look at this change in a moment. But first, let's look at what showimages() accomplishes. Function showImages() uses CSS to format the container for the images. It sets default values for the size requirements and uses glob to retrieve the images from the img folder. Then, if the images are the proper size, it formats the images using CSS and displays two images per row.

```
$out .= '<img src="'.$dir_name. '/' .$image.'" alt="'.$image.'"
title="'.$image.'"
```

The only change is the addition of the `alt` and `title` values. The administrator will now be able to scroll over the image to determine its file name. This will be useful as the administrator will soon be able to select an image to associate with a blog.

The navigation has also been updated to allow the administrator to select the viewing of all images.

***Listing 9-11.*** updated-admin-navigation.php

```php
<?php
//complete code for views/admin/updated-admin-navigation.php
$nav = "
<nav id='admin-navigation'>
    <a href='updatedadmin.php?page=updatedentries'>All entries</a>
    <a href='updatedadmin.php?page=updatededitor'>Editor</a>
    <a href='updatedadmin.php?page=updatedimages'>Image manager</a>
    <a href='updatedadmin.php?page=gallery'>Image gallery</a>
</nav>";
?>
```

This new navigation is now accessed in `updatedadmin.php`.

Once these updates have been saved, the gallery can be tested by loading `updateadmin.php` into a browser. Of course, some images must exist within the `imgs` folder before they are displayed. The display of the images is the same as in Chapter 4, except for the addition of the tool tip (scroll over the image) will display the image name.

**Exercise**: While our program does a great job of displaying images, it does not provide a delete function to remove unwanted images from the folder. Add links to the image manager to delete each image. Then use the unlink function to remove the image from the folder. The following function can be used to complete the process.

```php
if ( $deleteImage ) {
    //grab the src of the image to delete
    $whichImage = $_GET['delete-image'];
    unlink($whichImage);
}
```

You could format a URL string similar to the following to be used by the function.

```
<a href='admin.php?page=images&delete-image=img/coffee.jpg'>
   delete
</a>
```

See how a URL variable, page, is set to images and another URL variable, delete-image, is set to img/coffee.jpg? Clicking this delete link will load the images controller and then can use the if statement to determine if a request to delete the image is desired. Hint: Place the link within the loop so each picture has its own delete link.

# Using an Image in a Blog Entry

We can now make changes to our editor to allow the administrator to select which image they would like to use in their blog.

***Listing 9-12.*** Partial Listing of updated-editor-html.php

```
if ( $entryData->title !="") {
        $info .= "value='$entryData->title' ";
}

        $info .= "pattern='[A-Za-z]{,150}'
    title='Title can contain only alphabetic letters, no special
    characters. Title is required.'
     required />
     <p>Image<br>
     <select name='image'>";
     $dir_name = "imgs";
     chdir($dir_name);

     $images = glob("*.jpg");
     $info .="<option value='None'";
     if ($entryData->image =="") { $info .=" selected "; }
     $info .= ">None</option>";

     foreach($images as $value) {
     $info .= "<option value='$value'";
```

```
    if ($entryData->image == $value) { $info .=" selected "; }
        $info .= ">$value</option>";
    }
$info .= "</select>";
```

This partial listing from `updated-editor-html.php` shows a very commonly used algorithm to create an HTML select list using the contents from the `imgs` folder. The `glob` function creates a `$images` array. The foreach loop goes through the array and places the file names into the `option` statements for the `select` statement. If this is an update, the if statement will compare the contents of `$entryData->image` to the current file name from the folder. If they match, the selected value is also appended to the `option` tag to highlight the previous choice of image.

But wait, where did `$entryData->image` come from? Ah you caught me. Let's look at a few other changes.

First, we must add a column to the database table using `phpMyAdmin`. `phpMyAdmin` can be found in the `Adobe` dashboard. Simply enter `http://localhost/` into a browser. Then click the menu item on the right. Select the database (`simple_blog`) from the left side menu. Then select the table (`blog_entry`). Click the `structure` menu tab.

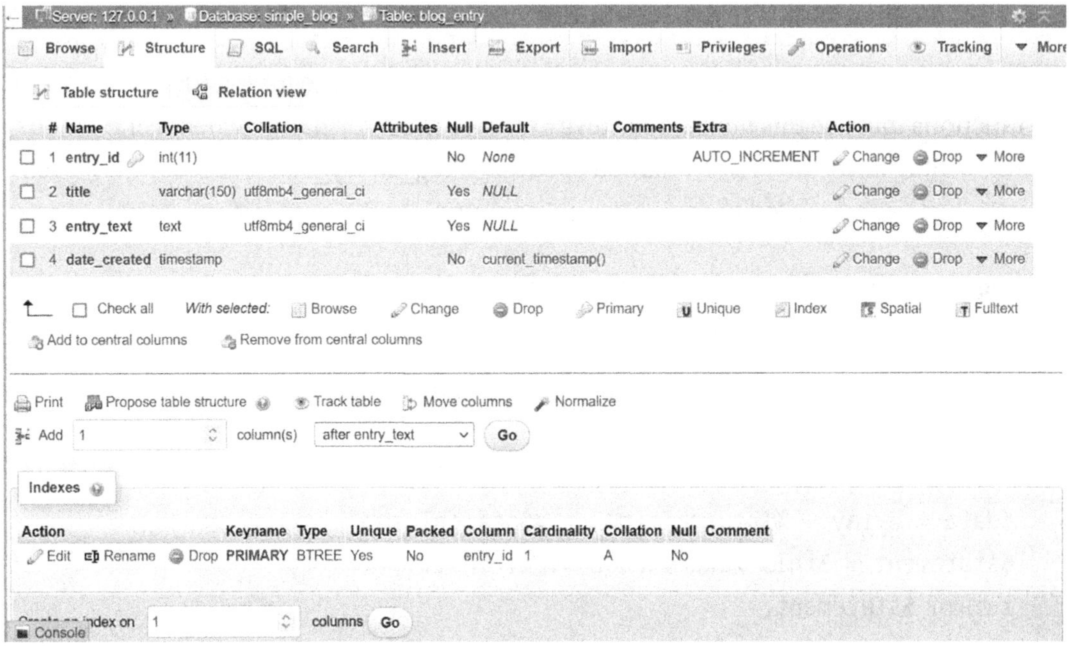

*Figure 9-2.* *phpMyAdmin*

Near the bottom of the window is an add area. In Figure 9-2, it indicates that one column will be added after the entry_text column. Click the Go button.

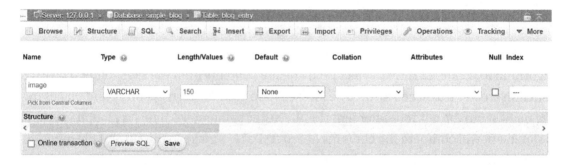

***Figure 9-3.*** *phpMyAdmin insert*

Enter the information shown earlier and click the Save button. The column will now be added to the table.

---

**Note**    In the examples in this chapter, a copy of the table (`simple_blog1`) has been produced with the new column to keep the integrity of the original table intact.

---

Now that we have the table adjusted, we need to make some minor adjustments to the functions that use this table, to retrieve and save the information whenever needed.

In the Blog Entry Table (now named `Updated_Blog_Entry_Table.class.php`), each function has been updated to access the new column.

***Listing 9-13.*** Partial Listing of Updated_Blog_Entry_Table.class.php

```php
public function searchEntry ( $searchTerm ) {
    $sql = "SELECT entry_id, title, image FROM blog_entry
            WHERE title LIKE ?
            OR entry_text LIKE ?";
    $data = array( "%$searchTerm%", "%$searchTerm%" );
    $statement = $this->executeSQL($sql, $data);
    return $statement;
```

For example, in Listing 9-13, the `searchEntry()` function has been updated to return the `image` column in addition to the other columns. Once we include these updates, the `select` list will be populated and the administrator can use it to create a new entry or update an existing entry. We can now enter `updatedadmin.php` program into a browser and click the `Editor` menu item to test the functionality.

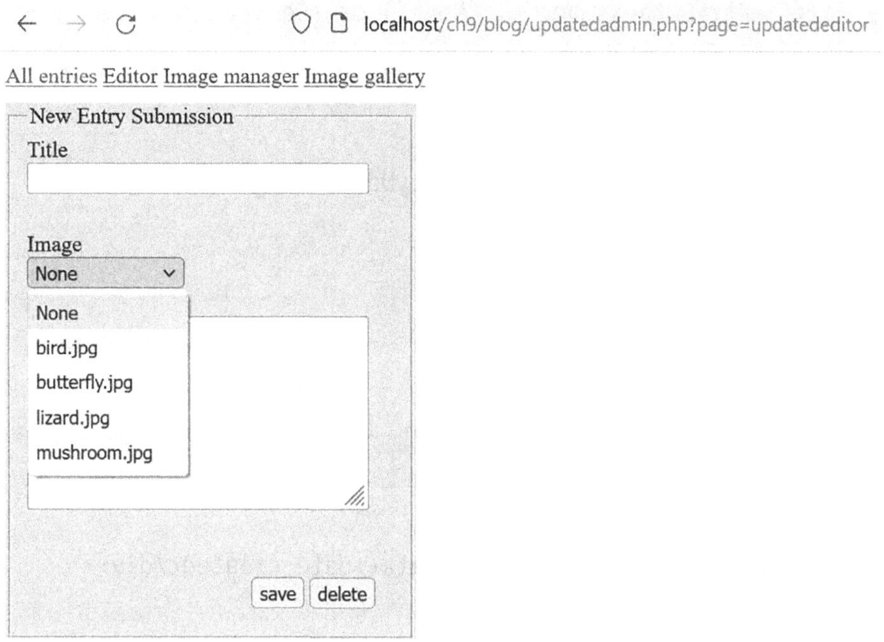

***Figure 9-4.*** *updatededitor.php*

OK, but how do we attach the image to the display of a blog?

Actually, now that everything else is working. That task is pretty straightforward.

***Listing 9-14.*** entry-html.php

```php
<?php
//complete source code for views/entry-html.php
$entryFound = isset( $entryData );
if ( $entryFound === false ) {
    trigger_error( 'views/entry-html.php needs an $entryData object' );
}
$info = "<h1>Detailed Blog</h1>";
```

```php
//properties available in $entry: entry_id, title, entry_text, image,
date_created
$info .= "<article>
    <h1>$entryData->title</h1>";
     if((isset($entryData->image)))
     {
          if(($entryData->image == "None") or ($entryData->image == "")) {
               $info .="";
          }
          else {
          $info .= "<img src='imgs/$entryData->image'
          alt='$entryData->image'
          style='height: 200px;
          width: 250px;
          border: 2px solid black;
          padding: 5px;
          margin: 5px;'/>";
     }
     }
    $info .= "<div class='date'>$entryData->date_created</div>
    $entryData->entry_text
</article>";
?>
```

In the entry-html.php program, we can determine if the blog has an associated picture. If the value in $entryData->image is None or "", this indicates the administrator did not assign a picture. If so, we will not make any changes. If the blog does have an associated picture, it will be displayed using the same CSS that was used to display the gallery. By placing the code in entry-html, the user will see the picture after clicking the Read more link. Test this process by entering index.php in a browser and selecting a blog with an image. Of course, you might need to create one first!

← → C        ○ □ localhost/ch9/blog/index.php?page=blog&id=18

# Detailed Blog

## New Mush

2022-05-13 10:58:21
Mushy!

Your name [＿＿＿＿＿＿]   Your Comment [＿＿＿＿＿＿] [post!]

[＿＿＿＿＿] [search]

***Figure 9-5.*** *entry-html.php*

Finally, it works! We have a blogging system with images!

**Exercise**: In entry-html.php, the if statement does not add anything to $info if there is no picture available. Create code to display a default image if the administrator has not chosen an image.

# Improving Security with Authentication

One of the last things we need to do is to close a big security hole. Our administration module is wide open and available for all users. Let us create a procedure which requires all administrators to log in before using the system. Creating this requires that we perform the following tasks:

- Create an admin table in the simple_blog database

- Use one-way hashing of passwords

- Create an HTML form for creating new administrators

- Create a login form for administrators

- Hide administration module from unauthorized users

- Use sessions to persist a login state across multiple HTTP requests

## Creating an admin_table in the Database

Enabling authorized administrators for our site requires that we create a table to store their data. We will create an admin table to store the following information about administrators:

> *admin_id*: A unique number identifying an administrator

> *email*: The administrator's email address

> *userid*: The administrator's userid

> *password*: The administrator's password

We will hash the password using BCRYPT (the default hash in PHP 8) which currently creates a string of 72 characters. However, future versions will expand this string. Consequently, we will create the password column using the VARCHAR data type and limit input to 255 characters for future expansion. We will also allow a userid with a VARCHAR data type and size of 255 characters. However, we will require a minimum size of eight characters, for both the userid and password, which will be verified using both HTML and PHP code.

To create the admin table, we will navigate to http://localhost/phpmyadmin in a browser, select the simple blog database, and open the SQL tab. Then we will enter the following command to create the table.

```
create table admin(
    admin_id INT NOT NULL AUTO_INCREMENT,
    email TEXT,
     userid VARCHAR(72),
    password VARCHAR(72),
    primary key (admin_id)
)
```

---

**Note**    You can also select the database, then scroll down to the create table area and enter the table name (`admin`). Then click the Go button. The system will then provide a form for completing the fields in the table. Entering the same information as shown in the preceding script will produce the same results, after you click the Save button.

---

# Hashing the Password with BCRYPT

Once we get around to inserting new users into the admin table, we will discover how to hash a string with BCRYPT. The BCRYPT algorithm provides one-way hashing.

Hashing passwords is an absolute requirement for strong security because a hashed password is harder to steal. Let us imagine the password is *Test*. If we hash it using BCRYPT, then *Test* becomes

```
$2y$10$xJN9J3cSlTp25rqS5MNYFepRs5Mkcs0y.zya6MFshLPDllWBTav4S
```

This certainly becomes a very difficult password to crack! Even if the database suffers a serious attack, and all usernames and passwords are exposed, attackers still will have a difficult time trying to misuse the usernames and passwords.

# One-Way Hashing

Passwords should always be protected through one-way hashing. If a password is hashed with a one-way hashing algorithm, it will be nearly impossible to determine the real password.

Any system that can recover a lost password is inherently unsafe. If the original password can be recovered, the system must have somehow remembered the password. If the password is remembered by the system, it is likely that system administrators can see the password. If the password can be seen, it is vulnerable. A secure system only stores hashed passwords. If someone forgets their password, a secure system will provide an opportunity to reset the password.

In the context of the blogging system, it means that administrator passwords are protected from all blog administrators. If a user loses their password, it cannot be sent to them again. Instead, the system could offer them a chance to reset the password.

## Sufficient Security

Always assume that even the most secure systems can be hacked. The question is how much time and effort are required from the attacker. Our task is to provide enough security to discourage attackers from trying to access the content of the database.

---

**Note**    For more information on hashing passwords with PHP, visit www.php.net/
manual/en/function.password-hash.php.

---

## Adding Administrators in the Database

We now have a database table to save administrator credentials; we are ready to start creating blog administrators. Our first step is to create a form that allows us to enter an email address, a userid, and a corresponding password. Once we accomplish this, we will store the information in the database for later use.

## Building an HTML Form

As we have already learned, it is best to create forms that provide feedback to users. We can prepare the form for user feedback right away. Let us look at the code.

*Listing 9-15.* new-admin-form-html.php

```php
<?php
//complete code for views/admin/new-admin-form-html.php
if( isset($adminFormMessage) === false ) {
    $adminFormMessage = "";
}

$info = "<form method='post' action='admin.php?page=users'>
    <fieldset>
        <legend>Create new admin user</legend>

        <label for='userid'>Userid</label>
        <input type='text' name='userid' id='userid'
         minlength='8' required>
```

```
            <label for='password'>Password</label>
            <input type='password' name='password'
        pattern='(?=.*\d)(?=.*[a-z])(?=.*[A-Z]).{8,}'
        title='Password must contain: at least one number, one uppercase
        letter, one lowercase letter, and 8 or more characters'  required>

            <label for='email'>e-mail</label>
            <input type='email' name='email' required/>

            <input type='submit' value='create user' name='new-admin'/>
        </fieldset>
        <p id='admin-form-message'>$adminFormMessage</p>
    </form>
    ";
    ?>
```

```
<label for='userid'>Userid</label>
        <input type='text' name='userid' id='userid'
    minlength='8' required>
```

The userid is set with a minimum length of eight characters and is required.

```
<label for='password'>Password</label>
        <input type='password' name='password'
    pattern='(?=.*\d)(?=.*[a-z])(?=.*[A-Z]).{8,}'
    title='Password must contain: at least one number, one uppercase
    letter, one lowercase letter, and 8 or more characters'  required>
```

The password is set with a required combination of one number, one uppercase letter, one lowercase letter, and at least eight characters.

```
<label for='email'>e-mail</label>
        <input type='email' name='email' required/>
```

The email input type will validate the email format.

All three entries will also soon be validated on the server side via PHP.

To display the form, we need a controller to load it and return it to the front door admin controller. We need to create a new navigation item and a corresponding controller. Let us begin by updating the navigation with an additional link.

***Listing 9-16.*** secure-admin-navigation.php

```php
<?php
//complete code for views/admin/secure-admin-navigation.php
$nav = "
<nav id='admin-navigation'>
    <a href='secureadmin.php?page=secureentries'>All entries</a>
    <a href='secureadmin.php?page=secureeditor'>Editor</a>
    <a href='secureadmin.php?page=secureimages'>Image manager</a>
    <a href='secureadmin.php?page=securegallery'>Image gallery</a>
    <a href='secureadmin.php?page=users'>Create Admin User</a>
</nav>";
?>
```

With the form's view and a new navigation item created, the next step is to create a controller to load the view. In the previous example, the href for the new link that requests a new page is called *users*. So, the system expects a controller called users.php.

***Listing 9-17.*** users.php

```php
<?php
//complete code for controllers/admin/users.php
include_once "views/admin/new-admin-form-html.php";
?>
```

We can now test our work by loading http://localhost/ch9/blog/secureadmin.php?page=users in a browser.

---

**Note**    The following files have been updated to access the new file versions: secureeditor.php, secureimages.php, secureentries.php, secure-editor-html.php, secure-entries-html.php, secure-images-html.php.

---

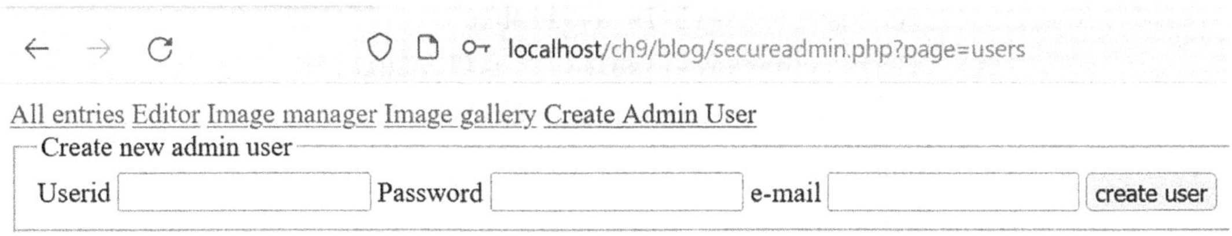

| ← → C | ○ ◻ o⊶ localhost/ch9/blog/secureadmin.php?page=users |
|---|---|

All entries Editor Image manager Image gallery Create Admin User

┌─Create new admin user─────────────────────────────────────────────────┐

Userid [            ] Password [                ] e-mail [              ] [create user]

└────────────────────────────────────────────────────────────────────────┘

***Figure 9-6.*** *Output from new-admin-form-html.php*

We should see a valid HTML form. We cannot really use it yet: it cannot insert new administrators into the database table. Let us work on that now.

# Saving New Administrators in the Database

Inserting new rows into a database table is a job for a *model* program. We have already made good use of the table data gateway design pattern a couple of times. We already have a base Table class, which we can extend to create a table data gateway for the admin table.

We want to avoid name conflicts, so before a new admin user is created, the code should check whether the email and/or userid is already used in the table. If the email and userid are not in use, the model script can insert a new entry into the admin table. We will create a new file which will inherit the information from the Table class.

***Listing 9-18.*** Admin_Table.class.php

```php
<?php
//complete code for models/Admin_Table.class.php
//include parent class' definition
include_once "models/Table.class.php";

class Admin_Table extends Table {

    public function create( string $email, string $userid, string
    $password ) {
        $valid_email = filter_var($email, FILTER_VALIDATE_EMAIL);
        if (($this->validate_password($password)) and ($valid_email) and
        (strlen($userid) >= 8)) {
```

```php
            //check if email is available
            if ($this->checkAvailable( $email, $userid )) {
                //hash password with BCYRPT
                $hashedpassword = password_hash($password, PASSWORD_
                DEFAULT);
                    $sql = "INSERT INTO admin ( email, userid, password )
                                    VALUES( ?, ?, ? )";
                    $data= array( $email, $userid, $hashedpassword );
                    $this->executeSQL( $sql, $data );   }
            else { throw new Exception("E-mail and/or Userid already
            used."); }
        }
      else { throw new Exception("Userid and/or Password not valid."); }
  }

  private function checkAvailable (string $email, string $userid) : bool {
      $sql = "SELECT email FROM admin WHERE email = ? OR userid = ?";
      $data = array( $email, $userid );
      $this->executeSQL( $sql, $data );
      $statement = $this->executeSQL( $sql, $data );
      //if a user with that email is found in database
      if ( $statement->rowCount() >= 1 ) {
              return false;
        } else {
              return true;
        }
  }
  private function validate_password(string $password) : bool {
      // Validate password strength
      $uppercase = preg_match('@[A-Z]@', $password);
      $lowercase = preg_match('@[a-z]@', $password);
      $number    = preg_match('@[0-9]@', $password);
      // Do not allow special characters
      $specialCharacters = !(preg_match('@[^\w]@', $password));
      $length = strlen($password);
```

```
        if ((strlen($length >=8)) and ($uppercase) and ($lowercase) and
        ($number) and ($specialCharacters)) {
                return true; }
          else {
          return false; }
      }

}
?>
```

```
$valid_email = filter_var($email, FILTER_VALIDATE_EMAIL);
```

The email is validated using the PHP function filter_var() with the parameter
FILTER_VALIDATE_EMAIL, which will return true if the email format is correct, false
otherwise.

---

**Note**   For more information on using the PHP function filter_var( ), visit www.php.
net/manual/en/filter.examples.validation.php.

---

```
      if (($this->validate_password($password)) and ($valid_email) and
      (strlen(userid) >= 8)) {
              //check if email is available
          if ($this->checkAvailable( $email, $userid )) {
```

The password is validated using a validate_password() function (which we will
look at shortly) and the userid is validated by using the PHP function strlen() to
determine that it has at least eight characters. The email was already validated. Also, the
database table is checked, via a checkAvailable() function to see if the email and userid
have been used before.

```
      //hash password with BCYRPT
          $hashedpassword = password_hash($password, PASSWORD_DEFAULT);
          $sql = "INSERT INTO admin ( email, userid, password )
                                    VALUES( ?, ?, ? )";
          $data= array( $email, $userid, $hashedpassword );
          $this->executeSQL( $sql, $data );   }
```

The PHP function password_hash() is used to create a hashed version using BCRYPT, which is the current default algorithm for PHP. We could have directly specified BCRYPT; however, by using the default parameter, the program will automatically use the latest version of hashing available. At this point, everything is valid and properly prepared. Thus, the email, userid, and password are inserted into the database table.

```
else { throw new Exception("E-mail and/or Userid already used."); }
        }
        else { throw new Exception("Userid and/or Password not valid."); }
    }
```

If the email and/or userid already exists in the database table, an exception is raised. If the userid and/or password is not valid, a different exception is raised. We will handle these exceptions soon.

```
private function checkAvailable (string $email, string $userid) : bool {
        $sql = "SELECT email FROM admin WHERE email = ? OR userid = ?";
        $data = array( $email, $userid );
        $this->executeSQL( $sql, $data );
        $statement = $this->executeSQL( $sql, $data );
        //if a user with that email is found in database
        if ( $statement->rowCount() >= 1 ) {
    return false;
    } else {
    return true;
        }
```

The function checkAvailable() uses an SQL SELECT statement to attempt to retrieve a record with a matching email or userid. If either of these matches, as indicated by one or more rows being found, then false is returned. Otherwise, true is returned.

```
private function validate_password(string $password) : bool {
    // Validate password strength
    $uppercase = preg_match('@[A-Z]@', $password);
    $lowercase = preg_match('@[a-z]@', $password);
    $number    = preg_match('@[0-9]@', $password);
            // Do not allow special characters
            $specialCharacters = !(preg_match('@[^\w]@', $password));
```

```
            $length = strlen($password);
        if (($length >=8) and ($uppercase) and ($lowercase) and
        ($number) and ($specialCharacters)) {
     return true; }
     else { return false; }
  }
```

The function `validate_password()` uses the PHP function `preg_match()` to determine if the password contains at least one uppercase letter, one lowercase letter, and a number. It does not allow special characters out of a concern the user might be attempting to do SQL Injection. If this format is correct, and the password is eight or more characters, `true` is returned. Otherwise, `false` is returned.

---

**Note**    For more information on preg_match, visit `www.php.net/manual/en/function.preg-match.php`.

---

**Exercise**: In the `create()` function, the userid is only checked to determine if it has eight or more characters. What other limits should we place on the userid? Update the function and the form to validate the userids with these new limits.

The preceding code is just waiting to be called from a controller. This code throws two exceptions. We now use a `try-catch` statement to capture the exceptions. If an operation fails, the code should fail gracefully, by catching the exception and providing relevant feedback to the user. Let us go back to the controller script and change some code to insert new admin userids.

***Listing 9-19.*** validusers.php

```php
<?php
//complete code for controllers/admin/validusers.php
//new code starts here
include_once "models/Admin_Table.class.php";

//is the form submitted?
$createNewAdmin = isset( $_POST['new-admin'] );
//if it is...
```

```
if( $createNewAdmin ) {
    //grab form input
    $newEmail = $_POST['email'];
    $newUserid = $_POST['userid'];
    $newPassword = $_POST['password'];
    $adminTable = new Admin_Table($db);
    try {
        //try to create a new admin user
        $adminTable->create( $newEmail, $newUserid, $newPassword );
        //tell user how it went
        $adminFormMessage = "New user created for $newEmail!";
    } catch ( Exception $e ) {
        //if operation failed, tell user what went wrong
        $adminFormMessage = $e->getMessage();
    }
}
//end of new code
include_once "views/admin/new-admin-form-html.php";
?>
```

Most of this code should look familiar. We have, however, included a try/catch block to handle any of the exceptions that might be raised. The HTML code will usually catch invalid attempts to enter new user information. However, we must expect that a hacker may try to bypass the input form. If an exception is raised, the message from the exception will be passed to the $adminFormMessage variable, which will be displayed on the create admin userid form.

---

**Note**   The following files have been updated to access the new versions: valideditor.php, validimages.php, validentries.php, valid-editor-html.php, valid-entries-html.php, valid-images-html.php.

---

Let us take some time to test it by running http://localhost/ch9/blog/validadmin.php?page=validusers in the browser. Try to create an admin user. You should get a confirmation message displayed in the form. Check in http://localhost/

phpmyadmin to see whether the admin user was in fact inserted into the admin database table. You should create at least one user, because you will need it to be able to create other users. Remember to write down the userid and password!

Once you have created a new admin user, try to create one more admin user using the same email address. It should not be allowed, and you should receive an error message in the form.

**Exercise**: Try to create a password with special characters. The current HTML will not catch this attempt. However, the PHP code will catch it and raise an exception. Adjust the HTML code to catch the attempt before it is passed to the server.

# Planning Login

Let us now use our userid and password for *authentication* to restrict access to the administration blog modules. We will need two *views*: a login form and a logout form. We will need a *controller* to handle user interactions received from these two views and a *model* to actually perform login and logout. The model should also remember a state: it should remember if the user is logged in or not.

# Creating a Login Form

We will begin with the login form. Our goal is to create a system in which a user must provide a valid userid and a matching password to be allowed access to the blog administration module. Thus, we need a userid and password field.

***Listing 9-20.*** login-form-html.php

```php
<?php
//complete code for views/admin/login-form-html.php
$info = " <form method='post' action='loginadmin.php'>
    <h1>Login to access restricted area</h1>
    <label>userid</label><input type='userid' name='userid' required />
    <label>password</label>
    <input type='password' name='password' required />
    <input type='submit' value='login' name='log-in' />
</form>";
?>
```

A very simple, straightforward form is all that is required. We can also create a simple controller to test our logic.

***Listing 9-21.*** login.php

```php
<?php
//complete code for controllers/admin/login.php
include_once "views/admin/login-form-html.php";
?>
```

The admin navigation does not provide a menu item for the login, and it shouldn't. We want the login form to be displayed as the default view of the front controller for the administration module. Only when a user is authenticated and logged in should the user be allowed to see the blog administration module.

# Hiding Controls from Unauthorized Users

It is very important that a login actually hides parts of a system from unauthorized users. So far, the administration module has been readily available to anybody visiting the front administration controller. We will fix this by making a few changes here:

- We will create an Admin_User object to remember login state.

- If a visitor is not logged in, we will show only the login form.

- If a user is logged in, we will show the admin navigation and the administration module.

To do that, we need to make some changes to the front controller for the administration module.

***Listing 9-22.*** loginadmin.php

```php
<?php
//complete code for blog/loginadmin.php
$nav = "";
$info = "";
//include_once 'views/admin/valid-admin-navigation.php';
include_once "models/Page_Data.class.php";
$pageData = new Page_Data();
```

```php
$pageData->setTitle("PHP/MySQL blog demo");
$pageData->setCss("<link rel='stylesheet' href='css/blog.css'>");

include_once "models/updateddatabase.php";

include_once "models/Admin_User.class.php";
$admin = new Admin_User();
//load the login controller, which will show the login form
include_once "controllers/admin/login.php";
$pageData->setContent($info);
//add a new if statement
//show admin module only if user is logged in
if( $admin->isLoggedIn() ) {
    include "views/admin/login-admin-navigation.php";
    $pageData->setContent($nav);
    $navigationIsClicked = isset( $_GET['page'] );
    if ($navigationIsClicked ) {
        $controller = $_GET['page'];
    } else {
        $controller = "loginentries";
    }
    include_once "controllers/admin/$controller.php";
    $pageData->appendContent($info);
} //end if-statement

include_once "views/page.php";
echo $page;
?>

include_once "models/Admin_User.class.php";
$admin = new Admin_User();
```

A new Admin_User class is included, and an instance is declared, $admin. This class will determine if the user is logged in or not. We will look at the code in a moment.

```php
include_once "controllers/admin/login.php";
$pageData->setContent($info);
```

The login page is displayed.

```
if( $admin->isLoggedIn() ) {
    include "views/admin/login-navigation.php";
    $pageData->setContent($nav);
    $navigationIsClicked = isset( $_GET['page'] );
    if ($navigationIsClicked ) {
        $controller = $_GET['page'];
    } else {
        $controller = "loginentries";
    }
}
```

If the user is logged in, the default entries page or the page selected by the user is displayed. This is the same code as before but is now controlled by the if statement.

## HTTP Is Stateless

Hypertext transfer protocol (HTTP) is the foundation of much data communication on the Internet. It is *stateless*, which means it treats each new request as a separate transaction. In practical terms, it means that all PHP variables and objects are created from scratch with every new request.

That has some consequences for us. When we submit the login form, we are making an HTTP request. PHP will run, and the $admin object will remember that we are logged in. If we try to click an entry, this will make a new HTTP request, and thus, a new $admin object will be created. PHP will not remember that we just logged in, because the new HTTP request is treated as an independent, separate transaction. The previous HTTP request is completely forgotten.

## Superglobal: $_SESSION

This stateless HTTP is bad news for our login. No matter how many times we log in, PHP will forget about it with every new request. It is very impractical, and of course, there is a solution: forming a persistent state across requests. We need a way to force PHP to remember that a given user is logged in. The PHP session will accomplish this task.

When a PHP session is started, the visiting user's browser will be assigned a unique identification number: a *session id*. The server will create a small, temporary file on the server side (by default). Any information we require for our application to remember across requests can be stored in this file. A PHP session duration can be configured in the php.ini file.

**Note**  Read more at www.php.net/manual/en/intro.session.php.

PHP provides a superglobal to make a session. Now, it is time for us to meet $_SESSION.

# Persisting State with a Session

To use a session, we must start a session. With that in place, we can create a *session variable*, which is a variable whose value is *stateful*, meaning a variable whose value can persist across HTTP requests.

Let us use a session variable to remember our login status.

*Listing 9-23.* Admin_User.class.php

```php
<?php
//complete code for models/Admin_User.class.php

class Admin_User {
    //declare a new method, a constructor
    public function __construct(){
        //start a session
        session_start();
    }

    public function isLoggedIn(){
        $sessionIsSet = isset( $_SESSION['logged_in'] );
        if ( $sessionIsSet ) {
            $out = $_SESSION['logged_in'];
        } else {
            $out = false;
        }
        return $out;
    }

    public function login () {
        //set session variable ['logged_in'] to true
        $_SESSION['logged_in'] = true;
    }
```

```
    public function logout () {
        //set session variable ['logged_in'] to false
        $_SESSION['logged_in'] = false;
    }
}

public function __construct(){
        //start a session
        session_start();
    }
```

The constructor starts a session when an instance of Admin_User is created.

```
    public function isLoggedIn(){
        $sessionIsSet = isset( $_SESSION['logged_in'] );
        if ( $sessionIsSet ) {
            $out = $_SESSION['logged_in'];
        } else {
            $out = false;
        }
        return $out;
    }
```

The isLoggedIn() function determines if the session variable has been created. If it has, the content is placed into $out. If it has not (not logged in), then false is stored into $out. Then $out is returned.

```
public function login () {
        //set session variable ['logged_in'] to true
        $_SESSION['logged_in'] = true;
    }

    public function logout () {
        //set session variable ['logged_in'] to false
        $_SESSION['logged_in'] = false;
    }
```

The login() function will set the contents of the session variable to true. The logout() function will set the contents of the session variable to false.

# Logging Users Out

It is customary to provide a logout option for logged-in users. It is also a good idea: we do not want administrators to stay logged in with no option for logging out. What if an administrator has to leave the computer to get a fresh cup of coffee? We would not want to leave the administration module exposed. Let us create a new view for logging out.

*Listing 9-24.* logout-form-html.php

```php
<?php
//complete code for views/admin/logout-form-html.php
$info = "
<form method='post' action='loginadmin.php'>
    <label>logged in as administrator</label>
    <input type='submit' value='log out' name='logout' />
</form>";
?>
```

This view should be displayed whenever a user is logged in. But simply showing a logout form will not actually log out users. If a user clicks the Logout button, this should run a script to log out the user. These are tasks for the controller.

Let us update the code for the login controller to allow logging out.

*Listing 9-25.* newlogin.php

```php
<?php
//complete code for controllers/admin/newlogin.php

$loginFormSubmitted = isset( $_POST['log-in'] );
if( $loginFormSubmitted ) {
    $admin->login();
}

$loggingOut = isset ( $_POST['logout'] );
if ( $loggingOut ){
    $admin->logout();
}
```

```php
if ( $admin->isLoggedIn() ) {
    include_once "views/admin/logout-form-html.php";
} else {
    include_once "views/admin/login-form-html.php";
}
?>

$loginFormSubmitted = isset( $_POST['log-in'] );
if( $loginFormSubmitted ) {
    $admin->login();
}
```

If the user arrived here by using the login form, then log-in will be set and the code will call the $admin->login() function.

```php
$loggingOut = isset ( $_POST['logout'] );
if ( $loggingOut ){
    $admin->logout();
}
```

If the user arrived here by using the logout form, then the logout will be set, and the code will call the $admin->logout() function.

```php
if ( $admin->isLoggedIn() ) {
    include_once "views/admin/logout-form-html.php";
} else {
    include_once "views/admin/login-form-html.php";
}
```

If logged in, the logout form will display. If logged out, the login form will display.

---

**Note**   The following files have been updated to access the new versions: newsessioneditor.php, newsessionimages.php, newsessionentries.php, new-session-editor-html.php, new-session-entries-html.php, new-session-images-html.php.

---

We can now take a break from coding and test the system. We can open up newsessionadmin.php in a browser. The system should jump to the login screen. Once a userid and password are entered, the newsessionadmin.php screen will display.

**Figure 9-7.** *newsessionadmin.php after login*

We now see our admin screen with an indication that we are logged in and an ability to log out. Clicking the Logout button will log the user out and display the login screen. Try any userid/password. Did you notice anything? The system accepts any value. Let us fix that next.

We have covered a lot. But soon it will be complete. Just hang in there. We now have the ability to have a login and logout using a session variable to determine the status. We are almost complete!

## Allowing Authorized Users Only

We now need to check whether the supplied userid and password match exactly one record in the database. The information is available in the admin table, and we already have a table data gateway called Admin_Table. We can create a new method to check whether submitted credentials are valid.

***Listing 9-26.*** New_Admin_User.class.php

```php
//partial  code for models/admin/New_Admin_Table.class.php
public function checkCredentials( $userid, $password ){
    $sql = "SELECT userid, password FROM admin
            WHERE userid = ?";
    $data = array($userid);
    $statement = $this->executeSQL( $sql, $data );
    if ( $statement->rowCount() === 1 ) {
     $userData = $statement->fetchObject();
     if((password_verify( $password, $userData->password))) {
         return "Valid";
         } else { return "Password not valid!";}
    } else { return "Userid not valid"; }
}

    $sql = "SELECT userid, password FROM admin
            WHERE userid = ?";
```

The function tries to match the userid and retrieves both the userid and password from the table, if one exists.

```php
if ( $statement->rowCount() === 1 ) {
    if((password_verify( $password, $statement->password)) {
                return "Valid";
        } else { return "Password not valid!";}
    } else { return "Userid not valid"; }
```

If one record is returned, then the password is verified using the PHP function password_verify(). A direct comparison cannot be done because the hash algorithm must be determined to compare the values. The function retrieves this, along with other information needed to do the comparison. If this comparison does not match, the string "Password not valid" is returned. If the userid was not found in the database, the string "Userid not valid!" is returned. If everything matches, the string "Valid" is returned.

---

**Note**   For more information on the PHP function password_verify(), visit www.php.net/manual/en/function.password-verify.php.

---

With this method declared, we are ready to call it from the login controller whenever a user tries to log in.

***Listing 9-27.*** completelogin.php

```php
<?php
//complete code for controllers/admin/completelogin.php
include_once "models/New_Admin_Table.class.php";
$loginFormSubmitted = isset( $_POST['log-in'] );
if( $loginFormSubmitted ) {
    $userid = $_POST['userid'];
    $password = $_POST['password'];
    $adminTable = new Admin_Table( $db );
    $message = $adminTable->checkCredentials( $userid, $password );
     if( $message === "Valid" ) {
                $admin->login();
           } else {
           $loginFormMessage = $message;
      }
    }

$loggingOut = isset ( $_POST['logout'] );
if ( $loggingOut ){
    $admin->logout();
}

if ( $admin->isLoggedIn() ) {
    include_once "views/admin/complete-logout-form-html.php";
} else {
    include_once "views/admin/complete-login-form-html.php";
}
?>

include_once "models/New_Admin_Table.class.php";
```

The newest version of the Admin Table class is included.

```php
$loginFormSubmitted = isset( $_POST['log-in'] );
if( $loginFormSubmitted ) {
    $userid = $_POST['userid'];
    $password = $_POST['password'];
    $adminTable = new Admin_Table( $db );
    $message = $adminTable->checkCredentials( $userid, $password );
     if( $message === "Valid" ) {
                 $admin->login();
         } else {
         $loginFormMessage = $message;
     }
```

The if statement checks to make sure that the user clicked the login button from the login form. If so, the userid and password are retrieved. Then an instance of the Admin Table class ($adminTable) is created, passing $db into the constructor. Then the userid and password are passed into the new checkCredentials() function. If "Valid" is returned, all is good, and the login() function is called. Otherwise, whatever message that was returned is placed into $loginFormMessage. The login form has been modified to accept and display this message.

***Listing 9-28.*** complete-login-form-html.php

```php
<?php
//complete code for views/admin/complete-login-form-html.php
if( isset($loginFormMessage) === false ) {
    $loginFormMessage = "";
}
$info = " <form method='post' action='completeadmin.php'>
    <h1>Login to access restricted area</h1>
    <label>userid</label><input type='userid' name='userid' required />
    <label>password</label>
    <input type='password' name='password' required />
    <input type='submit' value='login' name='log-in' />
</form>
<p id='login-form-message'>$loginFormMessage</p>";
?>
```

The format used is the same as the code in the create userid form.

Now that the userid and password can be validated, let us make a final change or two to the admin front controller.

***Listing 9-29.*** completeadmin.php

```php
<?php
//complete code for blog/completeadmin.php
$nav = "";
$info = "";
try {
    include_once "models/Page_Data.class.php";
    $pageData = new Page_Data();
    $pageData->setTitle("PHP/MySQL blog demo");
    $pageData->setCss("<link rel='stylesheet' href='css/blog.css'>");
    include_once "models/updateddatabase.php";
    include_once "models/New_Admin_User.class.php";
    $admin = new Admin_User();
    include_once "controllers/admin/completelogin.php";
    $pageData->setContent($info);

    if( $admin->isLoggedIn() ) {
        include "views/admin/complete-admin-navigation.php";
        $pageData->setContent($nav);
        $navigationIsClicked = isset( $_GET['page'] );
        if ($navigationIsClicked ) {
            $controller = $_GET['page'];
        } else {
            $controller = "completeentries";
        }
        include_once "controllers/admin/$controller.php";
        $pageData->appendContent($info);
    }
include_once "views/page.php";
echo $page;
}
```

```
catch(Exception $e) {
    echo "System Busy. Please come back later";
    $currentDateTime = date('Y-m-d H:i:s');
    $errorString = $currentDateTime . "-" . $e->getMessage();
    error_log($errorString, 3, "error-log.log");
}
?>
```

A try/catch block has been added to catch any unexpected errors or exceptions. In the catch block, a generic message is displayed to the user. They don't need to know any details of what occurred. We don't want to expose any potential security leaks.

```
$currentDateTime = date('Y-m-d H:i:s');
$errorString = $currentDateTime . "-" . $e->getMessage();
error_log($errorString, 3, "error-log.log");
```

The current time and date are gathered using the date() function with the format shown. This information is then appended to a string which includes the message. The string is then placed into an error log file using the error_log() function. You can test this by raising an exception inside of completeadmin.php and open the error-log.log file in a text editor to discover the message has been saved.

---

**Note**   For more information on the PHP error logs, visit www.php.net/manual/ en/function.error-log.php.

---

The use of the try/catch block, along with the logging of errors, properly prepares the system for real-world use. This would be a good point to invite users to beta test the system to completely check its vulnerabilities and usability.

The following files have been modified to access the new versions: completeeditor. php, completeimages.php, completeentries.php, complete-editor-html.php, complete-entries-html.php, complete-images-html.php.

We can now complete our final test by placing completeadmin.php into a browser to test the authentication and all other functionality of the system.

## Exercises

1. Unless you have already done so, the menu needs work before the program should be released. The CSS file `newblog.css` contains some code that could be used or create your own. Add the ability for the menu to use the new CSS.

2. Attempt to access other files in the system without logging in. Some files will just display blank pages; others will display exceptions for missing files. While the program is much more secure, it would be better if, whenever the user tries to access a page that requires administration access, they get redirected to the login page. Use some of the code from `completeadmin.php` to check the login status on each page and redirect them to the login page if they did not login.

# Summary

This was a long chapter. We covered a lot. Too much to list here. But some of the most important new skills we have gained include one-way encryption for privacy, a session for stateful memory, and effectively restricting access to the administration module of the blog. I hope you will agree it was very rewarding to implement a login system. As mentioned before, the blog is ready for beta testing. Have your significant other or a friend test the system out. It is not perfect, but close. Whatever potential problems the tester finds, take the time to fix them.

Remember, PHP programs can do more than manage websites. In the last chapter, we will diverge from creating websites to look at creating a data dashboard and the logic for a checkers game.

# Projects

1. Using the design practices from this and previous chapters, update the student registration system from Chapter 7. Provide the requirement that users must log in to the system before they can access student records.

2.  Update the blog application to provide the ability to recover from a lost password. The program should require that the user verify either the userid or password. Then, once verified, the user will have access to a form to change the password. For a bigger challenge, discover how PHP can send emails. Have the system send the user an email with a temporary passcode. Then require the user to enter the passcode before they can change the password.

3.  Update the blog application to provide the ability for the deletion of unused administrative userids from the system.

4.  Update the admin user verification system of the blog application to limit the number of attempts to sign in to four. After four, the system should reject all attempts from the same userid for ten minutes. This can be accomplished by creating another session variable to populate the last time attempted after four tries. Then clear the variable after ten minutes has expired. This is a common authorization requirement in the IT industry.

# CHAPTER 10

# Data Dashboard and Gaming

## Objectives

After completing this chapter, you will be able to

- Convert data from one data type to another

- Use the PHP function `json_encode()` to create JSON data

- Use the PHP function `fputcsv()` to create CSV data

- Use SQL statements to determine a database name, table name, and column names

- Use SQL statements to determine if the values in a column are numeric

- Convert a database table to a PHP array

- Use the PHP function `fopen()` to read and write to a file

- Use the PHP function `fgetcsv()` to convert a CSV file into an array

- Use the PHP function `file_get_contents()` to retrieve all the contents of a file at one time

- Use the PHP function `json_decode()` to convert a JSON file into an array

- Use the open source class `SIMPLEXLSX` to read data from a Microsoft Excel spreadsheet into an array

© Jason Lengstorf, Thomas Blom Hansen, Steve Prettyman 2022
J. Lengstorf et al., *PHP 8 for Absolute Beginners*, https://doi.org/10.1007/978-1-4842-8205-2_10

- Use the PHP function explode() to break a string into an array based on a delimiter

- Use the PHP function is_numeric() to determine if a value contains a number

- Use the PHP function is_string() to determine if a value is a string

- Use the PHP continue statement to skip an iteration of a loop

- Create a *Google Data Table* from a PHP array

- Use JavaScript and the *Google Charts Library* to create a data dashboard

- Create the logic for a checkers game using two-dimensional arrays

- Use a switch control to determine multiple outcomes from a single variable

In this final chapter, we will explore other tasks that PHP can accomplish besides controlling the interactivity of a standard website. Although PHP is not known as a tool for *data analysis* and gaming, we will demonstrate that it can be used for just that purpose. Let's first take a brief look at data analysis and discover how we can display a dashboard and related charts.

# Setting Up a Data Dashboard

*Data mining* and *data collection* are vital for both medium-size and large corporations. The ability to quickly analyze data can have a major impact on the bottom line for any company. Companies must be able to determine the best strategies using available information (such as sales data) to be successful. Data can be collected from multiple sources, including internally, externally (competition), environmentally (economics of a geographical area), and via the government. The ability to combine and compare this information is essential.

The popularity of the Python programming language is partially due to the number of available libraries within the language to manipulate and display data efficiently. However, there are techniques that other languages can use to accomplish similar goals. One of these tools is *Google Charts*.

Google Charts are JavaScript classes which are specially designed to interact with HTML5 web pages. This provides a natural ability for charts to interact with PHP, since PHP, HTML, and JavaScript work well together. Charts retrieve information from *Data Tables* (special types of arrays). Thus, any data source that can display data into an array can be a provider for a Google Chart.

We will build a *data dashboard* to display our charts. A data dashboard is simply a screen (web page) that displays data in multiple formats. Google has over 30 distinct types of *Charts* which can be placed within a dashboard. To demonstrate the ability to use different data sources, our example will allow the user to determine the source of the information. We will demonstrate this ability by allowing data to be pulled from a database table, *JSON file*, *CSV file*, or a *Microsoft Excel Worksheet*. The information will then be displayed in several charts within a dashboard.

Let us discuss some of the process before we begin the task. A Google Dashboard is defined using *google.visualization.Dashboard Classes*. The Dashboard instance uses a data table which contains the data to be displayed and distributes this data to all the charts that are part of the dashboard.

*Controls* provide the ability for the user to interface with data and to change the subset of data used within the charts. These controls are common widgets, pickers, sliders, and auto completers, which can easily be manipulated by the user.

Now that we have a general idea of what can exist within a dashboard, let us look at the steps needed to accomplish our goal.

- *HTML dashboard skeleton*: We will design an HTML framework which will position and hold charts to be displayed in the dashboard.

- *Libraries*: We must load two Google libraries (a *Google AJAX API* and a *Google Visualization Control Package*) to access the dashboard and charts.

- *Data*: We will retrieve the data from several sources, allowing the user to select which data source to use when displaying results within the dashboard. The selected data will be placed within a two-dimensional array which will be converted to a Google Data Table for easy use by the charts within the dashboard.

- *Dashboard*: We will use the *Google Dashboard Class*, by creating an instance of it (object) and by passing a reference to the location of the dashboard within the HTML (div tag location).

- *Controls/charts*: We will create controls for users to manipulate and charts which will display the data within the dashboard.

- *Dependencies*: We will bind together the dashboard and charts which will automatically update the data displayed when the user manipulates a control.

- *Display dashboard*: We will draw the dashboard and pass the data to it, which will, in turn, be displayed in the charts.

- *Programming*: We will finally include additional programming code to allow the charts within the dashboard to be updated whenever a user manipulates a control.

First, we will need to develop programs which will retrieve our information, which is dependent on the type of data the user selects. Remember, the key to successful program development is to not reinvent the wheel. We will use some existing open source code to make our program as reliable and simple as possible.

# Gathering Microsoft Excel, CSV, JSON, and Database Data

The code included with this chapter contains several data files (data.csv, data.json, and datatest.xlsx). The Excel spreadsheet provided was used to design the data format and contents used for our testing. The CSV file, JSON file, and database table were created by extracting the spreadsheet data and reformatting it for each data type. While these programs would not be used in production, it gives us examples of how to retrieve information from an Excel spreadsheet and reformat it to another data format.

***Listing 10-1.*** createCSV.php

```php
<?php
use Shuchkin\SimpleXLSX;

require_once __DIR__.'/simplexlsx-master/src/SimpleXLSX.php';

if ( $xlsx = SimpleXLSX::parse('testdata.xlsx') ) {
  $values = $xlsx->rows();
  $file = fopen("data.csv","w");
            foreach ($values as $value) {
                fputcsv($file, $value);
```

```
                                        }
                                        echo "data.csv created";
    fclose($file);
} else {
        echo SimpleXLSX::parseError();
}
?>
```

One of the popular ways to access Microsoft Excel data using PHP is with the open source *SimpleXLSX class* available on GitHub: `https://github.com/shuchkin/simplexlsx`.

This class can be downloaded from the link provided and placed within the `ch10` folder after decompression. Code examples are provided at the web location and within the comments of the class itself. For your convenience, the files are already included within the `ch10` folder on the publisher's website.

```
use Shuchkin\SimpleXLSX;
```

The class includes a *namespace* (which will make sure it does not conflict with other existing classes). The `use` statement declares that any classes or functions used will be accessible through the namespace (`Shuchkin`) and the class name (`SimpleXLSX`).

```
require_once __DIR__ .'/simplexlsx-master/src/SimpleXLSX.php';
```

The `require_once` statement includes the PHP constant `__DIR__` which returns the current directory location. Thus, the class is imported from the `simplexlsx_master` source (`src`) directory within the current directory.

```
if ( $xlsx = SimpleXLSX::parse('testdata.xlsx') ) {
  $values = $xlsx->rows();
```

The `parse()` method of the `SimpleXLSX` class will retrieve all data from an Excel spreadsheet. This data includes more than just the values with the cells. Since we only are using the values stored in the cells, we can use the `SimpleXLSX` function `rows()` to retrieve the data in all rows. This function creates a two-dimensional array containing only the data, which we have named `$values`.

```
$file = fopen("data.csv","w");
                foreach ($values as $value) {
```

```
                    fputcsv($file, $value);

                                }
                            echo "data.csv created";

    fclose($file);
```

Using the PHP function fopen(), we can create a new file (data.csv) and declare that we want to write (w) to the file. The foreach loop will now loop through each data item within the $values array. The PHP function fputcsv() will pass the information into the file in comma separated format. Finally, once all information has been written, the file is closed using fclose(). We changed the format of our data with just a few lines of code!

---

**Note**   Visit www.php.net/manual/en/function.fopen.php for more information on fopen(). Visit www.php.net/manual/en/function.fputcsv. php for more information on fputcsv().

---

***Listing 10-2.***   createJSON.php

```php
<?php
use Shuchkin\SimpleXLSX;

require_once __DIR__ .'/simplexlsx-master/src/SimpleXLSX.php';

if ( $xlsx = SimpleXLSX::parse('testdata.xlsx') ) {
  $netJSON = json_encode($xlsx->rows());
  file_put_contents("data.json", $netJSON);
  echo "data.json created";
} else {
    echo SimpleXLSX::parseError();
}
?>

  $netJSON = json_encode($xlsx->rows());
  file_put_contents("data.json", $netJSON);
```

The logic to creating the *JSON file* is similar to the previous logic. However, to convert the data, we use the PHP function `json_encode()`. Once the data has been changed into JSON format, we can copy the complete contents of the JSON formatted data into a file using the PHP function `file_put_contents()`. Pretty quick and efficient!

---

**Note**   For more information on file_put_contents(), visit `www.php.net/manual/en/function.file-put-contents`.

---

*Listing 10-3.*  populateDatabase.php

```php
$<?php
use Shuchkin\SimpleXLSX;

include_once "models/Table.class.php";
require_once __DIR__.'/simplexlsx-master/src/SimpleXLSX.php';

if ( $xlsx = SimpleXLSX::parse('testdata.xlsx') ) {

  $dbInfo = "mysql:host=localhost;dbname=studentresults";
  $dbUser = "root";
  $dbPassword = "";
  $db = new PDO( $dbInfo, $dbUser, $dbPassword );
  $rows = $xlsx->rows();
  foreach($rows as $row) {
        if($row[0]=="Last Name") {
                continue;
        }
  }

  $lastname = $row[0]; $firstname = $row[1]; $gender = $row[2];
  $assignmentaverage = $row[3];
  $discussionaverage = $row[4]; $researchaverage = $row[5];
  $semesteraverage = $row[6]; $semestergrade = $row[7];

        $entrySQL = "INSERT INTO student_data( lastname, firstname,
        gender, assignmentaverage, discussionaverage,
        researchaverage, semesteraverage, semestergrade) VALUES
        ( ?, ?, ?, ?, ?, ?, ?, ?)";
```

```
                    $formData = array($lastname, $firstname, $gender,
                    $assignmentaverage, $discussionaverage, $researchaverage,
                    $semesteraverage, $semestergrade);
        $statement = $db->prepare( $entrySQL );
        $statement->execute( $formData );
}
            echo "Database studentresults, database table student_data
            populated";
} else {
        echo SimpleXLSX::parseError();
}
?>
```

Most of the logic for this program should now look familiar, as the program retrieves the data from the Excel spreadsheet using the same logic as before. It then opens the database and inserts the information into the database table.

---

**Note**    In order to use a different set of data, the code in this program would need to be modified for the new format. To populate your database table for testing, you can use this program in combination with the spreadsheet data provided with the chapter files. However, first, you would need to create the database and table using *phpMyAdmin*. The following fields should be created in the `student_data` table (which is located in the `studentresults` database): `studentindex` (auto increment) `lastname` (varchar), `firstname` (varchar), `gender` (varchar), `assignmentaverage` (float), `discussionaverage` (float), `researchaverage` (float), `semesteraverage` (float), `semestergrade` (varchar).

---

Now we have four types of test data available that we can use to populate our charts! We are ready to move onto the next steps!

But before we look at more code, we need to decide on the logic of our program. Let us think about the steps required for the user to provide us the necessary information along with the process of creating the dashboard and the charts.

- *Choose a file format*: Database, Excel spreadsheet, JSON, or CSV.

- *If database is chosen*: Determine the database to use and determine the table within the database.

- *If Excel spreadsheet is chosen*: Select the spreadsheet to use.

- *If JSON is chosen*: Select the JSON file to use.

- *If CSV is chosen*: Select the comma separated file to use.

- *For any choice*: Determine which numeric column to use and one additional column. One column must be numeric for the population of a slider control to display a chosen subset of data.

- *For any choice*: Retrieve the columns selected (array) and format them into a Google Data Table, which can be accessed by the dashboard and charts.

- *Display the charts*: Create the chart wrappers, bind the data, and draw the dashboard and charts (the steps we previously mentioned).

We will also use our basic MVC logic that we have developed from the previous chapters. This includes the use of the `Page_data.class.php` model from Chapter 9 to organize our program flow. We will make only slight modifications to the class to only accept information related to the dashboard program. To see the modifications, copy the files for this chapter from the publisher's website. Then open the file in a browser. We will create another model next to retrieve our data. We will also create any necessary controllers and views to complete the design of our application.

# Creating the Model Data Class

From the list of tasks needed for the program, many of these require the ability to access the data selected. These tasks all belong in a model class which will include functions to return the requested data from the requested data source (database, spreadsheet, JSON file, CSV file). Let us look at the functions required for each task. All the functions will reside in the `accessData.class.php` file.

Let us look at the functions required when selecting database data first.

***Listing 10-4.*** Function returnDatabases from accessData.class.php

```
function returnDatabases() {
    $user = 'root';
    $password = '';
    $dbInfo = "mysql:host=localhost";
    $pdo = new PDO($dbInfo, $user, $password);
    $stmt = $pdo->query('SHOW DATABASES');
    $databases = $stmt->fetchAll(PDO::FETCH_COLUMN);
    $data = "<select name='columns' id='columns'>";
    foreach($databases as $database){
            if(($database=="information_schema" or
            $database=="mysql" or
                $database=="performance_schema" or
                $database=="phpmyadmin"))
                { continue; }
            $data .= "<option value='$database'>$database</option>";

    }
    $data .= "</select>";
    return $data;
}
```

The function `returnDatabases()` creates a drop-down list of databases.

```
$pdo = new PDO($dbInfo, $user, $password);
$stmt = $pdo->query('SHOW DATABASES');
$databases = $stmt->fetchAll(PDO::FETCH_COLUMN);
```

The MySQL/MariaDB database management system is opened using the provided location (`localhost`), userid (`root`), and password (""). The SQL command `SHOW DATABASES` is then executed to return the databases and related information. Since we want only the database names, we use the PDO function `fetchAll()` with the `FETCH_COLUMN` parameter to create an array (`$databases`).

```
foreach($databases as $database){
    if(($database=="information_schema" or $database=="mysql" or
        $database=="performance_schema" or $database=="phpmyadmin"))
```

```
        { continue; }
    $data .= "<option value='$database'>$database</option>";
```

We will skip any standard databases which are populated by MySQL/MariaDB by using the command `continue`, which skips an iteration of the loop.

Once we have selected the database, we need to select a table within the selected database for our chart information.

***Listing 10-5.*** Function returnDatabaseTables from accessData.class.php

```
function returnDatabaseTables($database){
    $user = 'root';
    $password = '';
    $dbInfo = "mysql:host=localhost;dbname=$database";
    $pdo = new PDO( $dbInfo, $user, $password );
    $stmt = $pdo->query('SHOW TABLES');
    $tables = $stmt->fetchAll(PDO::FETCH_COLUMN);
    $data = "<input type='hidden' id='database' name='database'
    value='$database'>";
    $data .= "<select name='columns' id='columns'>";
    foreach($tables as $table){
        $data .= "<option value='$table'>$table</option>";
    }
    $data .= "</select>";
    return $data;
    }
```

```
$pdo = new PDO( $dbInfo, $user, $password );
$stmt = $pdo->query('SHOW TABLES');
$tables = $stmt->fetchAll(PDO::FETCH_COLUMN);
$data = "<input type='hidden' id='database' name='database'
value='$database'>";
```

First, we open access to the database by creating a new PDP Object ($pdo). Then we submit the SQL query `SHOW TABLES` to retrieve all table information from the database. We use the `fetchAll()` function with the `FETCH_COLUMN` parameter to create an array of table names ($tables). We save the database name in a hidden variable so we can use it in the next function called.

```
foreach($tables as $table){
        $data .= "<option value='$table'>$table</option>";
}
```

We create a drop-down list of all table names using a foreach loop. Next, we need to retrieve the column names in the table selected.

***Listing 10-6.*** Function returnDatabaseTitles from accessData.class.php

```
function returnDatabaseTitles($database, $table, $title, $flag=false) {
// $flag == false - all columns, == true only numeric columns
        $user = 'root';
        $password = '';
        $dbInfo = "mysql:host=localhost;dbname=$database";
        $pdo = new PDO( $dbInfo, $user, $password );
        $sqlstring = "select * from " . $table . " limit 1";
        $result = $pdo->query($sqlstring);
        $data = "<input type='hidden' id='database' name='database'
        value='$database'>";
        $data .= "<input type='hidden' id='table' name='table'
        value='$table'>";
        $data .= "<input type='hidden' id='title' name='title'
        value='$title'>";
        $data .= "<select name='titles' id='titles'>";
        $fields = array_keys($result->fetch(PDO::FETCH_ASSOC));
        $column_count = 0;
        foreach($fields as $column) {
                if($column_count == 0) {
                    $column_count = 1;
                                        continue;
                        }
                        if($flag==true) {
                        $meta = $result->getColumnMeta
                        ($column_count);
                        if($meta["native_type"]=="VAR_STRING") {
                        // assume string or number only
                        $column_count++;
```

```
                                    continue;
                                          }
                                    }
        $data .= "<option value='$column'>$column</option>";
        $column_count++;
        } //foreach
    $data .= "</select>";
    return $data;
}
```

```
function returnDatabaseTitles($database, $table, $title, $flag=false) {
```

The function call accepts four parameters. The $flag parameter is set to the default (false) if the parameter is not passed.

```
$pdo = new PDO( $dbInfo, $user, $password );
$sqlstring = "select * from " . $table . " limit 1";
$result = $pdo->query($sqlstring);
```

Next, we connect to the database table. Then execute an SQL command to retrieve just the first line of the table requested within the database. This will also retrieve other information about the table, including the column names.

```
$fields = array_keys($result->fetch(PDO::FETCH_ASSOC));
```

The PDO fetch() function, with the FETCH_ASSOC parameter, will create an associative array containing table information including the column names. The PHP function array_keys() will create an array of only the keys (not the values). The keys are the actual column names. These column names are stored in the array $fields.

```
if($column_count == 0) {
    $column_count = 1;
    continue;
}
```

The first column contains the auto numbered id field, which we do not need for our data. Thus, it will increment the counter and skip the rest of the current iteration of the loop.

```
if($flag==true) {
```

```
$meta = $result->getColumnMeta($column_count);
if($meta["native_type"]=="VAR_STRING") {
    // assume string or number only
    $column_count++;
    continue;
}}
```

The user will select two columns, one that is numeric and one that can be any type. This function accepts a parameter ($flag) which will indicate if the call to the function will return only numeric columns ($flag==true) or all columns ($flag==false). If numeric only, the *metadata* for the current column is retrieved and placed into $meta. The associative array created includes a key "native_type" which provides the data type set for the column in the database table. If the value is "VAR_STRING", we skip it, increment the counter, and go to the next column.

```
$data .= "<option value='$column'>$column</option>";
$column_count++;
```

If the flag is true, and we found a numeric column, or the flag is false, we create an entry in the drop-down list for the current column. We now have the ability to select the columns. Let us retrieve the data for those columns.

***Listing 10-7.*** Function returnDatabaseData from accessData.class.php

```
function returnDatabaseData($database, $table, $row, $column){
        $user = 'root';
        $password = '';
        $dbInfo = "mysql:host=localhost;dbname=$database";
        $pdo = new PDO( $dbInfo, $user, $password );
        $sqlString = "SELECT " . $row . " , " . $column . " From "
        . $table;
        $results = $pdo->prepare($sqlString);
        $results->execute();
        $result = $results->fetchAll();
        return $result;
}
```

Hopefully, this listing is logical at this point. It is similar to what we have shown in the previous chapters.

**Exercise**: Function `returnDatabaseData()` and function `returnDatabaseTitles()` do not use prepared statements. Although it might be pretty safe in this circumstance, change both functions to use prepared statements, to provide the best security possible.

Now that we have the ability to retrieve database data, let us look at retrieving Microsoft Excel data. We will assume that we only have one spreadsheet within an *Excel workbook*. We will also assume the column titles are in the first row of the spreadsheet.

***Listing 10-8.*** Function returnExcelTitles from accessData.class.php

```php
function returnExcelTitles($file, $title, $title_Name, $flag=false) {
        //$flag==true return only numbers, $flag==false return all
        if ( $xlsx = SimpleXLSX::parse($file) ) {
                $rows = $xlsx->rows();
                $data = "<input type='hidden' id='numeric_Title'
                name='numeric_Title' value='$title'>";
                $data .= "<input type='hidden' id='numeric_Name'
                name='numeric_Name' value='$title_Name'>";
                $data .= "<input type='hidden' id='filename'
                name='filename' value='$file'>";
                $data .= "<select name='all_Columns' id='all_Columns'>";
                $count = 0;
                foreach($rows[0] as $column) {
                        if($flag==true) {
                if(is_string($rows[1][$count])) {
                //assume values numbers or strings $count++;
                continue;
                        }
                    }
            $value = $count . ',' . $column;
            $data .= "<option value='$value'>$column</option>";
            $count++;
        }
        $data .="</select>";
        return $data;
```

```
    } else {
        echo SimpleXLSX::parseError();
    }
}
```

Most of the logic from the function is similar to the database function, with a few exceptions.

```
if ( $xlsx = SimpleXLSX::parse($file) ) {
        $rows = $xlsx->rows(); }
```

The Excel spreadsheet is parsed using the SimpleXLSX class. The parse() function returns a standard object containing the spreadsheet and its related information. The rows() function will retrieve the data only from the object and create an array ($rows).

```
foreach($rows[0] as $column) {
        if($flag==true) {
                if(is_string($rows[1][$count])) {
                        //assume values numbers or strings
                        $count++;
                        continue;
                }}
```

The foreach loop will look at the first row only (which contains the titles of the columns). If $flag is true (only retrieves numerical columns), the PHP function is_string() will look at the next row (the first row of actual data), in the same column to determine if it is a string. If it is, the column is skipped.

```
$data = "<input type='hidden' id='numeric_Title' name='numeric_Title'
value='$title'>";
$data .= "<input type='hidden' id='numeric_Name' name='numeric_Name'
value='$title_Name'>";
$data .= "<input type='hidden' id='filename' name='filename'
value='$file'>";
$data .= "<select name='all_Columns' id='all_Columns'>";
$count++;
```

If the flag equals `true` and the column is numeric, or when the flag is `false`, the numeric title (which was passed into the function), the title (column) name, and the file name are saved for future use in hidden variables. The column name is placed into a drop-down box. The counter is then incremented.

```
} else {
   echo SimpleXLSX::parseError();
}
```

If there is a problem parsing the spreadsheet, the parsing error is displayed.

**Exercise**: In function `returnExcelTitles()` instead of echoing the error, raise and capture the error using `try/catch`. Also, adjust any other programs that need try/catch to capture problems.

We now have determined the columns; let us retrieve the actual data in the columns.

***Listing 10-9.*** Function returnExcelData in accessData.class.php

```
function returnExcelData($file, $row, $col) {

                    if ( $xlsx = SimpleXLSX::parse($file) ) {
                            $rows = $xlsx->rows();
                            $i = 0;
                            foreach($rows as $column) {
                                    $results[$i][0] = $column[$row];
                                    $results[$i][1] = $column[$col];
                                    $i++;
                            }
                        return $results;
                    } else {
                    echo SimpleXLSX::parseError();
                    }
            }

$i = 0;
foreach($rows as $column) {
        $results[$i][0] = $column[$row];
        $results[$i][1] = $column[$col];
        $i++;
}
```

The only actual change in the code from the previous example is what occurs within the foreach loop. The first column to retrieve is in $row, and the second column to retrieve is in $col. The column information is placed into the $results array, which is returned. The values for $row and $col will be set when the user selects the columns they want to use.

Let us move on to the *CSV file* and the ability to access its column names and column data.

***Listing 10-10.*** Function returnCSVTitles from accessData.class.php

```
function returnCSVTitles($file, $title, $title_Name, $flag=false) {
        //$flag==true return only numbers, $flag==false return all
        $file_to_read = fopen($file, 'r');
        if($file_to_read !== FALSE){
        $data ="<input type='hidden' id='CSV_Numeric_Title' name='CSV_
        Numeric_Title' value='$title'>";
                        $data .= "<input type='hidden' id='CSV_Numeric_
                        Name' name='CSV_Numeric_Name'  value='$title_
                        Name'>";
                        $data .= "<input type='hidden' id='CSV_
                        Filename' name='CSV_Filename' value='$file'>";
                        $data .= "<select name='columns'
                        id='columns'>";
                        $info = fgetcsv($file_to_read, 1000, ',');
                        $info2 = fgetcsv($file_to_read, 1000, ',');
                        for($i = 0; $i < count($info); $i++) {
                if($flag==true) {
                        if(!is_numeric($info2[$i])) {
                        continue;
                        }
                }
                $value = $i . ',' . $info[$i];
                $data .= "<option value='$value'>$info[$i]</option>";
                }
                $data .= "</select>";
                fclose($file_to_read);
```

```
                    return $data;
        }
}
```

The general logic is the same, but there are several differences from the previous example.

```
$file_to_read = fopen($file, 'r');
if($file_to_read !== FALSE){
```

The CSV file will be opened using the PHP function fopen(). The r parameter indicates that it is open for *read mode*. We now have a channel to access the file data. If we were able to open the file, we would retrieve the column titles.

```
$info = fgetcsv($file_to_read, 1000, ',');
$info2 = fgetcsv($file_to_read, 1000, ',');
```

We will grab two rows of information (up to 1000 characters). fgetcsv() will create an array, using the comma as the delimiter to determine what values are placed in each column in the array. $info will contain the column names (assuming the column names are in the first row). $info2 will contain the first row of data.

```
for($i = 0; $i < count($info); $i++) {

    if($flag==true) {
        if(!is_numeric($info2[$i])) {
        continue;
        }
}}
```

If the flag is set to true, we only want numerical data. The PHP function is_numeric() will look at the same column in the second row to see if it is numeric or not. If it is not numeric, the iteration of the loop will be skipped.

```
$data .= "<option value='$i'>$info[$i]</option>";
```

If the flag was set to true, and the data is numeric, or if the flag is set to false, the current column name is placed into the drop-down list.

Let us retrieve the CSV data.

***Listing 10-11.*** Function returnCSVData from accessData.class.php

```php
function returnCSVData($file, $row, $col) {

    $file_to_read = fopen($file, 'r');
    if($file_to_read !== FALSE){
        $lines = array();
    while(!feof($file_to_read) && ($line =
    fgetcsv($file_to_read)) !== false) {
        $lines[] = $line;
        }
        $i = 0;
        foreach($lines as $line) {
            $results[$i][0] = $line[$row];
            $results[$i][1] = $line[$col];
            $i++;
        }
        return $results;
            fclose($file_to_read);
        }
    }

$file_to_read = fopen($file, 'r');
if($file_to_read !== FALSE){
    $lines = array();
```

If we can open the file, an empty array, $lines, is created.

```php
while(!feof($file_to_read) && ($line =
fgetcsv($file_to_read)) !== false) {
    $lines[] = $line;
}
```

If we are not at the end of the file (feof) and we can read data from the CSV file, then we place that data into the $lines array. fgetcsv() will create an array of the data from the current line. That array is actually added to the $lines array. A lot in just two lines!

```php
foreach($lines as $line) {
```

```
        $results[$i][0] = $line[$row];
        $results[$i][1] = $line[$col];
        $i++;
}
```

However, we only want the two columns the user specifies, so we retrieve each column using the $row and $col as the indexes and create a new $results array which contains only the two columns.

Finally, let us look at the process for a JSON file.

***Listing 10-12.*** Function returnJSONTitles from accessData.class.php

```
function returnJSONTitles($file, $title, $title_Name, $flag=false) {
    // Read the JSON file
    $json = file_get_contents($file);
    // Decode the JSON file
    $json_data = json_decode($json,true);
    $data = "<input type='hidden' id='JSON_Numeric_Title' name='JSON_
    Numeric_Title' value='$title'>";
    $data .= "<input type='hidden' id='JSON_Numeric_Name' name='JSON_
    Numeric_Name' value='$title_Name'>";
    $data .= "<input type='hidden' id='JSON_Filename' name='JSON_
    Filename' value='$file'>";
    $data .= "<select name='columns' id='columns'>";
    // Display data
    $i = 0;
    foreach($json_data[0] as $title) {
            if($flag==true) {
                if(!is_numeric($json_data[1][$i])) {
                    $i++;
                    continue;
                }
            }
            $value = $i . ',' . $title;
            $data .= "<option value='$value'>$title</option>";
            $i++;
    }
```

```
        $data .= "</select>";
        return $data;
}
```

```
// Read the JSON file
$json = file_get_contents($file);
```

```
// Decode the JSON file
$json_data = json_decode($json,true);
```

We will use the PHP function file_get_contents() to retrieve the complete file at once and place it into $json. We will then use the PHP function json_decode() to convert the JSON data into a PHP array ($json_data).

```
foreach($json_data[0] as $title) {
    if($flag==true) {
        if(!is_numeric($json_data[1][$i])) {
            $i++;
            continue;
        }
    }
}
```

We will loop through the first row of data (where the titles are kept). If the flag is true, we will check the same column of the second row (the first row that actually has data) to see if it is not numeric. If it is not, we skip the result of the iteration of the loop.

```
$data .= "<option value='$i'>$title</option>";
```

If the flag is true and the data is numeric, or the flag is false, we save the column name in the drop-down box.

Let us retrieve the actual JSON data.

***Listing 10-13.*** Function returnJSONData from accessData.class.php

```
function returnJSONData($file, $row, $col) {

                    // Read the JSON file
                    $json = file_get_contents($file);

                    // Decode the JSON file
                    $json_data = json_decode($json,true);
```

```
                    $i = 0;
                        foreach($json_data as $column) {
                                $results[$i][0] = $column[$row];
                                $results[$i][1] = $column[$col];
                                $i++;
                        }
                        return $results;
            }
            }
```

This code is similar to the last example.

```
// Read the JSON file
    $json = file_get_contents($file);

            // Decode the JSON file
            $json_data = json_decode($json,true);
```

We first dump the complete contents of the file into $json. Then we use json_decode() to create an array of the JSON data ($json_data).

```
foreach($json_data as $column) {
        $results[$i][0] = $column[$row];
        $results[$i][1] = $column[$col];
        $i++;
}
```

For each row of data in the $json_data array, we pull the two columns of data requested by the user and place them into the array $result, which is then returned.

**Exercise**: Create a test program that will test each of the functions provided in the accessData.class.php program. Did you discover any problems? If so, correct those problems before moving on.

# Creating the Drop-Down and File Type Views

Let us create some views to handle our information we are requesting from the user. First, we need to request the file type of the data to be used. We can use a simple radio button collection to gather this information.

*Listing 10-14.* filetype-form-html.php

```php
<?php
//complete code for views/fileType-form-html.php

$info .= "
<form action='index.php?page=fileType' method='post' id='fileType-form'>

        <label>Select the data file type</label><br><br>
        <input type='radio' id='Database' name='file_type'
        value='Database'>
        <label for='Database'>mySQL/MariaDB Database</label><br>
        <input type='radio' id='Excel' name='file_type' value='Excel'>
        <label for='Excel'>Microsoft Excel</label><br>
        <input type='radio' id='JSON' name='file_type' value='JSON'
        <label for='JSON'> JSON - JavaScript Array</label><br>
        <input type='radio' id='CSV' name='file_type' value='CSV'>
        <label for='CSV'>CSV - Comma Separated</label><br>

    <input type='submit' value='submit' />
</form>";
?>
```

This form provides four selections for the data file type (Database, Excel, JSON, CSV). Whichever the user chooses, the value is saved into the file_type name and passed back to the index.php page, along with the page value which is set to filetype.

After the user selects the data file type, if they select "Database", the list of databases must be provided, followed by the list of tables within the database, finally followed by the list of numerical columns and all columns. If the user selects any of the other choices, after selecting the file to open, the logic will jump to listing the numerical columns and all columns.

In the functions created in the accessData class, drop-down boxes were already created. Our form(s) need only provide the form information and submit button along with the drop-down box. This process is the same for most of the views (except for gathering the name of any nondatabase file to open). Thus, we can create one shell HTML view which will accept the drop-down box code and display a form around it. This will reduce our coding from many forms to gather this information to just one.

***Listing 10-15.*** dropdown-form-html.php

```php
<?php
//complete code for views/dropdown-form-html.php

$idIsFound = isset($type);
$DDIsFound = isset($dropdown);

if( $idIsFound === false ) {
    trigger_error('views/dropdown-html.php needs an $type');
}
if( $DDIsFound === false ) {
    trigger_error('views/dropdown-html.php needs an $dropdown');
}
$info .= "
<form action='index.php?page=$type' method='post' id='comment-form'>

        <label>Select one $type</label><br>"
                . $dropdown .
        "<br><br><input type='submit' value='submit!' />
</form>";
?>
```

The code expects two values to be set ($type, $dropdown). $type will describe what type of data we are requesting ("Database", "Table", ...). If either is missing, the program will raise an error. If they are provided, then the form tag uses the $type value to set the page parameter. The code in $dropdown is displayed between the label requesting the user selection and the submit button. A simple shell that does a lot of work for us!

To complete gathering information from the user, we need a form to select any nondatabase file to open.

***Listing 10-16.*** file-form-html.php

```php
<?php
//complete code for views/admin/file-form-html.php

$idIsFound = isset($type);
$FTIsFound = isset($file_type);

if( $idIsFound === false ) {
```

381

```php
    trigger_error('views/file-form-html.php needs an $type');
}
if( $FTIsFound === false ) {
    trigger_error('views/dropdown-html.php needs an $file_type');
}

$info .= "<h1>Select $type Data File<h1>
<form method='post' action='index.php?page=$type'
    enctype='multipart/form-data'>
    <input type='file' name='filename' id='filename' accept='$file_type' />
    <input type='submit' name='submit' id='submit' value='upload' />
</form>
";
?>
```

If $type and $file_type are set, then the form will restrict the file type selection to the value in $file_type, and it will use $type to display the request for a file to open. $type will also be passed into the page parameter when the information is passed to the index file. We now have the ability to request all the required information from the user. Let us take a look at the main controller and the other controllers.

## Creating the Front Door Controller and the Subcontrollers

Most of the code for the front door controller (index.php) should look familiar.

***Listing 10-17.*** index.php

```php
<?php
//complete code for ch10/index.php
$info = "";
require_once __DIR__.'/simplexlsx-master/src/SimpleXLSX.php';
require_once "models/Page_Data.class.php";
$pageData = new Page_Data();
$pageData->setTitle("PHP Dashboard demo");

$pageRequested =  isset( $_GET['page'] );
//default controller file_type
$controller = "file_type";
```

```php
if ($pageRequested ) {
    $controller = $_GET['page'];
}
include_once "controllers/$controller.php";
$pageData->setContent($info);
include_once "views/page.php";
echo $page;
?>
```

Let us look at a couple of differences from our previous main controllers.

```php
require_once __DIR__ .'/simplexlsx-master/src/SimpleXLSX.php';
```

We will use the open source class SimpleXLSX to access our Excel file. Thus, we will retrieve the code from its folder location.

```php
$controller = "file_type";
```

Our default program will be file_type.php which requests the user to select the file type.

---

**Note**   This current version of the program requires the file which contains the data to exist within the same folder as the program. This can be adjusted by the reader to accept the full pathname.

---

Let us take a look at the other controllers. Once the file type is selected, the file type controller is called.

***Listing 10-18.*** filetype.php

```php
<?php
// complete code for controllers/fileType.php
if(isset($_POST['file_type'])) {
        $file_type = $_POST['file_type'];
        require_once "models/accessData.class.php";
        $dataObject =  new accessData();
        if($file_type == "Database") {
            $type = "Database";
```

```
                $dropdown = $dataObject->returnDatabases();
                require_once "views/dropdown-form-html.php";
        }
        else if($file_type == "Excel") {
                $type = "Excel";
                $file_type = ".xlsx";
                require_once "views/file-form-html.php";
        }
        else if($file_type == "JSON") {
                $type = "JSON";
                $file_type = ".json";
                require_once "views/file-form-html.php";
        }
        else if($file_type == "CSV") {
                $type = "CSV";
                $file_type = ".csv";
                require_once "views/file-form-html.php";
        }
}
?>

$file_type = $_POST['file_type'];
require_once "models/accessData.class.php";
$dataObject =  new accessData();
if($file_type == "Database") {
    $type = "Database";
    $dropdown = $dataObject->returnDatabases();
    require_once "views/dropdown-form-html.php";
}
```

If the file_type is populated, an instance of the accessData() class is created. If the file type chosen is "Database", then the $type variable is set to "Database" and the returnDatabases() function is called and passed to the dropdown-form-html.php, which will display the databases available to choose.

```
else if($file_type == "Excel") {
        $type = "Excel";
```

```php
    $file_type = ".xlsx";
    require_once "views/file-form-html.php";
}
```

If any of the other file types are chosen, the $type variable is set to the type of file, and the $file_type variable is set to the required file ending, which is then used in the file-form-html.php form to request the user pick a file of the set file type.

Once the database or file is selected, each type of file (Database, Excel, JSON, CSV) will require a controller which will be called when the particular file type is chosen. Let us look at each of these controllers.

***Listing 10-19.*** Database.php

```php
<?php
// complete code for controllers/Database.php
if(isset($_POST['columns'])) {
        $database = $_POST['columns'];
        require_once "models/accessData.class.php";
        $dataObject =  new accessData();
        $type = "Table";
        $dropdown = $dataObject->returnDatabaseTables($database);
        require_once "views/dropdown-form-html.php";
        }
?>
```

The columns variable (which contains the database selected) must be set. If it is, the database name is placed in $database. An instance of accessData() is created ($dataObject); the $type variable is set to "Table", which is then used by the returnDatabaseTables() function to create the drop-down list. It is then displayed using dropdown-form-html.php, which displays the tables within the database selected.

***Listing 10-20.*** Excel.php

```php
<?php
// complete code for controllers/Excel.php
use Shuchkin\SimpleXLSX;
if(isset($_FILES['filename']['name'])){
        $file =$_FILES['filename']['name'];
```

```
    require_once "models/accessData.class.php";
    $dataObject =  new accessData();
    $type = "Numeric_Column";
    $dropdown = $dataObject->returnExcelTitles($file,'','', true);
    require_once "views/dropdown-form-html.php";
    }
?>
```

If Excel was chosen as the file type, the if statement will verify that an Excel file was also chosen. If it was chosen, the file name will be placed into $file. An instance ($dataObject) of accessData() is created. The $type is set to "Numeric_Column", which will be used by the drop-down form. The function returnExcelTitles() is called, with the $file variable, and the Boolean value true is passed. This will cause the function to only retrieve numeric column names. The middle two parameters are set to "", because they are not needed in this process. The form including a drop-down list of the numeric columns is displayed for the user to make a selection.

Both the JSON.php and CSV.php controllers use similar logic to the Excel.php program. Once a numeric column has been selected, then another column must be selected. All the file types will call the Numeric_Column.php controller to request another column.

***Listing 10-21.*** Partial Listing of Numeric_Column.php

```
use Shuchkin\SimpleXLSX;
if((isset($_POST['table'])) and (isset($_POST['database']))and (isset
($_POST['titles']))){
    // database
    $columns = $_POST['table'];
    $database = $_POST['database'];
    $title = $_POST['titles'];
    require_once "models/accessData.class.php";
    $dataObject =  new accessData();
    $type = "Column";
    $dropdown = $dataObject->returnDatabaseTitles($database,
    $columns, $title);
    require_once "views/dropdown-form-html.php";
    }
```

If the database, the table, and the numeric column have been selected (as determined by the `if` statement), the table name, database name, and numeric column are stored in variables. An instance of the `accessData()` class is created, the `$type` variable is set to "Column", and this information is passed into the `returnDataTitles()` function. Because no value is passed into the fourth parameter, the function will set the flag to `false` to display all columns in the drop-down list. The drop-down form will then display the list for the user to select another column.

***Listing 10-22.*** Partial Listing of Numeric_Column.php

```
else if((isset($_POST['filename'])) and (isset($_POST['all_Columns']))) {
        // Excel
        $file = $_POST['filename'];
        $numeric_Column = $_POST['all_Columns'];
        require_once "models/accessData.class.php";
        $dataObject =  new accessData();
        $type = "Column";
        $numeric_Info = explode(",", $numeric_Column);
        $dropdown = $dataObject->returnExcelTitles($file,$numeric_
        Info[0],$numeric_Info[1]);
        require_once "views/dropdown-form-html.php";
}
```

If the Excel file type was selected, the function will verify that an Excel file has been selected, and a numeric column has been chosen. If so, the file name and numeric column name are stored in variables. The `$type` variable is set to `"Column"`. The information retrieved from the previous call to this function will pass back both the column number and column name. The PHP function `explode()` will create an array by breaking apart a string with a *delimiter* (,). This will place the column number in the zero position and the column name in the first position of the array. The file name, the column number, and the column name are passed into the function `returnExcelTitles()`. Again, since the fourth parameter is not passed, the function will create a drop-down list of all columns, which is displayed using the function `returnExcelTitles()`. The user can now select another column. The logic for the JSON and CSV code within the `Numeric_Column.php` file is the same as the Excel logic.

Once a second column has been selected, the program will finally have enough information to display the dashboard. Each of the file types will call the Column.php controller to finish the process.

***Listing 10-23.*** Partial Listing of Column.php

```
if((isset($_POST['table'])) and (isset($_POST['database'])) and
        (isset($_POST['titles'])) and (isset($_POST['title']))){
        // Database
        $columns = $_POST['table'];
        $database = $_POST['database'];
        $Label = $_POST['titles'];
        $RangeLabel = $_POST['title'];
        require_once "models/accessData.class.php";
        $dataObject =  new accessData();
        $Data = $dataObject->returnDatabaseData($database, $columns,
        $Label, $RangeLabel);
        require_once "views/googleDashboard.php";
        $info .= displayDashboard($Data, $RangeLabel, $Label);
        }
```

If the database, table, numeric column, and another column (as verified by the if statement) have all been determined, the program can finish the process of displaying the dashboard. All four of these values are placed into corresponding variables. An instance of the accessData() class is created. Then all the variables are passed into the returndatabaseData() function. This function will return a two-column array with the information requested. Now that the table has been created, the googleDashboard. php program will be included. This program includes the function displayDashboard() which will use the array ($Data) and the column names ($Rangelabel, $label) to create the dashboard.

***Listing 10-24.*** Partial Listing of Column.php

```
else if((isset($_POST['filename'])) and (isset($_POST['numeric_Title']))
and ($_POST['all_Columns']) and ($_POST['numeric_Name'])) {
                //Excel
                $file = $_POST['filename'];
```

```
        $numeric_Column = $_POST['numeric_Title'];
        $numeric_Name = $_POST['numeric_Name'];
        $columns = $_POST['all_Columns'];
        $columns_Info = explode(',',$columns);
        require_once "models/accessData.class.php";
        $dataObject =  new accessData();
        $Data = $dataObject->returnExcelData($file, $columns_
        Info[0], $numeric_Column);
        require_once "views/googleDashboard.php";
        $info .= displayDashboard($Data, $numeric_Name, $columns_
        Info[1]);
    }
```

If any of the nondatabase types are selected, similar logic is used to prepare for the display of the dashboard. The file name, numeric column name, numeric column number, and the column information for the other column are stored in variables. The information for the other column is transformed into an array using explode(). An instance of the accessData() class is created. The file name, numeric column name, and the other column name are all passed into the returnExcelData() function. This function will return a two-dimensional array containing the requested information. The Dashboard.php file is then imported. The displayDashboard() function is called, passing the array data ($Data), the name of the numeric column, and the name of the other column. This will display our dashboard.

It is finally time to display our dashboard! The code used to prepare our dashboard is a mixture of PHP, HTML, and JavaScript. To allow the learner ability to relate this example to other Google Dashboard examples, we borrowed code directly from the Google Charts website, with a few modifications.

---

**Note**   This exercise provides us practice in preparing data for display within graphical charts. The code, up until this point, is not actually dependent on using Google Charts for the actual display of information. The programmer (you) can modify this code to prepare data for any charting tool available. Google Charts is not designed for displaying large amounts of data (thousands of records). The actual data is uploaded into the Google Charts API (application programming interface) on the Google website. Thus, you would not want the inefficiency of trying to upload thousands of records. Also, because the data is sent to Google, we must consider security risks. If this data is intended to be public information (or not secure information), then Google Charts is a good choice. If the information needs to be secure, then another application should be used.

---

***Listing 10-25.*** Partial Listing of googleDashboard.php

```php
<?php
function displayDashboard($Data, $RangeLabel, $Label) {
$info = "<html>
  <head>
    <!--Load the AJAX API-->
    <script type='text/javascript' src='https://www.gstatic.com/charts/
    loader.js'></script>
    <script type='text/javascript'>

      // Load the Visualization API and the controls package.
      google.charts.load('current', {'packages':['corechart',
      'controls']});
      // Set a callback to run when the Google Visualization API is loaded.
      google.charts.setOnLoadCallback(drawDashboard);

      // Callback that creates and populates a data table,
      // instantiates a dashboard, a range slider, and charts,
      // passes in the data and draws it.
      function drawDashboard() {
              var data = new google.visualization.DataTable();
              // Add columns
              data.addColumn('string','" . $Label . "');
              data.addColumn('number','" . $RangeLabel . "');
              ";
```

We can now complete the requirements to display our dashboard. First, we will import the Google Charts JavaScript Loader code, which is an *AJAX API*. AJAX is a JavaScript code which provides asynchronous display of information within a web page. It allows portions of the page to be updated, without having to reload the complete web page (like we have been doing up until now). This allows the program to change chart information without affecting the rest of the page. Next, we call the Google Visualization API, with parameters that indicate which items will be displayed using AJAX. In this example, we include the charts and the controls. The `OnLoadCallback()` function redraws the dashboard every time an attempt is made to reload the page. The function `drawDashboard()` is a JavaScript function which creates the `DataTable` from the array and sets the parameters for the dashboard, slider, and charts. An instance of the `DataTable` (data) is created. Then the `$RangeLabel` variable (passed into the PHP function (`displayDashBoard()`) containing the numeric column name, which is added to the data table as a `'number'` column. The other column name (`$Label`) is also passed into the PHP function, as a `'string'` column.

***Listing 10-26.*** Partial Listing of googleDashBoard.php

```
$info .="data.addRows([";
        $count = 0;
        foreach($Data as $row) {
        if($count == 0) { $count++; continue; }
        $info .= "['" . $row[0] . "'," . $row[1] . "],";
        $count++;
        }
$info .= "]);
        // Create a dashboard.
        var dashboard = new google.visualization.Dashboard(
        document.getElementById('dashboard_div'));
```

Once the columns are defined, then we use PHP to `"addRows"` to our data table by pulling the information from the `$Data` array (passed into the PHP function). Once we have established the data table, we can complete the dashboard, controls, and charts information. We create an instance of the dashboard (`dashboard`) and define where it will exist in the web page (inside the HTML div tag identified as `'dashboard_div'`).

***Listing 10-27.*** Partial Listing of googleDashboard.php

```
// Create a range slider, passing some options";
        $info .="
        var donutRangeSlider = new google.visualization.ControlWrapper({
```

```
      'controlType': 'NumberRangeFilter',
      'containerId': 'filter_div',
      'options': {
        'filterColumnLabel': '" . $RangeLabel . "'
      }
    });

    var pieChart = new google.visualization.ChartWrapper({
      'chartType': 'PieChart',
      'containerId': 'chart_div',
      'options': {
        'width': 300,
        'height': 300,
        'pieSliceText': '" . $Label . "',
        'legend': 'right'
      }
    });

      var lineChart = new google.visualization.ChartWrapper({
      chartType: 'LineChart',
      options: {'title': '". $Label . "'},
     containerId: 'vis_div'
      });

      var columnChart = new google.visualization.ChartWrapper({
      chartType: 'ColumnChart',
      options: {'title': '" . $Label . "'},
      containerId: 'column_div'
      });

  var tableChart = new google.visualization.ChartWrapper({
    chartType: 'Table',
    containerId: 'table_div',
      options: {
                     'allowHtml': true,
                     'page': 'enable',
                     'width':'48%',
```

```
                        'height':'250px',
                        'pageSize': 10,
              'alternatingRowStyle' : true
                        }
      });
```

```
// Create a range slider, passing some options";
        $info .="
        var donutRangeSlider = new google.visualization.ControlWrapper({
          'controlType': 'NumberRangeFilter',
          'containerId': 'filter_div',
          'options': {
            'filterColumnLabel': '" . $RangeLabel . "'
          }
        });
```

We use *Control Wrappers* to set up each item we want to display in the dashboard. For the *range slider* (which the user can adjust and will automatically adjust the data displayed), we declare the div tag (`filter_div`) which will hold the slider, declare the actual range control to use (`NumberRangeFilter`), and declare that the numeric column name be displayed.

```
var pieChart = new google.visualization.ChartWrapper({
  'chartType': 'PieChart',
  'containerId': 'chart_div',
  'options': {
    'width': 300,
    'height': 300,
    'pieSliceText': '" . $Label . "',
    'legend': 'right'
  }
});
```

For the *PieChart*, we have similar settings, but also include some formatting, such as width and height. The label displayed will be the column name which is not specifically numeric. The *line chart* and *column chart* have similar settings.

```
var tableChart = new google.visualization.ChartWrapper({
```

```
chartType: 'Table',
 containerId: 'table_div',
  options: {
                    'allowHtml': true,
                    'page': 'enable',
                    'width':'48%',
                    'height':'250px',
                    'pageSize': 10,
                    'alternatingRowStyle' : true
          }
});
```

The *Table chart* has additional settings, including the ability to display HTML, paging ability (for more than ten rows), alternating row colors, and width and height settings.

***Listing 10-28.*** Partial Listing of googleDashboard.php

```
var formatter = new google.visualization.BarFormat({width: 120});
      formatter.format(data, 1); // Apply formatter to second column

    // Establish dependencies, declaring that 'filter' drives 'pieChart',
    // so that the pie chart will only display entries that are let through
    // given the chosen slider range.
     dashboard.bind(donutRangeSlider, [pieChart, tableChart,
     columnChart, lineChart]);
    // Draw the dashboard.
    dashboard.draw(data);
   }
 </script>
```

We can now *bind* the charts to the dashboard. This will cause all the charts bound to adjust (via AJAX) whenever the user slides the range bar. Finally, we can draw the dashboard. Of course, we need a place to display all the dashboard information.

***Listing 10-29.*** Partial Listing of googleDashboard.php

```
<body>
    <!--Div that will hold the dashboard-->
```

```
    <div id='dashboard_div'>
      <!--Divs that will hold each control and chart-->
      <div id='filter_div'
          style='display: flex;
            padding: 10px;
            justify-content: center;
            align-items: center;
            border: 3px solid black; '>
      </div>
      <div id='container_div' style=' width: 100%; margin-top: 20px;'>
      <div id='chart_div'
            style='
              justify-content: center;
              align-items: center;
              width: 48%;
              padding-left: 40px;
              margin-bottom: 20px;
              float: left;'>
    </div>
    <div id='table_div'></div>
    </div>
     <div id='column_div'
         style='float: clear;'>
     </div>
     <div id='vis_div'>
      </div>
    </div>
  </body>
</html>";
return $info;
```

The HTML code contains the div tags to define the location of the dashboard, slider, and charts. It also includes some formatting with CSS.

We can now run index.php from our browser, pick the data type, file (or database and table), and columns. Then our dashboard appears!

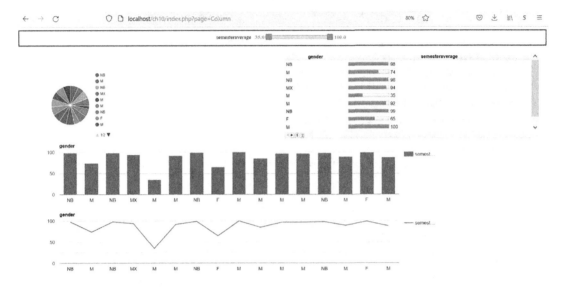

**Figure 10-1.** *Dashboard display from index.php*

Not a bad-looking dashboard! Play with the slider control. Select different columns. It is very interactive! There is a lot more that we can do and display. However, the formatting logic is similar for the over 30 charts you can use in a Google Dashboard.

---

**Note**   For more information on Google Charts, visit `https://developers.google.com/chart`.

---

Hopefully, this has increased your interest in what else PHP can do besides display web pages. When we receive data from outside sources, it can come in many formats. We used four common formats in this example. Sometimes, we need to merge data and eliminate any data that is invalid. While we can use one of PHP's many array functions (there are a lot) to merge our data, it will not be as efficient as using our source data platform to merge data. For example, if our data is all MySQL/MariaDB, we will have a much more efficient merging of data using the *SQL JOIN clause*.

---

**Note**   For more information on the SQL JOIN clause, visit `www.w3schools.com/sql/sql_join.asp`.

---

For multiple data sources that are Excel, we can use the *Consolidate Data Tool*.

> **Note**   For more information on the merging Excel spreadsheets, visit `https://support.microsoft.com/en-us/office/combine-data-from-multiple-sheets-dd7c7a2a-4648-4dbe-9a11-eedeba1546b4`.

For mixed data sources, we can either use an open source merging tool or transform our data using PHP into either MySQL/MariaDB or Excel data and use the methods we just mentioned. Anytime we want to merge data (even if we are using another programming language), we should use a data management system function, when available. They are efficient and, in many cases, can manage the merging of a lot of data. Always error on the side of efficiency!

**Exercise**: Using one of the techniques mentioned, merge data from multiple sources and then display the results using our Google Charts program.

One final note, the same should be said for any calculations we want to perform, such as creating averages, means, and modes. Use the tools available in the data management application to perform the math required, and then return the results back to the PHP program to be displayed in the dashboard. Using these techniques will improve the performance of data analysis using PHP.

Let us look at one last logical example before we close our last chapter.

# Creating the Logic for a Checkers Game

In this section, we will look at the logic in creating a checkers game. The intent is to demonstrate the important use of arrays to accomplish our mission. Hopefully, this example will demonstrate that an understanding of arrays is essential in becoming a good programmer. This exercise will also give us an opportunity to use embedded if/then/else structures and case statements. Along the way, we will also discover the use of the PHP substring function.

This example will provide several demonstrations on creating and updating a two-dimensional array which represents a checkerboard. It is not the intent of this example to provide the complete working code or the most efficient code. A more efficient example would include the use of recursive looping with objects. Something that is much more advanced than a beginning programmer should try to tackle. Once you have grasped this example (which might take a while to completely absorb), you can expand your knowledge by looking at the many examples on creating a checkers game on the Internet.

***Figure 10-2.*** *Empty checkerboard*

1. What is the first thing we do when we play checkers? Open the box and lay the board out on a table.

This would map directly to the first logical step in creating a checkers game. A `display_board()` function could be designed to show the initial board. Each time the user makes a move, the board will need to be redrawn to indicate a change in what is displayed. Thus, the `display_board()` function would be called every time the board must be redrawn.

Since the location of checkers on the board continuously changes, there needs to be a way to save these changes. As you can see from Figure 10-2, the checkerboard has rows and columns just like a two-dimensional array. We can use a two-dimensional array to represent the board and its contents.

The board has eight columns and eight rows. The red and black colors alternate by column and by row.

***Listing 10-30.*** Initial Checkerboard Array (checkerarray.php)

```php
<?php
$checker_board = array (
                array ( "black", "red", "black", "red", "black",
                "red", "black", "red" ),
                array ( "red", "black", "red", "black", "red" , "black",
                "red", "black" ),
                array ( "black", "red", "black", "red", "black", "red",
                "black", "red" ),
                array ( "red", "black", "red", "black", "red" , "black",
                "red", "black" ),
```

```
                array ( "black", "red", "black", "red", "black", "red",
                "black", "red" ),
                array (  "red", "black", "red", "black", "red" ,
                "black", "red", "black" ),
                array ( "black",  "red", "black", "red", "black", "red",
                "black", "red" ),
                array ( "red", "black", "red", "black", "red" , "black",
                "red", "black" )
);
?>
```

---

**Note**    In the image above the red and black squares are reversed from the image below. The arrays demonstrated are related to the images discussed.

---

Once the array has been created, as shown, the `display_board()` function can loop through the array, display the proper board, and color combinations using either a series of embedded if statements or a *switch* statement. While the switch statement was discussed in Chapter 5, we have not had an opportunity to demonstrate it. The following example shows how the switch statement can make it easier to understand the logic of the code.

*Listing 10-31.* display_board Function (display_board.php)

```php
<?php
function display_board() {

    foreach( $checker_board as $position) {

        switch ($position) {
                case "red" :
                // display a red square or image
                break;

                case "black":
                // display a black square or image
                break;
```

```
            default:
            print "Error displaying board";
            break;
            }
        }
    }
?>
```

The basic structure will loop through each position in the array, determine the color needed, and then display the color. Since there are many ways that the actual board image could be created, this code is left to the reader to determine.

We might create a two-dimensional table to contain each square. The squares then can be created using color blocks designed with HTML or we could insert small images for each position.

**Exercise**: Decide how you would like to display your red and white squares and add code to the switch structure to display the checkerboard.

2. After the player lays out the board on a table, the pieces are then placed in their proper positions. In an application, this can be done by replacing the positions in the array with the checkers pieces.

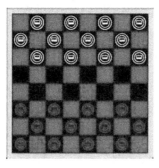

***Figure 10-3.*** *Checkerboard with pieces*

The programmer could choose to start the game with the pieces already on the board or require the user to indicate they are ready to play (such as clicking a 'start game' button). We will assume that the player must indicate they want to start a game (or a new game).

A start_game() function could execute each time the 'start game' button is clicked. This function places the checker pieces in the proper positions by updating the array containing the board and then calling the display_board() function to show the board with the checker pieces. As we know or can see from the previous image, all pieces go on the black squares. For the white pieces, the first-row pieces are in odd locations, the second row is even (assuming zero is even), and the third row odd again. The red pieces work in reverse.

*Listing 10-32.* start_game Function (start_game.php)

```php
<?php
function start_game() {
for ($I=0; $I < 8; $I++) {
if( ($I % 2 == 0 )&& ($I != 4 )) {
 for($J=1; $J < 8; $J = $J +2) {
        $checker_board[$I][$j] = ($J == 6) ? "red checker" : "white
        checker";
                }
        }
                else if(($I % 2 !=0) && ($I != 3)) {
                        for($J=0; $J < 8; $J = $J + 2) {
                        $checker_board[$I][$J] =  ($J == 1) ? "white checker" :
                        "red checker";
                        }
                }
        }
    }
    display_board();
}
?>
```

The outside for loop (containing $I) controls the rows. Then the initial if statement uses $I to determine if the row is even (again assuming that zero is even). If the row is even and not the empty row (4), then the $J for loop is called. This loop starts at column 1 (because a checker is not placed in column 0 on the zero row) and places a red or white checker in each black square on the board. If it is the sixth row, a "red checker" is placed. If it is any other row, a "white checker" is placed.

**Suggestion**: Either use a checkerboard or draw a checkerboard on paper and follow along with the logic of these examples.

---

**Note**   This example does not wipe out any checkers that are in the "blank" rows. This could be accomplished by coding a loop for the two rows involved and setting each usable position to "black".

---

The else part of the if statement manages the odd numbered rows. The logic is the same except $I start at 0 instead of 1. Also, if the row is 1, then a "white checker" is placed in the position. Otherwise, a "red checker" is placed. It skips the third empty row. After executing the start_game() function, the array would now contain the following.

***Listing 10-33.*** Checkerboard Array After Executing Start Game Function (game_ start_array.php)

```php
<?php
$checker_board = array (
        array ( "red", "white checker", "red", "white checker",
        "red",   "white checker", "red", "white checker" ),
        array ( "white checker", "red", "white checker", "red",   "white
        checker" , "red", "white checker", "red" ),
        array ( "red", "white checker", "red", "white checker",
        "red",   "white checker", "red", "white checker" ),
    array ( "black", "red", "black", "red", "black" , "red", "black",
    "red" ),
    array ( "red", "black", "red", "black", "red", "black", "red",
    "black" ),
    array ( "red checker", "red", "red checker", "red", "red checker" ,
    "red", "red checker", "red" ),
        array ( "red", "red checker", "red", "red checker", "red", "red
        checker", "red", "red checker" ),
        array ( "red checker", "red", "red checker", "red", "red
        checker" , "red",   "red checker", "red" )
);
?>
```

We will need to make some changes to the `display_board()` function to manage the addition of the checkers.

***Listing 10-34.*** Display Board Function Version 2 (display_board_version2.php)

```php
<?php
function display_board() {
foreach($checker_board as $position) {
        switch ($position) {
        case "red" :
            // display a red square or image
            break;

        case "black" :
             // display a black square or image
             break;

        case "white checker" :
             // display a white square or checker image
             break;

        case "red checker" :
             // display a reddish square or a checker image
             break;

         default:
             print "Error displaying board";
             break;
        }
    }
}
?>
```

We have added `case` procedures to manage the white and red checkers that now exist in the array. When the `start_game()` function calls this `display_board()` function, the board will display with the checkers in the proper positions.

3. It is now time for one of our players to move a checker. Let's only be concerned with trying to move a piece and not all the other factors that may affect our movement. We can always add to a working function after we determine the basic moves.

Top of board

| X | W | X | | W | X |
|---|---|---|---|---|---|
| W | X | **start** | | X | W |
| X | **a** | X | | **b** | X |

Using the preceding diagram, following the rules of checkers, if we want to move the 'start' white checker (not yet a king), it can only move to position 'a' or 'b'. All other positions are not valid. Notice that position 'a' is one row more than 'start'. Also notice that position 'b' is one more row than 'start'.

Thus, part of a valid move is movement only to the next row (we are not concerned with jumps yet). The column of 'a' is one less than the column of 'start'. The column of 'b' is one more than the column of 'start'. This indicates that a valid move is also determined if the column move is one less or one more than the original column. Try this logic and you will discover that this holds true for all moves from the top of the board toward the bottom of the board (until it becomes a king).

| X | **a** | X | | **b** | X |
|---|---|---|---|---|---|
| W | X | **start** | | X | W |
| X | W | X | | W | X |

Bottom of board

If we want to move a 'start' red checker, it moves in the reverse direction. The valid moves are indicated by positions 'a' and 'b'. Notice that the valid columns, again, are either one more or one less than the column of 'start'. The only difference is that the row will be one less than the row of 'start'. With the white 'start' checker, it was one more.

In order to determine valid moves, we will need to collect the original position (row, column) of the checker about to be moved and the location that the user is attempting to move the checker. Then we will need to make the comparison just described in the last couple of paragraphs.

---

**Note**   We could do the following collection of information by creating objects for each position in the board. However, to simplify this example, as much as possible, we will use a different technique.

---

If every black square on the board is a button and every red square is just an image, we eliminate the worry about the user trying to jump to a red square or even outside the board itself. We just have to concern ourselves with the restrictions already discussed.

Each black button will actually perform the same code, with one exception – the saving of its location in the $checker_board() array.

We can call a function from any of the buttons and pass the location in the array of that button.

```
make_move(3, 3);
```

Each button can pass the row and column of its location in the array into the make_move() function. The make_move() function will then determine if this is the first click (selecting the checker) or second click (indicating where the checker will move).

***Listing 10-35.*** Make Move Function (make_move.php)

```php
<?php
$first_click = false;
$first_row = -1;
$first_column = -1;
$second_row = -1;
$second_column= -1;
function make_move($row,$column) {
        If ($first_click == false) { // first click
            $first_click = true;
            $first_row = $row;
            $first_column = $column;
        }
        else { // second move because $first_click is true
            $first_click = false; // clears flag even if move is not
                                    valid to allow user to try again
            $second_row = $row;
            $second_column = $column;
            valid_move($first_row, $first_column, $second_row, $second_
            column);
        }
}
?>
```

The make_move() function must determine if it is the first click or second click. If it is the first click, the $first_click flag is set to true. Then the row and column that were passed into the function are saved into $first_row and $first_column. That is all that is needed with the first click. If it is a second click, then $first_click is set back to false, the values for the row and column are saved in $second_row and $second_column, and the four row and column values are passed into a valid_move() function.

***Listing 10-36.*** Valid Move Function (If Statement) (valid_move.php)

```php
<?php
function valid_move($first_row, $first_column, $second_row, $second_
column) {
If (($checker_board[$first_row] [$first_column] ==   "white checker") &&
    (checker_board[$second_row] [$second_column] ==  "black")){
    If(($second_row - $first_row == 1) &&
        (($second_column - $first_column == 1) ||
          ($second_column - $first_column == -1))) {
            $checker_board[$second_row][$second_column] = "white checker";
            $checker_board[$first_row][$first_column] = "black";
        }
    }
}
?>
```

The valid_move() function must determine what type of checker we are moving to determine the direction. If it is a white checker, we are moving from top to bottom. It must also make sure that the second clicked area is empty ("black" square). The second row must be one more than the first row. The second column must be one more or one less than the first column. If this is true, the "white checker" is placed in the array at the location of the second click. The position of the first click is changed to be empty ("black" square).

***Listing 10-37.*** Partial Valid Move Function (Else Statement) (valid_move_with_ else.php)

```php
} else {
```

```
        If ( ($checker_board[$first_row] [$first_column] ==  "red
        checker") &&
              ($checker_board[$second_row] [$second_column] ==  "black"))
          {
           If(($second_row - $first_row == -1) &&   (($second_column -
           $first_column == 1) ||
              ($second_column - $first_column == -1))) {
              $checker_board[$second_row][$second_column] = "red checker";
              $checker_board[$first_row][$first_column] = "black";
           }
       } // if both if statements fail it is not a valid move
     }
   display_board();
}
```

If the red checker is moved and the second clicked area is empty ("black" square), the valid_move() function will determine if the second row selected is one less than the first row. It will also determine if the column is one more or one less than the first column. If this is true, then the "red checker" is moved into the array at the position of the second click. The first click position is set to empty ("black" square).

If any of the following happens, the function will not make a move:

- The first click selected an empty space.

- The second click selected an occupied space.

- The second click did not select a proper square to move.

If a move is not made, the user can try again, because the $first_click flag was already set to false. The board is redisplayed (display_board()) whether or not a move took place. If it did take place, the display_board() function will show the changes.

4. Let us now consider the process of a checker becoming a 'King'. This would occur if a red checker reached row zero or a white checker reached row 7. We can add some if statements within our valid_move() function to determine this situation. Also, a king can move in a forward or backward direction. However, they still must follow the other rules.

***Listing 10-38.*** Valid Move Function Version 2 (If Statement) (valid_move_
version_2.php)

```php
<?php
function valid_move($first_row, $first_column, $second_row, $second_
column) {
        If (($checker_board[$first_row][$first_column] !=   "red
      checker") &&
           (checker_board[$second_row][$second_column] ==   "black")){
      If(($second_row - $first_row == 1) &&  (($second_column - $first_
      column == 1) ||
         ($second_column - $first_column == -1))) {
         If((second_row == 7) &&  ($checker_board[$first_row][$first_
         column] == "white checker"))
         {
            $checker_board[$second_row] [$second_column] = "white
            king"; }
            else {
               $checker_board[$second_row] [$second_column] =
               $checker_board[$first_row] [$first_column]; }
               $checker_board[$first_row] [$first_column] = "black";
         }
      }
   }
?>
```

Instead of checking for a white checker, white king, or red king to allow movement
down the board, it is a much shorter code to look for any object that is not a red checker.
Only red checkers cannot move down the board. However, when we check for row 7 to
determine if we need to crown a checker, we also need to make sure it is a white checker
in row 7. We cannot crown a red checker and do not need to crown a white or red king! If
we are not crowning a white checker, we are moving either a white checker, white king,
or red king to a new location. Since we do not know what is moving, we can take the
value from the first clicked location and copy it into the second clicked location. This will
move the proper item.

***Listing 10-39.*** Partial Valid Move Function Version 2 (Else Statement) (valid_move_version_2_with_else.php)

```
} } else {
      If ( ($checker_board[$first_row] [$first_column] !=  "white
      checker") &&
           ($checker_board[$second_row] [$second_column] ==  "black"))
           {
             If(($second_row - $first_row == -1) &&
               (($second_column - $first_column == 1) ||
                ($second_column - $first_column == -1))) {
                If((second_row == 0) &&
                  ($checker_board[$first_row] [$first_column] == "red
                  checker"))  {
                    $checker_board[$second_row][$second_column] =
                    "red king";
                    } else {
                    $checker_board[$second_row] [$second_column] =
                    $checker_board[$first_row] [$first_column];
             } // else
                  $checker_board[$first_row] [$first_column] = "black";
             } // end if $second_column - $first_column == -1
          } // not white checker - if both if statements fail it is not a
             valid move
      }
   display_board();
}
```

To move up the board, only a white checker is restricted. If a red checker reaches row 0, it is time to become a "red king". Now that we have movement down, we need to make an adjustment to our display_board() function to allow it to display "red king"s and "white king"s.

***Listing 10-40.*** Display Board Function Version 3 (display_board_version_3.php)

```php
<?php
function display_board() {
              foreach( $checker_board as $position) {
                    switch ($position) {
                          case "red" :
                              // display a red square or image
                          break;

                          case "black" :
                              // display a black square or image
                          break;

                          case "white checker" :
                              // display a white square or checker image
                          break;

                          case "red checker" :
                            // display a reddish square or a checker image
                          break;

                          case "white king" :
                                // display a king color square king
                                    checker image
                          break;

                          case "red king" :
                                // display a king color square king
                                    checker image
                          break;

                          default:
                            print "Error displaying board";
                          break;
                    }
              }
}
?>
```

410

As you can see, it only became necessary to add two additional `case` statements for the "white king" and the "red king".

5. Of course, there is no way to win this game unless we can jump the opponent and remove the piece from the board.

```
} // end if $second_column - $first_column == -1
} // not white checker - if both if statements fail it's not a valid move
}
display_board();
}
```

In the `valid_move()` function, if the flow of the code falls between the last two brackets, it is not a valid move. However, it might be a valid jump.

```
}
    } else { // not white checker, could it be a jump?
        valid_jump(($first_row, $first_column, $second_row, $second_
        column);
        }
    }
    display_board();
}
```

Instead of adding more code within the `valid_move()` function, it makes sense to instead create a `valid_jump()` function and call it if there was not a valid move.

Top of board

| W | X | W | X | W | X | W |
|---|---|---|-------|----|---|---|
| X | w | x | start | x | w | x |
| W | x | ar | x | br | x | w |
| X | a | x | w | | b | x |

Two valid jumps for the white 'start' checker would land the checker on 'a' or 'b'. One additional concern is that a red checker or red king must exist in the 'ar' or 'br' positions (the checker being jumped over). If a king does exist, in some checkers rules, it is not a valid jump. However, we will assume it is valid.

Logically, most of this is similar to the move process. Looking at this example, a valid jump for a white checker's row is two more than the original row. The column of a valid jump is two less or two more than the original column. If the checker jumps to 'a', we also need to check the position that is one less row and one more column than position 'a' to determine if a red checker or red king exists. If the checker jumps to 'b', we need to check the position that is one less row and one less column than position 'b' to determine if a red checker or red king exists. If the jump is valid, the 'start' position changes to an empty square, the 'ar' (or 'br') position changes to an empty square, and the 'a' position or 'b' position will now contain the checker that did the jumping.

***Listing 10-41.*** Partial Valid Jump Function (Right Side) (valid_jump.php)

```
function <?php
function valid_jump($first_row, $first_column,  $second_row, $second_
column) {
        if (($checker_board[$first_row] [$first_column] != "red
        checker") &&
           (checker_board[$second_row] [$second_column] ==  "black")){
            if($second_row - $first_row == 2) {
                if($second_column - $first_column == 2) {
                    // right side jump attempted
                        if(((($checker_board[$first_row + 1][$first_
                        column + 1] !=
                            "black") && // not jumping empty space
                            (substr(
                            $checker_board[$first_row +1] [$first_
                            column + 1],0,3) !=
                            substr(
                            $checker_board[$first_row] [$first_
                            column],0,3))))
                            // not jumping its own color
                            {
                                    if((second_row == 7) &&
                                    ($checker_board[$first_row] [$first_
                                    column] ==
```

```
                            "white checker")) { $checker_
                            board[$second_row][$second_
                            column] =
                              "white king";
                   } else {
                           $checker_board[$second_row]
                           [$second_column] = $checker_
                           board[$first_row][$first_column];
                   }

                             $checker_board[$first_row]
                             [$first_column] =
                          "black";
                              $checker_board[$first_row + 1]
                              [$first_column + 1] =
                          "black";
                     }
                } // end not jump own checker and not
                     jump empty
              } // end right side jump attempted
     else {
         if  ($second_column - $first_column == -2) {
             // left side jump attempted
                 if((($checker_board[$first_row+1][$first_
                   column-1] !=
                 "black") &&
                 // not jumping empty space
                 (substr(
                 $checker_board[$first_row+1][$first_
                 column-1],0,3) !=
                  substr(
                 $checker_board[$first_row][$first_
                 column],0,3))))
                 // not jumping its own color
             {

                 if((second_row == 7) &&
```

```
($checker_board[$first_row][$first_column] ==    "white checker"))  {
                                                $checker_board[$second_
                                                row][$second_column] =
                            "white king";
                                    } else {
                            $checker_board[$second_row][$second_
                            column] =
                            $checker_board[$first_row][$first_
                            column];
                }

                            $checker_board[$first_row] [$first_
                            column]= "black";
                            $checker_board[$first_row + 1][$first_
                            column - 1] =
                            "black";
                    } // end not jump own checker and not jump empty
                    } // end left side jump attempted
            } // end jumped two rows
        } // end not red and empty place to jump
}
?>
```

This is a lot of code. Take your time and break it down. Try to follow the logic discussed here. Looking at this half of the code, the logic (in order) that occurs is

1.  If the checker is not red, it can make a jump down the board. The place it is jumping to must also be empty ("black").

2.  If the jump is two rows more than the original position and two columns more than the original position, then a right side of the board jump is being attempted. (See #7 for left side jump.)

3.  If the checker did not jump over an empty ("black") space and the checker did not jump its own kind, then it is a valid jump. The code looks at the first three characters to match "red" or "white" for both the checkers and kings.

4.  Did the jumper checker land on row 7? If so, and the checker is
    white, then make it a king. If not, move the checker from the first
    position to the second position.

5.  Set the first position to empty ("black").

6.  Set the position jumped to black.

7.  Did the checker jump two columns to the left? If so, it is
    attempting to jump on the left side of the board.

8.  If the position jumped not empty (not "black") and not the
    checkers own type, then the jump is valid.

9.  Did the jumper checker land on row 7? If so, and the checker is
    white, then make it a king. If not, move the checker from the first
    position to the second position.

10. Set the first position to empty ("black").

11. Set the position jumped to black.

***Listing 10-42.*** Partial Valid Jump Function (Left Side) (valid_jump_with_
else.php)

```php
else {
    if (($checker_board[$first_row] [$first_column] != "white
    checker") &&
    (checker_board[$second_row] [$second_column] ==  "black")){
        if($second_row - $first_row == -2) {
        if($second_column - $first_column == 2) {
        // right side jump attempted
            if(((($checker_board[$first_row-1] [$first_
            column+1] !=
                    "black") && // not jumping empty space
        (substr(
        $checker_board[$first_row-1] [$first_
        column+1],0,3) !=
        substr(
        $checker_board[$first_row] [$first_column],0,3))))
```

```
                            // not jumping its own color
                            {
                                if((second_row == 0) &&
                                ($checker_board[$first_row] [$first_column] ==
                                "red checker"))  {
                                            $checker_board[$second_row]
                                            [$second_column] =
                                    "red king";
                                            } else {
                                    $checker_board[$second_row] [$second_
                                    column] =
                                    $checker_board[$first_row] [$first_column];
                                                                }
                            $checker_board[$first_row] [$first_column] =
                            "black";
                            $checker_board[$first_row-1] [$first_column+1] =
                                    "black";
                        } // end not jump own checker and not jump empty
                    } // end right side jump attempted else
                    }
                    if  ($second_column - $first_column == -2) {
                    // left side jump attempted
                                    if((($checker_board[$first_row-1]
                                    [$first_column-1] !=
                            "black") &&
                                            // not jumping empty space
                            (substr(
                            $checker_board[$first_row-1] [$first_
                            column-1],0,3) !=
                            substr(
                                $checker_board[$first_row] [$first_
                                column],0,3))))
                            // not jumping its own color
                            {
                            if((second_row == 0) &&
```

```
            ($checker_board[$first_row] [$first_column] ==
            "white checker")) {
                    $checker_board[$second_row] [$second_
                    column] =
                "white king";
                            } else {
                    $checker_board[$second_row] [$second_
                    column] =
                $checker_board[$first_row] [$first_column];
}

            $checker_board[$first_row] [$first_column] = "black";
            $checker_board[$first_row-1] [$first_column-1] = "black";
            } // end not jump own checker and not jump empty
                    } // end left side jump attempted
        } // end jumped two rows
        } // end not white and empty place to jump
}
```

You thought we were done with the logic? That was only half the fun. The else part of the main if statement manages the jumping from the bottom of the board toward the top of the board. The logic is the same except for minor changes. The second row must be two less than the first row (instead of two more).

There are no requirements to change in the display_board() function to manage jumps because all changes occur in how items are positioned in the array. There are no new items in the array.

As stated at the beginning of this example, the goal is to show the necessity of arrays, especially in the gaming industry. There are more efficient ways to design this type of application with object arrays and recursion. However, these techniques are beyond the scope of this book.

To complete the coding of a checkers game, additional code would be required to enforce the following rules and techniques. Try designing some of the logic to see how well you are doing. Remember, the Internet has plenty of examples to help you be successful:

1. A scoring ability must keep track of the number of checkers and be reduced each time a checker is removed from the board. A player wins when all the other opponents' checkers are removed.

However, a player also wins when the opponent cannot make any other moves. This would require the program to look at all possible moves a player can accomplish. A technique to keep track of the number of wins for each player is needed.

2.   A technique to keep the wrong player from trying to move a piece when it is not their turn is necessary.

3.   Depending on the version of checkers, some versions do not allow checker pieces to jump kings. Some versions do not allow checker pieces to jump at all. The code shown does allow checker pieces to jump kings.

4.   A recursion technique is needed to allow multiple jumps in the same turn. Depending on the version of checkers, players may be required to jump if they can. This would require coding to determine all jumps after the player selects a piece to move.

# Summary

Another long chapter! We covered a lot. We now know we can use PHP to access many data types and to display dashboards and charts, via an open source class. We also began to look at the logic of game development, by using arrays to set up a checkers game.

It's time to depart from our adventure. We hope that you learned a lot and realize how much PHP can accomplish. We have barely skimmed the surface of possibilities. Keep up your learning process by working through free tutorials and viewing free videos on the Web. Good luck. You are on your way to becoming a great programmer!

# Projects

1.   Using the design practices (MVC) from this and previous chapters, complete the programming and design for the checker's game. First test the example functions provided and link them together. Attack one part at a time, test the logic and code, then tackle the next part.

2. Update the Google Dashboard program to display the file type request. Then once it is selected, display it again, along with the next requirement for the user (either the database name or file name). Continue this process to display all the drop-down lists when the user has selected all requirements. Allow the user to change selections and redisplay the changes.

3. Investigate the ability for PHP to access other database types. Make changes to the Google Dashboard program to allow the user to select a type of database, and then select the databases available for the type selected. Continue the process to select the table and columns from the new database type(s).

# Index

## A

© Jason Lengstorf, Thomas Blom Hansen, Steve Prettyman 2022
J. Lengstorf et al., *PHP 8 for Absolute Beginners*, https://doi.org/10.1007/978-1-4842-8205-2

# E